The Lost Peace

HENRIK DAHL

THE LOST PEACE

How the West Won the Cold War
and Never Understood the New Dangers

GRØNNINGEN 1

The Lost Peace
How the West Won the Cold War
and Never Understood the New Dangers

ISBN: 9788785536181
Omslag: Harvey Macauley/Imperiet
Forfatterfoto: EPPGroup-MLahousse
1. udgave

This book is a translated and updated edition of *Den tabte fred*, first published in Denmark in 2025 by the publishing house Grønningen 1.

Forlaget Grønningen 1
Store Kongensgade 68, 3. sal
DK-1264 København K
www.gronningen1.dk

CONTENT

PREFACE

Political television series such as *The West Wing*, *Yes, Prime Minister*, and *Borgen* are rarely watched because viewers wish to master the intricacies of American, British, or Danish constitutional arrangements. Their careful grounding in a specific national setting serves an artistic function: it makes identification possible and sustains the suspension of disbelief. Yet their lasting appeal lies elsewhere. They endure because they capture recurrent features of democratic governance: the exercise of power under institutional constraint, the interplay between elected officials and permanent bureaucracies, the influence of expertise and media, and the persistent tension between political ideals and political necessity.

In that sense, such series are less national case studies than dramatizations of general political dynamics. The scenery changes; the logic does not. The forms differ, but the grammar of power remains strikingly similar across democratic systems.

This book should be read in the same spirit.

What follows is not a study of Danish politics as a curiosity, nor an attempt to trade on insider anecdotes. It is an analysis of how European and Western political elites, in the decades after the end of the Cold War, repeatedly misread their strategic environment—and how those misreadings gradually solidified into policy orthodoxies that proved resistant to revision even when empirical reality began to contradict them.

The argument is structural rather than national. It concerns the presence—and frequent absence—of realism; the limits of institutional thinking; the seductive force of optimistic assumptions about convergence, cooperation, and inevitable progress; and the tendency of political systems to privilege short-term coherence over long-term strategic clarity. These tendencies are not confined to any single country. They are characteristic of Western democracies operating in conditions of relative security, economic confidence, and diminishing attentiveness to classical power politics.

It is true that much of the empirical material draws on Danish examples. This is a practical and methodological choice rather than a normative one. Denmark functions as a closely observed case within a broader Western context. Many of the processes examined here unfolded in parallel across Europe and the wider transatlantic community. I use Danish material because I encountered these debates at close range and because parliamentary records and policy documents are readily accessible to me. The examples should therefore be read as illustrations, not as claims of Danish uniqueness. Comparable patterns could be demonstrated in other Western democracies with little difficulty. The dynamics are transferable; the national setting is contingent.

At the same time, a word must be said about timing—and about the temptation to keep rewriting.

The Danish manuscript was, in all essentials, completed in August 2025. That is not long ago. Yet in international politics "not long ago" can already feel like an earlier era. Events accelerate; alignments shift; positions harden; doctrines once considered stable become negotiable. It is therefore intensely tempting—especially when new ruptures occur—to "improve" a book that has only just been finished: to add a new chapter, to rewrite a conclusion, to let the most recent episode dictate the architecture of the whole argument.

The temptation is understandable. It is also dangerous.

A book such as this is not a live blog. Its purpose is not to keep pace with the news cycle, but to explain why the news cycle has become so violent and unstable. If the argument is sound, new developments should not require a wholesale rewrite; they should, rather, appear as further evidence of the underlying dynamics the book describes. That is the standard I have tried to hold myself to while preparing this international edition.

This revision therefore follows a restraint principle.

First, I have not attempted to retrofit the entire narrative to whatever has happened since August 2025. To do so would not only risk making the book opportunistic; it would also risk making it fragile. A book that constantly "updates itself" to the last headline becomes hostage to the next one.

Second, I have made adjustments where the international reader legitimately needs them: to clarify context, to reduce reliance on Danish shorthand, and to sharpen the distinction between what is merely Danish scenery and what is, in fact, a Western pattern. The goal has been continuity rather than reinvention. A reader who reads both editions should recognise the same book—because it *is* the same book.

Third, where I have tightened or nuanced formulations, it has been done to improve analytic precision, not to change the thesis. A recurring hazard in political writing is that moral temperature drifts upward just as explanatory clarity drifts downward. Indignation is sometimes justified; it is rarely illuminating. In revising, I have tried—without pretending to neutrality in matters that are not neutral—to make claims in a way that maximises their explanatory force and minimises their dependency on rhetorical heat.

The book's central claim remains simple. The peace following the Cold War was not undone primarily by unforeseeable external shocks. It was gradually weakened by a sequence of decisions rooted in misjudgment, wishful thinking, and an enduring reluctance to confront uncomfortable strategic realities. This is not, in any substantive sense, a book about Denmark. It is a book about how Western democracies understood—and misunderstood—the world they inhabited after 1989.

The idea for the book began to crystallize in the summer of 2017. I had been asked by a newspaper to comment briefly on two books that had left a lasting impression on me. Space was limited, but I wrote that one was Francis Fukuyama's *The End of History and the Last Man*, because for a time it seemed that everyone believed its thesis to be correct. The other was Samuel Huntington's *The Clash of Civilizations*, because there, I suggested, one could find something closer to the enduring realities of international relations. I submitted the text in haste, as I was preparing to serve as a delegate to the United Nations General Assembly in New York, and did not reflect much further on it—until the Assembly convened and the then President of the Czech Republic, Miloš Zeman, unexpectedly expressed almost the same judgment from the podium.

At that moment it occurred to me that this juxtaposition might be worth more than a short column. Perhaps it could become a longer essay—or even a book. Nine years later, here it is.

I have not spent all nine years writing it. Yet the project has accompanied me throughout much of that period. From the formation of the ill-fated centre-right government—at the insistence of the party I represent—at the end of 2016 until my departure from the Danish Parliament in 2024, I served as my party's spokesperson on foreign affairs. With the exception of the years 2019–2022, when we lacked the number of seats required for representation, I was also a member of the Danish Foreign Policy Committee. The arguments developed in these pages were therefore shaped not only by retrospective reflection but by direct engagement with contemporary policy debates.

The central question is how the West, after the fall of the Wall, could expose itself to such substantial strategic risk. Europe's dependence on Russian gas reached a level at which the European Union imported approximately 40 percent of its gas from Russia—an exposure that proved catastrophic when Russia, following Vladimir Putin's Munich speech, began to employ energy as a geopolitical instrument. At the same time, Europe's economic interdependence with China deepened to an extent that must likewise be described as strategically unsound: the European Union relied on China for roughly 90 percent of its rare earth elements and up to 80 percent of certain critical technological components. Measured against the risks of political coercion and the potential consequences of such coercion, these figures illustrate the magnitude of the strategic miscalculations examined in this book.

The purpose of the analysis is not to assign blame. Decision-making is rarely difficult in the abstract; the difficulty lies in making the right decisions under conditions of uncertainty. I have myself supported majorities that believed they were acting prudently, only later to question whether that confidence was justified. What interests me is not whether any single decision was defensible in isolation. Rather, it is why a series of increasingly problematic decisions was not reconsidered when their underlying premises eroded. Why do competent individuals persist on a given course even as mounting evidence suggests that it may be dangerous?

Part of the answer lies in psychology and group dynamics: the social incentives that reward conformity, the career penalties attached to dissent, the comfort of established orthodoxies, and the tendency of institutions to prefer continuity over correction. Another part lies in interests: the political and economic costs of changing course are often immediate and concentrated, while the benefits are delayed and diffuse. In such a setting, even well-informed actors can end up behaving rationally in the short term—and irresponsibly in the long term. The book returns repeatedly to this dilemma: not merely how errors were possible, but why they were *stable*.

My own relationship to these events changed in 2015, when I was elected to the Danish Parliament. Before that point, my perspective was that of an observer; thereafter, it became in part that of a participant. I do not claim ownership of Denmark's foreign policy after 2015. But my contributions are recorded in the parliamentary archives, and readers may consult them. The account that follows therefore combines analytical distance with a measure of personal involvement.

A brief orientation may be helpful. The first seven chapters, together with a short interlude, provide a historical analysis informed by theoretical reflection. Chapter 8 presents ten proposals for improved leadership. The epilogue offers ten recommendations for future policy.

Responsibility for the arguments advanced here rests solely with me. I am, however, indebted to many for discussions and assistance: the secretariat of the Danish Foreign Policy Committee, the Parliamentary Library, my friend Mikkel Andersson, my editor Truels Præstegaard Sørensen, and my wife, Christina, whose patience and encouragement have been constant throughout the long gestation of this book.

Finally, a small promise to the reader: if you sense, at times, that the world continues to move faster than the printed page can follow, you are not imagining things. But the remedy is not constant rewriting. The remedy is to understand the structural forces that make our era volatile: the return of power politics, the limits of institutional optimism, the strategic use of economic interdependence, and the increasing fragility of cohesion within Western societies. If the book succeeds, it will remain readable even as the headlines change—because it is, at bottom, an attempt to explain why the headlines have become what they are.

Chapter 1

STRUCK BY REALISM

Wir erleben eine Zeitenwende

Federal Chancellor Olaf Scholz, 27 February 2022

With this book, I seek to tell the story of the paradoxes that came to shape the West's management of the world after the Cold War.

When the Berlin Wall fell in 1989, many Western leaders and intellectuals believed that history had come to an end, and that democracy and the liberal international order would spread inevitably and effortlessly. Today we know that this assumption was a dangerous illusion.

In reality, the West was confronted with new and complex threats that were underestimated or ignored. In the West, the geostrategic and geopolitical thinking of earlier eras was replaced by a mode of thought that might be described as "geoeconomic."

This entailed the mistaken belief that economic globalisation was a guarantee of political stability and democratic development—a belief that remained largely unchallenged even when it should have been clear that China and Russia had never abandoned their great-power ambitions or their authoritarian systems of governance.

At the same time, Islamist radicalisation was gaining ground, facilitated by failed military interventions and by an inability—and an unwillingness—to engage seriously with the historical, cultural, and religious dynamics that fundamentally distinguish the Middle East from the West and drive developments in the region.

With this book, I aim to show that warnings against these illusions were repeatedly issued—not by marginal or sensationalist analysts, but by the most competent and experienced voices of the time. The near-systematic disregard of such insightful warnings led the West, from the 1990s to the present day, time and again to make decisions based on wishful thinking and short-term politics rather than on realistic assessments and strategic foresight.

The book demonstrates how this systematic blindness contributed to the weakening of NATO, to an energy-policy dependence on Russia, to a dangerous underestimation of China's strategic ambitions—and, last but certainly not least, to a loss of influence and soft power in the Middle East and the Global South, which may prove more than difficult to reverse in the years ahead.

Through counterfactual analyses, the book also explores how a more realistic and strategically grounded approach might have altered the course of history. As noted, the aim is not to assign blame, but to learn from the repeated misjudgments that have rendered the West vulnerable and the world more unstable. The book is therefore both a critical diagnosis and a call for a clearer-eyed foreign policy capable of securing peace and stability in a world in which the struggle over the future is far from over.

Turning point

In 2014, Russia annexed the Ukrainian peninsula of Crimea. That same year, parts of Ukraine's Luhansk and Donetsk regions were proclaimed independent states by pro-Russian separatists, with political and military support from Russia. After that, the front line froze for many years.

But on 24 February 2022, Russia invaded Ukraine with a force estimated at between 150,000 and 200,000 troops. From the early morning hours, strategic key points across the country were attacked by aircraft and missiles. Within a short time, Russian forces were positioned outside the capital, Kyiv, and for a period there was a real danger that Ukraine's lawful government could be captured and a Russian puppet government installed.

That did not happen. But no one could know or take for granted that it would not in the first days of what Russia consistently called "the special military operation"—its unlawful war of aggression.

Three days after the invasion, Germany's then chancellor, Olaf Scholz, delivered one of the most important speeches of his career in the Bundestag in Berlin. In this speech, Scholz stated unequivocally that responsibility for the war lay solely with Russia; that the war marked a rupture in Europe's history; and that the continent therefore stood at a crossroads. Are we to return to the power politics of the nineteenth century? Or are we, on the basis of international law, to hold on to the dearly bought lessons of the Second World War and the subsequent effort to build a rules-based international order?

The central passage of the speech ran as follows:

> *24 February 2022 marks a turning point in the history of our continent. With the attack on Ukraine, Russian President Putin has cynically launched a war of aggression—for one reason only: Ukrainians' freedom challenges his own oppressive regime. This is inhumane, it violates international law, and it cannot be justified by anything or anyone. We are experiencing a turning point. And that means: the world after is no*

> *longer the same as the world before. At its core, this is about the question of whether power may break the law; whether we allow Putin to turn back the clock to the era of the great powers of the nineteenth century—or whether we can muster the strength to set limits on warmongers like Putin.*[1]

What has made the speech famous in retrospect is the phrase *"wir erleben eine Zeitenwende"*—in English: *we are experiencing a turning point.* In the period leading up to the Russian attack, Germany had been subjected to increasingly frustrated criticism for sending only small and largely symbolic contributions to Ukraine's defence. The speech quite literally became a turning point for Germany. Shortly after Scholz delivered it, Germany began sending large consignments of increasingly heavy weaponry to Ukraine.

The speech earned Olaf Scholz widespread recognition and praise. For instance, Simon Tisdall wrote this in *The Guardian* the following day:

> *Scholz's speech marks a historic turning point for Germany, abandoning decades of military restraint. [...] It's a bold, necessary move that reshapes Europe's response to Putin's aggression.*

At first, I too was among the many who were impressed by Scholz's speech. But then something began to dawn on me. Hadn't Mitt Romney already warned about Russia during the U.S. presidential campaign in 2012? And wasn't there circulating on social media a video of John McCain from 2015 in which he, in a prophetic manner, described where Russia's imperial ambitions would lead? The answer to both questions was yes. Political voices that it would have been plainly unwise to ignore had for years been saying that what had just happened in Ukraine was in the making.

When I reflected more deeply on Olaf Scholz's speech, I came to understand that it was an example of what psychology calls projection. Put simply, this means camouflaging a statement about oneself by pretending to speak about the surrounding world.

It is a harmless and everyday projection to say, "It is cold," when one really means, "I am freezing." It is far less harmless when the German chancellor says, "The world has entered an entirely new phase," in order to conceal the core of the matter: "Not only I myself, but the SPD and the entire political elite in Germany were overtaken by reality three days ago."

I am about to write something here that I will repeat later, because it is important: Olaf Scholz was not a fool. On the contrary. He was one of the most competent, experienced, and strategically minded politicians in Germany, with a long and impressive curriculum vitae. But that is one of the central arguments of this book: it is uninteresting to study the disasters that thoughtlessness and incompetence can bring about. For it is, in any case, the most plausible assumption that organisations and states will come to grief if they are led by thoughtless and incompetent people.

What is genuinely interesting—and one of this book's most important points—is that since the end of the Cold War the West has, to a large extent, been led by people who were just as capable and serious as Olaf Scholz. Not always and without exception, but by and large. Yet this has not prevented serious policy errors from being made—errors that in our own time have led to the loss of the peace after the Cold War.

For that reason, we must take a closer look at the principles and mechanisms that can both lead competent people to make poor decisions and cause organisations and states led by capable individuals to come to grief as a result of bad decisions.

Consultant or spin doctor?

One thinker who offers a valuable explanation for why people are slow to revise their assumptions is the American psychologist Jonathan Haidt. He presents this argument in *The Righteous Mind.*

Haidt's point of departure is a classic question in psychology: Does reason govern the emotions? This, Haidt writes, was above all the view of Plato. Or do emotions govern reason? That was the view of the philosopher David Hume, who lived in the eighteenth century. Or is it the case that reason and emotion are co-regents of the human mind as a whole, each with its own delimited sphere of responsibility? This was the view, among others, of the learned American president and co-author of the Declaration of Independence, Thomas Jefferson (admittedly, he developed these ideas in order to justify being in love with a married woman—but they may still be valuable for all that).

Haidt explains that he initially believed in a modified Jeffersonian model: intuition (which he then regarded as a feeling) and rational thinking are more or less equal partners. But after many years of research, he came to understand that it is wrong to classify intuition as a feeling. The correct way to understand it is to see it as part of the human cognitive apparatus—in other words, as part of the total package of rationality and reason, if one simplifies the argument somewhat. Intuition is the human capacity for "rapid cognition," which is necessary if we are to make decisions at the pace required by ordinary daily life. It draws on many sources: experience, instinct, and the ability to recognise patterns.

Haidt ultimately concludes that around 90 per cent of human decisions are driven by intuition, leaving only 10 per cent to slow and careful rational deliberation. He expresses this through an image: intuition corresponds to a large and powerful elephant, while reason corresponds to its rider, seated on the elephant's back and attempting to direct its movements:

> *In* The Happiness Hypothesis, *I called these two kinds of cognition the rider (controlled processes, including "reasoning-why") and the elephant (automatic processes, including emotion, intuition, and all forms of "seeing-that"). I chose an elephant rather than a horse because elephants are so much bigger—and smarter—than horses.*[2]

As a rule, the elephant does what it has learned once before. In such cases, the rider can do little more than rationalise after the fact—if he is required to offer an explanation at all. But occasionally the elephant does what the rider wants. That is, in reality, the only genuinely rational decision out of ten. The rest are made by the elephant—that is, by intuition.

This is why a politician often clings to a failed policy long after the facts have demonstrated its unsustainability. For example, Angela Merkel could not let go of her intuition that economic engagement with Russia would inevitably produce peace and stability—even after the invasion of Georgia in 2008 sent a clear warning signal.

Jonathan Haidt's specialty is moral decision-making. What makes him relevant to politics, however, is his own observation that politics and morality are closely related. It matters, in this respect, that he himself has at times been close to American politics as an adviser to the Democrats. And as a professional politician, one pricks up one's ears at this point—because it is, in fact, a perceptive observation.

On paper, politics—so one learns in political science—is about allocating scarce resources in a legitimate manner. In reality—so one learns as a politician—most decisions (including economic ones) are the consequence of one's fundamental value-based politics.

Haidt argues that human beings fundamentally operate with six moral templates:

- Is this an expression of care or of harm?
- Is this fairness or cheating?
- Is this loyalty or betrayal?
- Is this respect for authority or the undermining of it?
- Is this respectful of the sacred, or does it undermine it?
- Is this an expression of freedom or of oppression?

These are the building blocks of morality. But, says the incisive psychology professor after spending considerable time in political environments, this is also how politics works.

If we take Haidt seriously—which is hereby recommended—it provides a powerful and persuasive explanation for why even the most capable politicians find it so difficult to change course. Even when a wealth of authoritative information and analysis indicates that they should. The refined analyses remain the tiny rider, attempting to explain to the large, intuitive elephant what it ought to do. And that succeeds only one time out of ten.

When the map is right and the terrain is wrong

As individual human beings, we must learn—if we have the stamina—to protect ourselves against the tendency to make insufficiently considered decisions and then, afterwards, to cosmetically embellish them with reason and rhetorical skill so that they appear more carefully thought through than they actually are.

Poor decisions entail, at best, an economic risk and, at worst, real danger. For that reason, organisations in particular must invest heavily in avoiding them—for example by ensuring that leadership establishes mechanisms and routines that help prevent bad decisions from being made.

Yet just as there are psychological mechanisms that prevent the individual from realising that they are making worse decisions than considerations of economy or peace of mind would warrant, there are also social-psychological mechanisms that prevent organisations from recognising when they are going astray. The most important of these will be reviewed below.

Once a group has been established with a formal leadership and formal roles set out in the organisational chart, as well as an informal leadership and informal roles that arise from the spontaneously emerging hierarchy, a consensus will also develop within the group on a wide range of questions: What is its task? How should it be solved in a commendable way? Where is it solved in a blameworthy way? And, more toxically: Who are the culture-bearing individuals in the group? And who are its black sheep?

In the academic literature, this mechanism is known as *groupthink*. Groupthink is necessary if a group is to become cohesive and solve its tasks to perfection, because it is groupthink that creates all the unwritten rules that allow a group to hold together and perform.

But it also has a dark side: criticism of, and challenges to, the consensus are often deeply unpopular and unwelcome. As a result of groupthink, individuals who challenge a group's fundamental assumptions and unwritten rules are more likely to be ostracised than to be listened to and taken seriously.

One of the factors most frequently contributing to groups becoming blind to the mistakes they are in the process of making is what is known as *confirmation bias*.

Confirmation bias operates by causing members of a group to notice only information that confirms their pre-existing views, while information that contradicts those views is either ignored or rationalised away.

The final key concept we must address when examining how groups think is *cognitive dissonance*.

Cognitive dissonance arises when events in the real world contradict one's deeply rooted beliefs about how the world works. The payoff of cognitive dissonance is that it spares one the need to revise those fundamental beliefs. But that is also precisely where the danger lies. Cognitive dissonance leads people actively to suppress information that could potentially undermine their worldview. In the seminal reference work *When Prophecy Fails* on the concept, written in 1956 by the social psychologist Leon Festinger, we can read about the American sect *The Brotherhood of the Seven Rays*, which awaited the end of the world and the sect's own rescue by extraterrestrials—and systematically disregarded all signs that something might be amiss with their worldview. The example drives the point home.

It is thus the interaction between groupthink, confirmation bias and cognitive dissonance that causes members of an organisation to ignore information they ought to take note of when moving through the terrain of reality, and instead to continue trusting the map. Of these three, however, cognitive dissonance is the most dangerous factor. It is the mechanism responsible for censoring warning signals from the outside world before they can even be subjected to rational consideration.

During the spring of 2025, the Danish newspaper *Berlingske* published a series of articles illustrating how warnings about Russia had been suppressed or ignored at the highest political level[3]. One of the most interesting contributions was an interview with

General Peter Bartram, who served as Denmark's Chief of Defence from 2012 to 2017.

In the interview, Bartram explains that when Russia invaded Crimea in 2014, he initiated an internal analysis within the Armed Forces to clarify what Denmark lacked in order to be able to fight an adversary of the kind represented by Russia.

The analysis concluded that Denmark was very far from being able to fight an opponent in that weight class, and it also identified a cause: for many years, the Armed Forces had been subject to severe cuts in the pursuit of the so-called peace dividend.

In the *Berlingske* interview, Bartram describes how, in 2015, he arrives at a meeting at the Ministry of Defence attended, among others, by the Minister of Defence, Nicolai Wammen, and his permanent secretary, Lars Findsen. At this meeting it becomes clear to Bartram that, on the political side, there is no interest whatsoever in engaging with the analysis he has commissioned. The minister is dismissive, and the permanent secretary relies on an assessment from the military intelligence service which, conveniently for the government, concludes that Russia poses no risk to Denmark and that there is sound military-professional justification for continuing to cut defence spending. Taken together, Bartram characterises the episode ten years later to *Berlingske* by saying that he received a "dressing-down."

The outcome was that Bartram was pressured—or at least felt pressured—into accepting continued cuts, even though his analysis demonstrated that these reductions would place Denmark in an unnecessarily dangerous position. In retrospect, Bartram believes that he was effectively gagged by the system within which he worked.

It is a piquant story that *Berlingske* tells. With the benefit of hindsight, we can see that Bartram and his staff were right and therefore had done nothing blameworthy. On the contrary, they had exercised the timely diligence one would expect of a general with overall responsibility for Denmark's military security.

The Ministry of Defence reacted as an organisation with all the hallmarks of groupthink, confirmation bias and cognitive dissonance. With a receptiveness to the political level that is regrettably not unique, the Defence Intelligence Service produced a threat assessment that both confirmed what the government wished to hear and suppressed information that contradicted this wishful thinking (for example, Vladimir Putin had already stated in practice at a conference in Munich in 2007 that Russia would henceforth pursue the foreign policy of the Soviet Union—more on this later). In this way, it became both easy and convenient for the minister to shoot the messenger rather than listen to the message.

For anyone not afflicted by the social-psychological mechanisms discussed above, the terrain had already, for most of a decade, looked very different from what the map claimed when Peter Bartram was pushed aside by the Danish government in 2015. Unfortunately, there was nothing unusual about this sequence of events across the Western world in the mid-2010s. That is what my next example will show.

From Russia with love

In the spring of 2018, I travelled to Berlin with the Danish Parliament's Brexit subcommittee. As one might expect, the visit was largely devoted to Germany's position in the negotiations on the United Kingdom's withdrawal from the EU, which at the time were in full swing.

But another topic also found its way into many of the conversations: the German–Russian cooperation on building the Nord Stream 2 gas pipeline. What made the issue particularly sensitive—seen from a Danish perspective—was that the project at that point envisaged a route passing through Danish territorial waters southeast of the island Bornholm.

This placed Denmark in an acute dilemma. At the highest level, our most important political and economic partner in Europe—Germany—expressed a clear desire that Denmark should not place obstacles in the way of the project. This was linked to the fact that Germany had already, in 2011, taken a principled decision to phase out its nuclear power plants and therefore had an urgent need for energy from Russia.

Conversely, our most important political and economic partner overall—the United States—was equally explicit in its wish that the Nord Stream 2 project should be halted. That wish was based on the assessment that the project would create a dangerous dependence on Russian energy, which could later be used for political coercion by Russia. Such coercion was something the United States could under no circumstances ignore. By virtue of NATO's Article 5, the United States was the ultimate guarantor of Europe's security.

My personal interest in the matter was considerable. At the time, my party leader was Denmark's foreign minister, and I was the party's foreign policy spokesperson. Any criticism the issue might provoke in the Danish Parliament, or commentary in the press, could very easily end up on my desk.

The Danish embassy had put together an excellent program. It included an informal dinner with the German deputy foreign minister, high-level meetings at the *Kanzleramt* and meetings with representatives of the parties in the Bundestag.

It quickly became apparent that no one within the very highest political elite in Germany felt able to voice criticism of, or even reservations about, the Nord Stream 2 project.

Germany had a special relationship with Russia, we were told. And implicitly: something the U.S. State Department had failed to understand. Russia had never violated agreements concluded with Germany, we were also told. Not even in the darkest days of the Cold War. The long and short of it—repeated to us in various formulations over the course of a couple of days—was that there was nothing to worry about when it came to the gas agreement with Russia.

I returned to Denmark in deep reflection over the massive political consensus in Berlin. How could the few hundred kilometres between the capitals of Germany and Denmark feel like a journey between two different worlds?

It was not as clear to me then as it is now. But something had clearly happened to the German elite in Berlin: it had ended up inside a kind of information bubble. Much like the Danish Ministry of Defence a few years earlier. In both cases, the result was produced by the social-psychological ingredients we have discussed, compounded by deficient leadership.

The political elite – a sociological perspective

I have already used the term "elite" several times. It is therefore appropriate to define it. Because my original training is in sociology, I have a particular fondness for understanding elites, as a starting point, more or less in the way one of the founding figures of sociology, Max Weber, understood them.

When sociologists speak of political elites, this is not meant pejoratively or as a politically charged label. It is simply a shorthand term for the people who work on preparing and implementing decisions within the institutions that support those who hold power in a given country.

According to Max Weber, to exercise power is to be able to impose one's will despite what others may think or wish. That is precisely the privilege politicians possess in a democracy. Ultimately, even a government in a democratic country can enforce its decisions by the use of power.

But democratically elected politicians do not exercise power in a vacuum—both because doing so would be undemocratic and because it would be impossible.

They depend on the existence of ministries and agencies. This is partly because decisions must be prepared in a proper and substantive manner by people with the relevant education and qualifications, and partly because decisions, once taken, must be implemented in a way that balances many considerations: efficiency and prudent use of taxpayers' money; fidelity to both the spirit and the letter of the decision that has been made; and, of course, consideration for the people who are affected by the decision in one way or another.

In a democratic country, the ideal is that individual employees in ministries, agencies, and similar bodies are hired on the basis of their qualifications and promoted because they have demonstrated, in practice, that they are capable of managing the processes and projects they are employed to lead. The ideal is also that power is not exercised arbitrarily, but according to specific principles. Those who implement decisions in practice must have a legal mandate to do so. They must not have personal interests in whether a decision is implemented (or, for that matter, delayed). More generally, power should be exercised by the office, not by the individual person.

Max Weber subsumed all these principles of the exercise of

power under the concept of bureaucracy. This term, too, was not intended as a pejorative or critical one, but simply as an observation that in highly developed societies—whether democratic or not—power is exercised most efficiently by a bureaucracy that operates more or less in accordance with the guidelines I have outlined.

With regard to the broader understanding of political elites, there are two extreme positions, both of which I consider incorrect.

One extreme can be described as the conspiracy theory. According to this thesis—which is false—elites are organised in a clandestine manner. They are given names such as "the deep state," or it is imagined that covert activities take place when they meet at mythologized venues such as "Davos" or "the Bilderberg Group."

The argument against the conspiracy theory is, in a sense, banal: the world is far too complex to be governed by a conspiracy. Murphy's Law applies to too great an extent for this to be possible.

There will always be unforeseen events that cannot be controlled. There will always be people who make a mess of things at absolutely crucial moments. And there will always be people who simply cannot keep quiet about all the alleged secret plans. For these reasons, conspiracy theories do not make sense.

The second extreme position is the theory of the entirely disinterested bureaucracy. This thesis—also false—reveals itself when even quite perceptive people imagine that if only we were better at planning, conflicts in society would not arise.

The first problem with that assumption is that one cannot plan one's way out of conflicts of interest. A park can never occupy the same space as a motorway, or vice versa. Consequently, a choice must be made—one that some people will be unhappy about. It really is that simple. The second problem consists of the social-psychological factors we have already discussed, which prevent groups from taking the maximally rational view of a situation.

The heavy weight of past decisions

We still lack a single, widely shared concept for understanding why political systems so often continue along tracks that were laid down long ago. That concept is *path dependency*. In essence, path dependency means that past decisions exert an influence on present decisions. It can arise in two ways, which I will outline below.

One source of path dependency is that the costs of changing strategy can be very high. The more money that has already been invested in a given project, the harder it becomes to abandon it. This is why poor projects so often end up being completed, even when it is clear to most observers that they are far from optimal.

The second source of path dependency is more curious. Once politicians have decided that problem X should be remedied by means of Y (for example: lack of social mobility should be addressed through education), most of them tend to argue as follows: if problem X has not yet been solved, despite our having identified Y as the remedy, then the reason must be that we have done too little of Y.

Most people would think differently. They would think: I initially believed that Y was an effective means of solving problem X. But it clearly is not. Therefore, I must try something else—for example, Z. Politicians, however, are a special branch of humanity (or else they develop certain bad habits over time). As a result, they usually insist quite stubbornly that what is needed is a much larger dose of Y to remedy X, if the small dose of Y has proved insufficient.

I suspect that politicians' tendency to claim that too little has been done of what they themselves regard as the best solution is reinforced by the necessity of compromise. When one enters into a compromise, the solution will of course not look the way it would have if one had been allowed to decide everything alone. Claiming that too little has been done of what one would have preferred is therefore also a diplomatic way for politicians to say that it is their partners' fault that this or that initiative has gone off the rails.

Where the first form of path dependency is triggered by economic considerations, the second is triggered by political ones. Yet they have the same effect: decisions made in the past continue to shape the framework within which we act today and in the future.

How is power exercised in practice?

I have always regarded the television series *Yes Minister* and *Yes, Prime Minister* as the best description of how politicians and political elites interact and exercise power—especially after I was elected to the Danish parliament. It took some time, however, before I understood how Antony Jay and Jonathan Lynn, the two scriptwriters, achieved their comic effect.

For anyone who has never seen the series, or remembers it only vaguely, the main characters are, first, the politician James Hacker. We meet him in the opening episodes as an inexperienced minister; later he becomes an inexperienced prime minister. Second, there is the permanent secretary, Sir Humphrey Appleby. As a matter of principle, he always wants his own way—which is also the will of the civil service. At the same time, again as a matter of principle, he never openly contradicts the minister, even though he regards most of the minister's ideas as, at best, foolish and, at worst, dangerous. Hence the title of the series and its comic effect. "Yes, Minister" almost always means: "You must have lost your mind, Minister."

When I eventually began to look more closely at who had created the series, it dawned on me that Antony Jay was a great connoisseur of Niccolò Machiavelli, and had written a book in which he was a pivotal figure.

Machiavelli's working life unfolded in early-sixteenth-century Florence, where among many other things he wrote *The Prince*. It is a kind of handbook on the exercise of power, which he dedicated to the young prince Lorenzo de' Medici. Machiavelli's point is always the same: the long-term interests of the state take precedence over everything else. Consequently, when it comes to safeguarding the interests of the state, the end will always justify the means. This leads to one observation after another that sensitive people today find horrifying, but which are regrettably true. For example, if it is unavoidable to take some harsh action against political opponents, one should unleash the entire arsenal of severe measures at once. Much of it will be forgotten, and the rest will be perceived as evidence that those in power have grown much milder over the years. If one is harsh all the time, Machiavelli says, one is not perceived as a ruler who has become milder with age; one is simply perceived as a tyrant.

Using an example from modern history, one might say that if, for instance, one has grown thoroughly tired of an Ernst Röhm-type constantly running around causing trouble, then one should remove the entire leadership of his Sturmabteilung in one stroke—and then refrain from purges thereafter. People will of course shudder at the Night of the Long Knives. But they will also think that it was a one-off measure, and that their Führer may even have become more relaxed with time. That was what Adolf

Hitler took from Machiavelli, and it produced both calm and false hopes in Nazi Germany in the latter half of the 1930s.

If one understands all this, one also understands that *Yes Minister* and *Yes, Prime Minister* are simply lessons in Machiavelli. The minister is the young, inexperienced, idealistic Prince Lorenzo. And the permanent secretary is Machiavelli—disguised in Oxbridge manners and tweed.

Most modern people shudder when they read Machiavelli's recommendations. At the same time, they chuckle with laughter when they watch a modern Machiavelli explain to the young, naïve minister that education has absolutely nothing to do with improving social mobility ("But, Minister, education is for the teachers"), that it would be far too controversial to appoint a devout Christian as Archbishop of Canterbury, or that strengthening the EEC runs counter to five hundred years of British foreign policy:

Sir Humphrey Appleby: *Minister, Britain has had the same foreign policy objective for at least the last 500 years: to create a disunited Europe. In that cause we have fought with the Dutch against the Spanish, with the Germans against the French, with the French and Italians against the Germans, and with the French against the Germans and Italians. Divide and rule, you see. Why should we change now, when it's worked so well?*
James Hacker: *That's all ancient history, surely?*
Sir Humphrey Appleby: *Yes, and current policy. We had to break the whole thing [the EEC] up, so we had to get inside. We tried to break it up from the outside, but that wouldn't work. Now that we're inside we can make a complete pig's breakfast of the whole thing: set the Germans against the French, the French against the Italians, the Italians against the Dutch. The Foreign Office is terribly pleased; it's just like old times.*
James Hacker: *But surely we're all committed to the European ideal?*

Sir Humphrey Appleby: *Really, Minister.*
James Hacker: *If not, why are we pushing for an increase in the membership?*
Sir Humphrey Appleby: *Well, for the same reason. It's just like the United Nations, in fact; the more members it has, the more arguments it can stir up, the more futile and impotent it becomes.*
James Hacker: *What appalling cynicism.*
Sir Humphrey Appleby: *Yes. We call it diplomacy, Minister*

One might be tempted to say that after the victory in the Cold War, there were too many Hackers and too few Humphreys. Yet the deeper problem was not a shortage of clever officials or well-meaning politicians. It was the gradual disappearance of strategic seriousness.

What were the reasons why Western elites committed so many strategic errors?

I cannot imagine that it is possible to identify a single cause that excludes all others for why Western elites, over the course of roughly thirty years, committed an entire series of strategic mistakes. I will therefore examine some of the more obvious explanations before focusing on the one I personally believe carries the greatest weight: ideology.

One very obvious reason why Western elites failed to think clearly and realistically in the first years after the end of the Cold War is, in my view, the elementary fact that they were blinded by their own success.

I will not present myself as better than I am. In the years around the end of the Cold War, I was a grown man of around thirty. And I clearly remember that the prevailing mood resembled that of a successful football World Cup far more than that of ordinary political events when the Eastern Bloc collapsed. The communists gave up in Hungary. The communists gave up in the GDR. The communists were forced to give up in Romania. And finally, they gave up in the Soviet Union itself. It was hard not to feel triumphant.

And if the mood was not already intoxicating when the Eastern Bloc collapsed, it became so for many when, in 1991, a coalition of the willing led by the United States put Saddam Hussein in his place and restored Kuwait to its rightful rulers.

In those years, a sense emerged that the Western world could do no wrong—a feeling that, in hindsight, lingered far too long. The interventions in the Balkans throughout the 1990s were not as successful as they were portrayed at the time. The Good Friday Agreement on Northern Ireland in 1998 was sound and later served as an excellent reference point during the Brexit negotiations many years afterward. But the interventions in Afghanistan and Iraq were disastrous policy failures, which likewise stemmed from the erroneous belief that the West had discovered a formula that worked—leading to a dangerous hubris.

Another problem was that the then-popular theory of interdependence was simply wrong. Today, the theory has very few advocates. But in the years following the end of the Cold War, many who regarded themselves as insightful believed that interdependence—a refined term for countries becoming mutually dependent—would prevent wars and conflicts, especially if buttressed by multilateral organisations and treaty systems such as the WTO. When we traded with other countries, they would gradually begin to change. Implicitly: toward becoming like us—liberal democracies with high living standards and a pronounced degree of personal freedom.

A third partial explanation is conflict aversion. I have no doubt that throughout the central administrations of Western countries there were many capable and articulate individuals who were perfectly able to read statistics and other forms of evidence and conclude that China was not even attempting to comply with WTO rules. Likewise, there were people who noted that Russia had in fact returned as an imperial great power following its invasion of Georgia in 2008.

It was courageous of the Chief of Defence, Peter Bartram, to tell his superiors that the entire security doctrine he had been tasked with administering rested on a fragile and questionable foundation. But let us be honest: ninety-nine out of a hundred senior civil servants would not have done so. For no matter how unrealistic the policies they are instructed to administer may be, they are extremely realistic when it comes to the prospects for their own future careers.

The explanation to which I personally attach the greatest weight, however, is, as mentioned, the significance of ideology.

An ideology is something different from a political objective. The political objectives that guided Western policy toward the rest of the world in the decades after the Cold War were, first, to cooperate economically as much as possible under a market regime that was as liberal as practicable. Second, to expand existing and establish new multilateral organisations and institutions to regulate the growing volume of global trade. And third, to pursue non-economic objectives such as reducing CO_2 emissions through binding international agreements.

Without being stated very loudly, Western countries also wished to enforce this world order by force (globalisation is concretely based on maritime shipping, and maritime shipping presupposes dominance over international waters).

Finally—and this was expressed only in a muted tone—Western countries wished to remove the most provocative or irritating dictators around the world, as long as this appeared to be a manageable task from a military standpoint.

All of these objectives can be evaluated. And once that has been done, one can decide whether, since the previous evaluation, one has moved closer to them or further away.

If objectives turn into ideology, however, that is a different matter. An ideology is a coherent set of ideas—or a narrative, if you will—and it is carried by values. An ideology is not promoted because it is rational. It is promoted because it is the path to a better society or a better world. Conversely, those who place obstacles in the way of the ideology must be restrained or impeded, because they are, in reality, working to make society or the world worse.

I would call the political objectives that guided Western elites during the first three decades after the end of the Cold War the ideology of globalisation.

There is no official exposition of this ideology. But in 1999, Anthony Giddens published a concise popular-science account, *Runaway World*[4]. When the book appeared, it functioned as a manifesto for globalisation—and it still does when reread today. Why globalisation cannot be avoided. And why we should be happy about it. In the book, globalisation is presented almost as a force of nature. But the fact that it is difficult to control, Giddens argues, should not trouble us. Over time, it will lead to greater prosperity, more personal freedom, and more countries embracing fundamental democratic values.

The ideology of globalisation was, with little serious opposition, the dominant narrative among political elites prior to the attack on the World Trade Center on September 11, 2001.

It did not have to be so. For example, Benjamin Barber had already published *Jihad vs. McWorld* in 1995[5], in which he showed how globalisation also generates a dangerous backlash that deserves attention. But this line of argument was not accorded nearly the same weight by elites as that of Anthony Giddens.

The September 11 attack became, in a macabre way, an illustration of the very title of Barber's book. And further warnings followed, most notably the financial crisis of 2007–08. Nevertheless, the ideology of globalisation continued to dominate among political elites in the years that followed. Russia and China were still regarded as partners (Russia was not suspended from the G8 until it invaded Ukraine for the first time in 2014). Nation-building in the Middle East continued to sound like a good idea. So did the construction of an energy infrastructure that created dependence on Russia, and a green transition that created dependence on China.

With the benefit of knowing the consequences of these decisions, it is striking how close to our own time we must come before individuals in positions of real authority in Western countries begin to sense that something is wrong and start to question whether the chosen course is, in fact, the right one.

A dangerous cocktail: Hubris, idealism, and carelessness

What I will argue in this book is that the many political mistakes made in the roughly thirty years following the fall of the Wall were due to three factors. First, hubris after victory in the Cold War. Second, idealism—because, in the enthusiasm of the moment, the importance of realistic assessments of the world beyond the West, and of our own capabilities, was overlooked. And third, sloppiness with figures and information that did not fit the prevailing strategy. The elites failed to guard against the error of believing that the map still corresponded to reality, even though it manifestly did not.

It is far from my intention to claim that the world should be interpreted as a Greek tragedy. That said, we now find ourselves facing nemesis in the form of a Western international position that is far more weakened and challenged than it needed—or ought—to have been.

How matters could deteriorate so badly is something I will seek to demonstrate through two main analytical strands.

The first strand I call the counterfactual strand. It concerns what political elites might hypothetically have based their assessments and actions on with regard to Russia, China, the Middle East, and energy, had they listened to experts other than those they in fact chose to trust.

Or what the political elites themselves might have reasoned their way toward, had they not been blinded by banal yet dangerous social-psychological mechanisms.

I will focus in particular on the counterfactual strand in Chapters 2–5 and 7.

The second strand I call the critical strand. It addresses why political elites chose to focus on how institutions—especially the UN and the WTO—ought to function in theory, rather than on the evidence that told a different and more truthful story: namely, that both the UN and the WTO had been weaponised by adversaries of the Western order.

This weaponisation—so I argue—turned the UN (along with its subsidiary bodies) and the WTO into a kind of Trojan horse: organisations in which Western countries voluntarily engaged and invested, but which primarily served to undermine those same Western countries.

As part of the critical strand, I will also take a closer look at what was fundamentally flawed about nation-building beyond the

West: the belief that all societies are held together and governed by institutions. This critical analysis of the faith placed in institutions and multilateral organisations will be developed in particular in Chapter 6.

The elite perspective — and why it is appropriate

When one looks closely at concrete historical processes—and this can be done by reading primary sources, memoirs of key actors, and general historical accounts—it always becomes clear that what ultimately became the official decision was, at the time, both criticised and opposed.

That decisions are subject to criticism and resistance is the normal state of affairs in democratic states and organisations. But within the political world there will, sooner or later, be someone who decides that this will be the official line, which we will defend to the last minister, both before parliament and before the public.

The focus of this book is what ended up becoming the official line in the Western countries: we buy gas from Russia; we invade Iraq; we trust China.

However, in this introductory chapter I would like, as a matter of principle, to point out two things. First, there are many reasons why the official line becomes the official line. Second, there will always be some who hold views different from those expressed by the official line.

Almost all democratic governments find themselves in a parliamentary situation in which they cannot do exactly what is written in their party manifesto, or whatever the prime minister might desire. There will be coalition partners who demand their due in return for backing the prime minister. There will be a ministry of finance that points out that resources are scarce and that money can only be spent once. And there will be interest groups whom, for one reason or another, one prefers not to antagonize. The official line will always reflect such constraints.

Almost all decision-makers are in the position that they actually have a choice. Take, for example, the construction of a new motorway connecting cities A and B. There will always be different proposals for the route. Behind these proposals there will be persistent and strong-willed individuals who fight hard for their own view while disparaging that of their opponents. But in the end, a decision has to be made. Otherwise, no motorway will ever be built. And this is why almost all major decisions end up being controversial to some degree.

In this book I will very often deal with the fact that this or that position ended up becoming the official line of the government of country X. But one should always bear in mind that this is the result of an extensive "filtering" of analyses and opposing viewpoints and interests—something one can often gain insight into through memoir literature, even though that genre is not without its own problems.

It is in order to illustrate how major leaders could in fact have reacted differently to the events that unfolded between the fall of the Wall and the present day that I have written the counterfactual Chapter 7, in which I attempt to consider how other, but plausible, candidates for leading positions in the Western world might have responded to the challenges of their time.

Chapter 2

THE FATAL EUPHORIA

Potentially, the most dangerous scenario would be a grand coalition of China, Russia, and perhaps Iran, an 'antihegemonic' coalition united not by ideology but by complementary grievances against the hegemonic power of the United States.

– Zbigniew Brzezinski in The Grand Chessboard[6]

In this chapter, I focus on the West's misjudgments in the 1990s, following the fall of the Berlin Wall and the dissolution of the Soviet Union. It was a period marked by a complacent assumption that world history had reached its final stage, characterised by Western dominance. This outlook was largely the result of Western political elites being influenced by Francis Fukuyama's idea of the end of history with the triumph of democracy, while warnings from realists such as Samuel Huntington and Zbigniew Brzezinski about an impending clash of civilisations and great powers were ignored.

The optimism of the 1990s fostered a belief that economic integration would steer authoritarian regimes such as Russia and China toward democracy. This was a dangerous illusion. It underestimated China's strategic ambitions, ignored Russia's resentment over NATO's eastward expansion, and failed to recognise that globalisation also generated counter-reactions in the form of Islamist radicalisation.

Despite clear warning signs—such as the international community's impotence in the face of resurgent nationalism in Yugoslavia, the genocide in Rwanda, the UN's failure in Bosnia, and the difficulties of integrating East Germany—Western leaders continued to base their policies on wishful thinking rather than realism. In this way, the errors of the 1990s set a course that led to many of the geopolitical crises with which the West continues to struggle today.

The final conclusion of the Second World War – without clear plans

In 1990, the so-called Potsdam Agreement ceased to apply. This was the result of the negotiations that paved the way for German reunification.

The Potsdam Agreement was concluded in 1945, immediately after the end of the Second World War. It was entered into by the United States, the United Kingdom, and the Soviet Union—that is, the three undisputed victors of the war.

For better and for worse, the Potsdam Agreement constituted a plan for the peace that was to prevail after the Second World War. On the positive side, with certain exceptions—Spain and Portugal—Western Europe was now unequivocally set on a course toward liberal democracy. On the negative side, Eastern Europe was recognised by the victorious powers as a Soviet sphere of influence. This meant that liberal democracy faced very far-off prospects in that part of the continent.

When the Potsdam Agreement lapsed, the Soviet Union still formally existed. It did so in a severely weakened form, however, because the country was left without the sphere of influence of neighboring states that had always been a core component of Russian and Soviet foreign policy. Many people in 1990 probably also thought that it was difficult to imagine an outcome that the Soviet Union would regard as satisfactory to the chaos that followed the fall of the Berlin Wall and Gorbachev's many reforms and liberalisations.

What was—and remains—striking about the peace after the Cold War is that it was never accompanied by anything resembling a Potsdam Agreement. That is, there was no political settlement or centrally directed political process that led to a clarification of the most elementary question: What now? What was NATO to do after the dissolution and disappearance of the Warsaw Pact? Who was to take the Soviet Union's seat on the UN Security Council? How were all the countries of Eastern Europe that stood outside European economic and political integration to relate to it in the longer term? And what security architecture was this same group of countries to become part of?

For most countries, these questions eventually found answers. Even so, the wounds left by the civil war in Yugoslavia have not healed to this day, and the economic, political, and security situation across much of the Western Balkans therefore remains unresolved.

Yet the peace after the Cold War ultimately became far more shaped by improvised decisions than the peace after the Second World War—marked by trial and error rather than by overarching strategies comparable to those pursued in the aftermath of 1945.

That the 1990s were characterised by political hesitation regarding how to integrate the former Eastern Bloc—and after 1991 also the former Soviet republics outside Russia—into Western Europe's economic, political, and security architecture is hardly surprising. It was a vast and difficult task, even for the most capable statesmen of the time.

With the necessary caveats, the problem can be compared to the one that arose when empires across Europe and on its periphery collapsed after the First World War. What does one do with enormous territories and populations that, at catastrophic speed, fall out of all existing economic, political, and security structures and institutions simultaneously? Solving such problems in a constructive manner requires an exceptional degree of political skill.

Academic thinking in the 1990s on the fall of the Wall and the dissolution of the Soviet Union

While political elites across Western capitals were, for understandable reasons, treading water, academics and intellectuals were engaging in deep reflection on the fall of the Berlin Wall and the dissolution of the Soviet Union, and on the consequences of these events.

The first major interpretive contribution appeared as early as 1992 in the form of Francis Fukuyama's famous book *The End of History and the Last Man*[7]. I shall return to it shortly. First, however, I would like to discuss *The Age of Extremes* by the historian Eric Hobsbawm, which was published in 1994[8].

Hobsbawm advances a view shared by many political historians. According to this view, an era is a period during which there are no significant changes in the security policies of the great powers. From this perspective, the period from the Congress of Vienna in 1815 to the First World War constitutes an era. Although Italy and Germany were unified (the former between 1861 and 1870, the latter between 1870 and 1871), the security policies of the other great powers remained broadly stable throughout this long period of almost a hundred years.

For this reason, Hobsbawm argues, the twentieth century was extremely short: from the collapse of the European security order in 1914 until it collapsed again with the dissolution of the Soviet Union in 1991. The twentieth century, in his view, was about the Soviet Union. Therefore, the twentieth century ended when the Soviet Union ended. And the task of inventing and establishing a new security architecture for large, medium-sized, and small states alike had to begin anew.

But what should be the premises of the new security architecture made necessary by the fact that the Soviet Union no longer existed? This was the great question that scholars and statesmen (of both sexes) in the 1990s set out to address.

As mentioned, one highly prominent proposed solution appeared already in 1992, put forward by the philosopher and political scientist Francis Fukuyama.

To make a long story short, Fukuyama was inspired by the German philosopher Georg Wilhelm Friedrich Hegel, who was active during the first three decades of the nineteenth century.

Hegel believed that history was driven by what he called the *world spirit*—that is, a governing principle which, through a series of successive stages, unfolded towards an ever more perfect realisation of itself.

This can be difficult to grasp at first glance. But it may help to see how Hegel's most famous interpreter, Karl Marx, applied this line of thought. Marx believed that all history was the history of class struggle. In other words, he placed class struggle where Hegel spoke of the world spirit.

For the Hegel-inspired Karl Marx, the motor of history was

thus class struggle. Over time, through a series of new stages, it would move societies towards a condition in which class struggle itself dissolved, and a classless society would become a reality.

This principle was called *dialectics* by Hegel—and by Marx. It is a difficult concept to understand, but it implies that any given historical stage always contains the seed of a new one. If one needs a mnemonic to grasp the concept of dialectics, one might think of the expression "a blessing in disguise." It captures the essence of dialectics, because it suggests that the seed of good fortune may lie within misfortune.

For Fukuyama, it was the development towards more democracy and more civil rights that drove history forward. Once democracy and civil rights no longer had any enemies, history would be complete. That stage, he argued, had been reached with the fall of the Wall and the dissolution of the Soviet Union.

Just as there can be no further class struggle after the emergence of a classless society, there can be no further resistance to democracy and civil rights once history has come to an end.

Fukuyama summarized his thesis as follows:

> *What we may be witnessing is not just the end of the Cold War, or the passing of a particular period of postwar history, but the end of history as such. That is, the end point of mankind's ideological evolution and the universalization of Western liberal democracy as the final form of human government*[9].

What humanity was supposed to occupy itself with after the end of history remains unclear in Fukuyama's work. But among his disciples in the political elites of the West—who may not have absorbed all the nuances of his book—it became a widespread view that the West should appoint itself the handmaiden of historical necessity and spread democracy to the last parts of the world where it had not yet taken root.

If, according to Fukuyama, all other forms of government belonged on the scrapheap of history, the role of the West was closer to that of a caretaker than to that of a genuine political actor. The consequences of this Fukuyama-inspired analysis were often formulated in Western capitals in terms of the world having become unipolar in the 1990s. There was only one center of power, and it was the collective West.

However, it was not the case that Fukuyama and the thinking about a unipolar order he inspired went unchallenged. As early as 1996, Margaret Thatcher—who had been involuntarily retired from her position as British Prime Minister since 1990—warned: *We have to be very careful that we do not take steps that recreate the Russian threat in a new form*[10].

This warning was nevertheless dismissed by many, presumably because Thatcher was by then regarded as a historical relic of the Cold War era, on a par with her old partner Ronald Reagan.

Yet others with considerable authority also warned during the 1990s against assuming that Russia would tolerate anything. The renowned diplomat George F. Kennan, who as early as the late 1940s had formulated the United States' so-called containment policy towards the Soviet Union, stated in a 1998 interview with Thomas Friedman: *I think it is the beginning of a new cold war (...). The Russians will gradually react quite adversely*[11]. The occasion was the expansion of NATO already underway in the 1990s, which Kennan viewed with great skepticism.

The most famous critic of Francis Fukuyama, however, was the political scientist Samuel Huntington. In 1996 he published *The Clash of Civilizations*[12], an explicit critique of Fukuyama's assumptions and conclusions.

Huntington has often been criticised for his use of the concept of "civilisation." Yet this criticism seems to me largely marked by an unscientific approach to how one ought to deal with flaws and inaccuracies in theories that are otherwise rich in perspective. Let me give an example.

Strictly speaking, Copernicus's model of the solar system is "wrong." Why? Because he claimed that the planets orbit the sun in circular paths. But this is never how it is presented. Instead, one says that Copernicus's theory was groundbreaking, even though it contained certain inaccuracies, and that Johannes Kepler completed the theory by calculating the correct elliptical orbits.

Huntington's theory should be approached in the same way. The core idea is important and groundbreaking, but it needs refinement by scholars with competences other than Huntington's—anthropologists, sociologists, and scholars of religion, for example.

That is how Huntington's theory should be treated: important and valid, but not complete. At any rate, that is how I regard it.

The core of Huntington's critique was that Fukuyama and his disciples completely underestimated the importance of culture. He put it this way:

> *The great divisions among humankind and the dominating source of conflict will be cultural. Nation states will remain the most powerful actors in world affairs, but the principal conflicts of global politics will occur between nations and groups of different civilizations*[13].

Huntington was thus saying that it is a grave mistake to project Western, culturally based values onto the rest of the world. Human rights, for example, were not universal; they were Western—and therefore not something that seriously concerned rulers in, for instance, Russia, China, or states with Islamic constitutions (such as Iran or Pakistan).

One should therefore not believe that all countries in the world were converging towards liberal democracy. If Russia was heading anywhere, it was towards the fulfillment of traditional Russian objectives. If China was heading anywhere, it was towards the fulfillment of traditional Chinese objectives—and so on.

On this basis, Huntington predicted that China would never come to accept human rights or liberal democracy in a broad sense. Countries with Islamic constitutions or Islamic-majority populations would likewise never accept human rights and liberal democracy—albeit for reasons different from those of China. Similarly, Russia would never embark on such a course. It was therefore sheer hubris—combined with elementary ignorance of cultural conditions—that led Western elites to project their own ideas of the ideal society onto the rest of the world.

Remarkably, Huntington also foresaw that Ukraine would be a likely battleground for the clash between Western and Russian values.

Huntington was in academic terms basically a realist—and he was not alone. The year after the publication of *The Clash of Civilizations*, Zbigniew Brzezinski (who had served as National Security Advisor to U.S. President Jimmy Carter) published *The Grand Chessboard*. In that book, he too predicted that the world after the fall of the Wall and the dissolution of the Soviet Union would be unstable. He wrote almost prophetically:

> *Potentially, the most dangerous scenario would be a grand coalition of China, Russia, and perhaps Iran, an 'antihegemonic' coalition united not by ideology but by complementary grievances against the hegemonic power of the United States.*[14]

That is precisely where we have ended up today—and thus an impressive analysis, considering that it was presented almost thirty years ago.

In the 1990s, however, there were also other critical perspectives on Fukuyama's thinking—and that of his disciples—beyond those based on the concept of culture.

Starting from the rather banal observation that pressure generates counterpressure, Benjamin Barber had already in 1995 predicted that if globalisation created a culturally homogenized world, which he called "McWorld"—a clear reference to a well-known fast-food chain and its global market dominance—this would inevitably provoke a backlash. According to Barber, this backlash would take the form of either a literal or a metaphorical "jihad": an intense resistance in which local groups would fight to defend their own cultural, religious, or national distinctiveness against the homogenizing forces of globalisation.

Barber himself formulated it this way: *the planet is falling precipitously apart and coming reluctantly together at the very same moment*[15].

The idea, then, was that globalisation had a positive side in the form of international division of labor, economic growth, and increasing purchasing power for individuals. But it also had a dark side in the dissolution of traditional cultural communities and of old professions and industries that ceased to be profitable around the world.

In Barber's thinking, it was not a given that globalisation would prevail. It could just as easily be the protests against it that, in many countries, would draw the longest straw.

A similar line of thought appeared a few years later in the work of the sociologist Manuel Castells. In 1996, in *The Rise of the Network Society*, he wrote that the entire question of identity and belonging would become explosive in the twenty-first century. He expressed it as follows:

> *In a world of global flows of wealth, power, and images, the search for identity, collective or individual, ascribed or constructed, becomes the fundamental source of social meaning. Identity is becoming the main, and sometimes the only, source of meaning in a historical period characterised by widespread destructuring of organisations, delegitimation of institutions, fading away of major social movements, and ephemeral cultural expressions*[16].

Globalisation, in other words, would not be a leisurely stroll in the park. It could just as easily become a source of political protest and resistance—initiated by those segments of the population who suffered from globalisation rather than experienced its benefits.

During the 1990s, then, some experts believed that the world had become unipolar and that liberal democracy no longer had any opponents. Others, however, concluded that neither Russia, China, nor the Islamic world (exemplified by Iran) would quietly accept being steamrolled by the West.

But what were the political elites in the West thinking?

Here we can begin with the political elite in the country I know best: Denmark. Over many years, successive Danish governments have submitted a foreign policy statement to the Folketing. As a result, from the period following the fall of the Wall up to the present day, we have a series of statements from the governments in office at different times—albeit not in a uniform format—describing how they viewed the world from their perspective. I will allow myself to regard the perspective adopted in these statements as that of the highest national political elite. I consider this reasonable, since they articulate the worldview that the government and its civil servants, after careful deliberation, have chosen to present publicly and to be held accountable for before the Folketing.

In 1993, the Minister for Foreign Affairs was Niels Helveg Petersen. In his foreign policy statement to the Folketing, he explained how the newly appointed Poul Nyrup Rasmussen government perceived Denmark's international environment:

> *A development can be observed towards greater acceptance of the view that the interaction between democratic systems of government, respect for human rights, and a socio-economic order based on market-economy principles and a sound ecological foundation constitutes the synergy necessary to create the basis for positive societal development—nationally as well as internationally*[17].

It is not unfair to claim that Denmark's government at the time, with few reservations, embraced a popularised version of Fukuyama's argument. Peace had broken out. The task now was to roll out the Western model of society to as many countries as practically possible.

The Danish governments of the 1990s—led from 1993 to 2001 by Poul Nyrup Rasmussen—were by no means alone in promoting this popularised version of Fukuyama.

In 1994, Bill Clinton defined the objectives of U.S. foreign policy as the promotion of democracy throughout the world:

> *Ultimately, the best strategy to ensure our security and to build a durable peace is to support the advance of democracy elsewhere. Democracies don't attack each other*[18].

In 1995, the then Secretary-General of the United Nations, Boutros Boutros-Ghali, followed up on the 1992 programme declaration *An Agenda for Peace* and stated in that context:

> *Peace-keeping, in the sense of operations designed to monitor and consolidate peace processes, remains an indispensable instrument for the United Nations in its efforts to maintain international peace and security.*[19]

And in 1999, in a speech delivered in Chicago, Tony Blair declared that Britain's objective was to help spread democracy across the world—if necessary by force:

> *We are all internationalists now, whether we like it or not. [...] We cannot turn our backs on conflicts and the violation of human rights within other countries.*[20]

All of this was a consequence of the popularisation of Francis Fukuyama's ideas that Western elites championed in the 1990s.

There are many more examples than those already cited of how political elites thought in the 1990s. But they amount to little more than a repetition of what we have already seen: optimism and faith in a liberal world order were virtually unassailable.

What these statements have in common is the assumption that democracy, the market economy, and human rights had not only triumphed historically, but also represented a universal truth that now merely awaited global dissemination. What had been forgotten or overlooked—in the intoxication following the fall of the Wall—was that history never stops, and that other actors might have different plans and visions.

In retrospect, it seems almost astonishing that so many capable and experienced decision-makers could, with such confidence, overlook the clear signs that the global reality was far more complex and far less predictable than their idealistic visions allowed them to acknowledge. This fundamental error—interpreting the world as one wished it to be, rather than as it actually was—would in the decades that followed prove very costly for Western countries.

Political reactions to the fall of the Wall and the dissolution of the Soviet Union

The 1990s were, for better and for worse, a great era for the European Union. On the positive side, within a very few years the EU transformed itself from a political community into a political union. This included, among other things, the establishment of the single market and a common currency. But it also included the accession of ten new countries in a process that began in 1993 and was completed in 2004 (with the accession of two latecomers in 2007).

Thus, part of the answer to what was to happen to the countries in Eastern Europe that around 1990 found themselves without integration into any international systems or structures was that they were to be brought into the EU.

The less positive aspect was that, after this feat of strength, it was as if the EU had run out of steam and needed to catch its breath. As an active Member of the European Parliament writing these lines in 2025, I would say that it still feels as though the EU has not fully recovered from the dramatic years between 1993 and 2004.

The accession process began at the EU summit in Copenhagen in 1993. There, the EU member states at the time agreed that the requirements for EU membership could be formulated such that an applicant country had to possess fully developed democratic state institutions. It had to have a functioning market economy. And it had to be able, in practice, to assume the obligations that follow from EU membership.

In the years that followed, a total of twelve countries applied for membership: Estonia, Latvia, Lithuania, Poland, the Czech Republic, Slovakia, Hungary, Slovenia, Cyprus, Malta, Romania, and Bulgaria. The latter two were told to wait somewhat longer than the first ten, which were admitted in 2004. But by the end of 2007, all countries from the mid-1990s application round had become members of the EU.

More recent research suggests something many have probably suspected: in practice, compliance with the Copenhagen criteria was weighed against geostrategy[21]. Or, put more colloquially: had it not been for overarching political considerations, the big bang of twelve new EU member states by the end of 2007 would have been somewhat smaller.

With the enlargement of the EU, a very large share of the countries that either lay within the Soviet Union's sphere of interest or were directly part of it were politically and economically integrated into the old Western Europe. Those that were not included, but which in our own day have expressed an interest in EU membership, were Georgia—before the Georgian Dream party became overtly totalitarian—Moldova, and Ukraine.

Security integration took longer and ultimately became a greater source of friction with Russia than political and economic integration.

To this day, it remains contested whether the United States promised the Soviet Union not to expand NATO eastward when the issue arose in connection with German reunification and the lapse of the Potsdam Agreement.

Russia has asserted with increasing force that such a promise was given, as relations between Russia and the West have deteriorated following Vladimir Putin's famous speech at the Munich Security Conference in 2007.

Conversely, for example, former U.S. Secretary of State James Baker has argued that the United States at no point promised the Soviet Union not to expand NATO eastward.

Be that as it may, the first countries from the former Eastern Bloc (setting aside the GDR), namely Poland, the Czech Republic, and Hungary, were admitted to NATO in 1999. They were followed in 2004 by Estonia, Latvia, Lithuania, Slovakia, Slovenia, Romania, and Bulgaria.

Subsequent enlargements brought in Croatia, Albania, Montenegro, and North Macedonia. And in response to Russia's invasion of Ukraine, Sweden and Finland applied for NATO membership and were admitted in 2023–24. NATO thus reached a total of 32 member states.

However, it turned out that George F. Kennan had been right in 1998: this development did not go unnoticed in Russia. After Vladimir Putin formally came to power in 2000, it has been a significant driving force behind the radicalisation he has undergone.

Whether the incorporation of such large parts of Russia's sphere of interest into the political West is the cause of Russia's aggressive imperialism, or whether it is more accurate to say that it is merely the pretext for it, is today a contested question.

Many adherents of the so-called realist school in the study of international politics will tend to say that it is the cause. By contrast, those inspired by Samuel Huntington (who was, in fact, also a realist before layering cultural analysis onto his research) will be more inclined to say that it is a pretext. If Russia could not justify its imperialism by pointing to Western expansion eastward, it would simply find another way to legitimise its—metaphorically speaking—hereditarily conditioned behaviour.

The naïve belief in Russia's integration into the West

Throughout the 1990s, it was not difficult to understand the confidence—bordering at times on complacency—with which Western countries integrated large parts of the former Eastern Bloc economically, politically, and militarily. This approach rested on a widely shared premise, articulated clearly by the Danish government: that democracy, human rights, and a market economy grounded in sustainable principles were mutually reinforcing forces and that, together, they would generate a self-sustaining trajectory of positive development at both the national and international levels.

The consensus that prevailed in the EU and NATO during the 1990s—that eastward enlargement was not merely desirable but historically necessary—rested on variations of this same assumption. Across the Western world, there was a genuine belief that Russia itself was moving, perhaps unevenly but unmistakably, toward liberal democracy and a market-based economy. On that basis, Russia was admitted to the G7 in 1998, transforming it into the G8.

Had Western elites been less naïve—and perhaps placed greater weight on Huntington and Brzezinski than on Fukuyama—they might have given far more serious consideration than they actually did to the political and social consequences of the "shock therapy" prescribed for the fragile Russian society under Boris Yeltsin by the American economist Jeffrey Sachs.

Sachs—who advised Russia with the backing of both the U.S. government and the International Monetary Fund (IMF)—had, on the basis of earlier experience with reforming Eastern Bloc countries, designed the so-called shock therapy. It entailed extremely rapid privatizations and market liberalisations, as well as the withdrawal of state subsidies from Russian enterprises.

The shock therapy reforms, however, had dramatic consequences. They triggered hyperinflation and economic collapse, and they enabled the rise of the so-called oligarchs, who came to control large parts of the Russian economy during the 1990s.

In 2000, Vladimir Putin was formally appointed president of Russia. Support for him rested in part on the belief that he was the man capable of restoring order and putting an end to the turmoil that had followed the economic reforms.

There is an almost morbid dialectic embedded in the fact that it was precisely the belief that Russia would become a normal Western country that paved the way for one of the Western world's greatest enemies: Vladimir Putin.

China's true intentions

Deng Xiaoping is widely credited with restoring stability after the turmoil Mao Zedong left behind and with opening China to the outside world, including the West.

He is often remembered for his remark that he did not care whether a cat was black or white, as long as it caught mice. The comment is frequently taken to suggest that he was not deeply committed to communism. Yet this interpretation is misleading. Deng was, beyond doubt, a committed communist—while also being a strikingly pragmatic political actor.

The events of 1989 offered a sobering illustration of that combination. When the regime chose to suppress the youth uprising on Tiananmen Square with extreme violence, it underscored both

Deng's resolve and the limits of the reforms he was willing to tolerate. From his consolidation of power in 1978 until his death in 1997, no major political development in China occurred without his approval.

If one is to characterise the West's relationship with China in the 1990s, the most reasonable description is that policymakers in capitals across the West were well aware that the country was somewhat rough around the edges when it came to human rights and democracy. Yet trade with China held such promising economic prospects that these concerns about the country's political conditions were set aside—especially concerns about whether China might exploit any resulting economic dependence for its own political advantage.

As a consequence, it is difficult to find documents from Western political elites in the 1990s that seriously considered the possibility that China might act in bad faith. It is equally challenging to identify authoritative discussions of the risks associated with strategic dependence.

It was, to be sure, stated clearly and explicitly by Samuel Huntington that China was not a country that wanted the same things as the Western states. But this analysis left little mark on the decision-making processes in the West that led to China's accession to the WTO in 2001 and to the massive integration of China into the international division of labor, the first steps of which were taken in the 1990s.

The belief that trade over time would make countries resemble one another (implicitly: that it would make non-Western countries resemble Western ones) was so pervasive that it bordered on a religious dogma. It was not even considered that this belief might be unfounded.

False hopes in the Middle East

It was not only developments in Europe that, in the 1990s, nourished the Fukuyama-popularised belief that the world was inevitably moving toward greater peace and democracy.

In 1991, a coalition of Western countries liberated Kuwait from Iraqi occupation. This represented something as rare as a Western military presence in the Middle East that was actually welcomed by parts of the region.

Unfortunately—one might say with the benefit of hindsight—this was widely interpreted in the West as a mandate to intervene in the world's hotspots and use military force to alter political conditions. This is one of the misunderstandings that has most severely eroded the Western countries' soft power outside the political West since the fall of the Berlin Wall.

Why Western countries, even at the time, could have interpreted their own role as peace-brokers in a more nuanced way is an issue I shall return to at the end of the chapter.

In 1993, an agreement was concluded in Oslo between the PLO and Israel which, on paper, paved the way for peace between Israel and Palestine and for the establishment of a Palestinian state.

And the following year, Israel and Jordan concluded a peace treaty. This made Jordan the second country in the region to make peace with Israel, after Egypt had become the first in 1979.

Just as the geostrategic analysis of China in Western capitals during the 1990s had been inadequate and largely unaffected by the insights of thinkers such as Huntington and Brzezinski, so too was the geostrategic analysis of Iran and of global jihadism.

There was no shortage of signs at the time that could have indicated to a senior civil servant or politician in a Western country that Iran and global jihadism were developments worth close attention.

As early as 1981, a precursor to al-Qaeda—Egyptian Islamic Jihad—assassinated Egypt's leader, Anwar Sadat. This was done to punish Sadat (and Egypt's political elite) for the peace he had concluded with Israel a few years earlier, and for his generally accommodating attitude toward Western countries.

The leader of Egyptian Islamic Jihad was none other than Ayman al-Zawahiri, who later became Osama bin Laden's deputy in al-Qaeda.

In 1989, the regime in Tehran issued a fatwa—an Islamic religiously grounded death sentence—against the author Salman Rushdie for blasphemy. In the years that followed, the Iranian regime actively persecuted not only Rushdie himself, but also individuals who collaborated with him.

Finally, an extremely bloody civil war was fought in Algeria during the 1990s, between the country's secular government and the so-called Islamic Salvation Front. At the time, this conflict largely flew under the radar of Western media. Yet one is entitled to expect that people who work professionally with foreign-policy analysis and formulate recommendations on that basis take note of such developments.

The Algerian civil war was the event that political elites could—and should—have studied in order to better understand the political dynamics of the Middle East in the 1990s. It contained a very large share of the ingredients that have characterised the region since then: the destabilisation of secular governments and global jihadism in the form of financial support and direct participation in warfare by sympathisers already radicalised by other conflicts.

The only element missing from the civil war, compared to the present day, was a clear connection to Iran. That this connection was absent was no doubt due to the fact that the Islamic Salvation Front was not Shiite, but Sunni.

The course toward today's energy policy is set in Kyoto

The Fukuyama-inspired (but also highly popularized) narrative that Western political agendas would come to dominate the entire world after the fall of the Berlin Wall made political elites in the 1990s blind to the problems that could arise from integrating China into international trade—and thus into the Western economy and division of labor. In much the same way, it blinded political elites to developments that contradicted the story that the Middle East, too, was on its way to becoming a more peaceful and democratic region.

A third area in which Western countries in the 1990s projected their own values and priorities onto the rest of the world was energy policy.

Energy policy and global warming truly entered the international agenda at the summit in Rio de Janeiro in 1992. And at another summit in Kyoto in 1997, it was agreed that industrialized countries should reduce their emissions of greenhouse gases by 5.2 percent by 2012, relative to 1990 CO_2 levels.

This was to be achieved, among other things, through new mechanisms such as emissions trading, joint projects in which highly industrialized countries could cooperate to reduce emissions where it was most efficient, as well as projects outside the highly industrialized countries that would promote reductions in emissions.

But once again, the devil was in the details. A number of very large countries—and very large emitters—such as Brazil, India, and China succeeded in having themselves defined as developing countries. This exempted them from binding reduction targets. Moreover, enthusiasm for reducing CO_2 emissions was—and remains—limited in the United States.

The truth few have dared to tell the public in Europe is that the green transition is primarily something Europe cares about. At the same time, the continent accounts for only 6–7 percent of total global CO_2 emissions.

This honest discussion could well have been held in the 1990s, because it was in fact introduced by the Danish economist Bjørn Lomborg. But instead of taking Lomborg's warnings seriously, the political elite chose to kill the messenger of bad news.

European energy policy has ended up becoming one of the most self-destructive activities the EU has ever embarked upon, as documented, among other places, in the Draghi Report of 2024.

There have been serious critics of the energy ideology that has guided European energy policy for nearly thirty years, without political elites ever listening to them. The result has been, first, very high energy prices that undermine economic growth in Europe. Second, political division—on this point surpassed only by the immigration policy desired by political elites. And third, Europe has ended up making itself vulnerable to political blackmail from countries such as Russia and China, which either control the raw materials Europe lacks or the technologies necessary to carry out a green transition.

The lesson that was not learned from the civil war in Yugoslavia

After the successful intervention in Kuwait, an ideology emerged during the 1990s according to which it was the mission of the Western world to go out into the world to create peace and introduce democracy by violent means.

As I have noted earlier, this was the essence of doctrines articulated by both Bill Clinton and Tony Blair—and doctrines to which Denmark subscribed.

The dissolution of Yugoslavia was, at the time, regarded as an exemplary case of how the Western world could create peace.

The background was that Josip Broz Tito, after the Second World War, had assembled a number of heterogeneous states into the political entity of Yugoslavia. Some were Catholic and Western-oriented (Slovenia and Croatia). Some were Orthodox and Eastern-oriented (Serbia and Montenegro). And some were Muslim (Kosovo and, in part, Bosnia).

This construction was held together solely by Tito's personal authority. When he died in 1980, it was therefore only a matter of time before Yugoslavia would fall apart. That process began in 1991 and continued over the following years.

In Western Europe, the civil war in the former Yugoslavia was perceived as unacceptable—especially as it escalated in Bosnia-Herzegovina from 1992 onwards.

However, it soon became clear that the peacekeeping forces deployed by the United Nations were toothless and incapable, for example, of preventing the massacre in Srebrenica in 1995, which at the time was the worst massacre in Europe since the Second World War.

Eventually, NATO intervened in 1995 and bombed the Bosnian Serbs. This led to the so-called Dayton Agreement, concluded in November 1995.

At the time, the end of the civil war on Western terms in 1995 was interpreted as a major success for the Western countries' civilising mission across the globe. Consequently, for many years the intervention in the former Yugoslavia was regarded by Western elites as a model example of how the West ought to fulfil its historical task.

In reality, the Western intervention in the former Yugoslavia was problematic.

First, it demonstrated that the United Nations was a paper tiger. Second, that Europe was helpless when it came to the use of hard military power. Third, that the only security guarantees that truly count are American. Fourth, that nationalism—even in a globalised age—was alive and well. What the Yugoslavs had under Tito was a borderless country that closely resembled the most fervent dreams of an EU federalist. What the citizens wanted, by contrast, were good old nation-states of the kind that had existed before the world went off the rails.

And fifth, the Western intervention showed that there will always be too many loose ends in a "coerced peace." The problems of Bosnia-Herzegovina have never been resolved. In Serbia, a hostility toward the West thrives that is deeply damaging to future cooperation. And with the exception of Slovenia and Croatia, it has not truly succeeded in integrating the Western Balkans economically and politically into Europe (even though Montenegro and North Macedonia are members of NATO). This means, first, that these parts of Europe are falling further and further behind in terms of general social and economic development. And second, that both Russia and China find it far too easy to assert their influence.

A sixth and final point worth noting is that the West should have learned that one cannot "bank goodwill" in relation to the Islamic world.

The truth about the Western effort in the former Yugoslavia is that Western countries bombed Christian Serbs in order to save Muslim Bosniaks for purely humanitarian reasons.

This has never earned Western countries so much as a single positive point in the Islamic world. By contrast, Bosnia became a place where jihadists from all over the world both gained practical experience with weapons and armed combat and became radicalised to a significant degree.

Two stories of 1989 – and four warnings from the 1990s

By the end of the 1990s, the dominant narrative about 1989 was that it had been a kind of jubilee year, in which the dictatorships of Eastern and Central Europe collapsed under the weight of their own internal contradictions and their populations' thirst for democracy and freedom. It is a narrative that encourages a critically unreflective understanding of what kind of year 1989 actually was.

It is true that for the people who lived in Eastern and Central Europe, 1989 was a wonderful year (unless they had been members of the Communist Party and now faced the risk of ostracism). But 1989 was also a year that clearly demonstrated the existence of strong and determined alternatives to liberal democracy.

As already mentioned, 1989 was the year in which the student uprising in Tiananmen Square was crushed with brutal violence, and the year in which Ayatollah Khomeini issued a globally binding order to all faithful Shiite Muslims to kill Salman Rushdie.

On closer reflection, the story of 1989 should therefore have been that it was a year in which the dictatorial Soviet state did indeed give up in Eastern and Central Europe, but in which the rising dictatorial states of China and Iran, in return, demonstrated what they were made of: ruthless exercises of power across the globe. I will return to the discussion of the competing narratives about 1989 in Chapter 6.

As Western commentators toward the end of the 1990s were

drafting their articles about the decade that was drawing to a close, they would have been wise to dwell on four warning signs. Four signals that the world order one had dreamed of at the beginning of the decade might prove harder to establish than anticipated. I myself was among them, and I did not do so either. I therefore write these lines not to point fingers. It is difficult, in the present, to grasp what will prove important in the future.

The first two warning signs concerned the United Nations. If there was any lesson to be drawn from the genocide in Rwanda in 1994, it was that the UN was a weak organisation, lacking the ability to create and sustain peace. And what was the lesson of the civil war in the former Yugoslavia? The same. Despite solemn declarations that the UN had assumed responsibility for protecting civilians, and that the town of Srebrenica was a safe zone, a Bosnian Serb force under the command of Ratko Mladić was able to march unhindered past the UN troops tasked with protecting the civilian population of Srebrenica and murder between 7,000 and 8,000 Bosniaks.

After these events in the 1990s, it is puzzling that it remained a widespread belief that the UN was an important instrument for securing peace and stabilising fragile societies.

The third warning sign has already been mentioned: if the civil war in the former Yugoslavia demonstrated anything, it was the significance of nationalism. The driving force was that people did not wish to live in a borderless (albeit communist) mini-EU, but in a genuine nation-state with a flag, an anthem, and old traditions (which may not be all that old, but that is another story).

The fourth and final warning sign was the partially failed merger of the GDR with the Federal Republic of Germany. Already in the 1990s it was clear that there were many problems involving residents of the former East Germany who looked askance at their new compatriots in the former West Germany — and vice versa. This should have led more reflective members of the political elites to consider whether it could really be true that, if one simply pushed ahead with economic interaction and institution-building, support for the Western societal model would follow automatically.

I will return to these warning signs and to the consequences of ignoring them in the 1990s in Chapter 6. But it seems clear to me that even for those who did not follow closely the experts' discussions of the consequences of the fall of the Wall, a considerable body of practical evidence had already accumulated by the end of the 1990s suggesting that several of the period's standard assumptions about how the world worked were in fact highly problematic.

Already by the close of the 1990s, it should have been evident that the optimism and belief in a global liberal world order that had characterised the decade after the fall of the Wall rested on an uncertain and flawed foundation.

The inability and unwillingness to recognise this had major consequences in the years that followed. Russia's growing frustration over NATO's eastward expansion, China's deliberate strategy of exploiting globalisation to strengthen its own authoritarian regime, and the rising Islamist radicalisation in the Middle East demonstrated that the West's idealistic policies were not merely inadequate, but directly counterproductive. Thus, the foundations for the lost peace were already laid in the 1990s.

INTERLUDE

Denmark's development cooperation must form an integral part of an interest-based foreign policy. Anchored in the Sustainable Development Goals, Denmark should, through its development cooperation, invest in a world of progress and sustainable growth. This will benefit the Danish welfare state and business sector and help counter crises abroad that have direct consequences for security and prosperity in Denmark.

— Ambassador Peter Taksøe-Jensen, 2016[22]

How can perpetual peace best be secured? That question has presumably preoccupied decision-makers for as long as organised societies have existed. The expression "perpetual peace" itself, however, is first and foremost associated with the German philosopher Immanuel Kant, who in 1795 published a treatise entitled *Zum ewigen Frieden* (*Perpetual Peace*).[23]

If one is to simplify Kant's ideas, his main points are that the preconditions for lasting peace are national sovereignty, non-interference in the internal affairs of other states, the rule-of-law organisation of individual states, respect for human dignity, disarmament, free trade, and supranational cooperation. One need not be an expert in political science to recognise that these were remarkably farsighted ideas at the end of the eighteenth century.

The point of this brief detour is simple. Lasting peace is among the noblest goals a politician can pursue. But it is never enough to desire peace oneself; one must also reckon with the possibility that others do not share that ambition. Love and friendship require two willing parties. Discord requires only one.

In the academic circles in which Woodrow Wilson moved before entering politics, Kant's reflections on the foundations of peace were hardly obscure. They belonged to the educated background of the time—familiar even to scholars who were not Kant specialists, much as a working knowledge of Marx or Freud later became part of the intellectual air of the twentieth century.

It is therefore unlikely to be accidental that Wilson's Fourteen Points—the foundation of the American position in the negotiations that culminated in the Treaty of Versailles in 1919—echoed key elements of Kant's thinking.

The following of Wilson's points could almost have been written by Kant himself:

· Open diplomacy
· Freedom of the seas
· Free trade
· Disarmament
· Establishment of the League of Nations

And if one had combined the remaining nine points (which concerned the future of specific countries) into an overarching one called "national sovereignty," one could also claim that it derived directly from Kant.

I will not go into further detail about Kant's treatise on perpetual peace—only establish two things. First, that the very aim of a lasting peace is undoubtedly among the most worthy goals a politician can strive for. Second, that the notion that some form of supranational structure is necessary to secure that lasting peace comes close to having the finest pedigree any political-science idea could possibly have.

For that reason, I cannot at all subscribe to the assessment that there was anything wrong with the objectives that politicians in the 1990s set themselves, or with the means they regarded as best suited to achieving those objectives. A very broad cross-section of politicians from the Clinton era—himself included—wished to attain the old and venerable goal of lasting peace. And an equally broad cross-section—again with Clinton himself among them—believed that peace should be guaranteed by multilateral organisations that all countries could see an advantage in joining.

Nor was the idea that the UN could serve as a framework that gathered and focused efforts to create a better and more just world pulled out of thin air.

In 2000, a summit was held in New York that resulted in the so-called Millennium Declaration.[24] Here, all UN member states and 22 international organisations committed themselves to working to achieve eight goals by 2015.

The baseline against which progress was to be measured was 1990, and the eight goals were:

· Eradicate extreme poverty and hunger.
· Education for all.
· Promote gender equality.
· Reduce child mortality.
· Improve maternal health.

- Combat HIV/AIDS, malaria, and other diseases.
- Ensure environmental sustainability.
- Develop a global partnership for development.

When, fifteen years later, the UN took stock, the results looked like this:

- ***Poverty:*** The number of people living in extreme poverty (under USD 1.25 a day, later adjusted to USD 1.90) had fallen from 1.9 billion in 1990 to 836 million in 2015 (one should also recall that the world's population in the period rose from 5.3 billion to 7.4 billion. Measured as a share of the world's population, the decline is therefore drastic).

- ***Education:*** Primary-school enrolment increased from 83% in 2000 to 91% in 2015.

- ***Gender equality:*** Two thirds of developing countries achieved gender parity in primary education, and women's access to paid employment and political representation increased (though not to the Millennium target).

- ***Child mortality:*** Mortality among children under five fell from 90 to 43 deaths per 1,000 live births between 1990 and 2015—a reduction of 49% (some way short of the Millennium target, but a large drop nonetheless).

- ***Maternal health:*** Maternal mortality fell by 45% globally, with major progress in South Asia (a 64% reduction). Again a large drop, even if the Millennium target was not reached.

- ***Diseases:*** More than 6.2 million malaria deaths were averted between 2000 and 2015, and tuberculosis treatment saved an estimated 37 million lives between 2000 and 2013. The spread of HIV/AIDS was slowed, and access to treatment increased.

- ***Drinking water and sanitation:*** In 2010, the world reached the target of halving the proportion of people without access to clean drinking water, with 2.1 billion people gaining access to improved sanitation.

- ***Global partnership:*** Official development assistance rose by 66% between 2000 and 2014, and debt service in developing countries fell from 12% to 3% of export revenues. Access to the internet and mobile phones grew dramatically.

There are many reasons why the advances across the eight goals became as substantial as they did. But the economic growth that globalisation unleashed in parts of the world that had previously been very poor (for example China and India) was a strongly contributing reason why things went so well.

Before anyone makes sport of how great the hopes were that 1990s politicians attached to multilateral organisations like the UN—and to the socially beneficial side effects of globalisation—they should remember that for a long period after the end of the Cold War, experience and the cool numbers suggested that these were effective strategies for creating peace and a better world.

Imagine, for a moment, that someone from 2025 could step into a meeting room in 2000 or 2005 and say: "I'm from the future. We need to talk."

The reaction would be predictable. Charts would appear. Growth curves would be cited. The visitor would be told that the strategy was working. The numbers were sound.

The relevant question, however, would not concern the logic behind the policy, but the risks embedded in it. Not: *Why are you doing this?* But: *What is the worst that could happen within this framework?*

The answer might come quickly: "Worst case? This is globalisation. It benefits everyone."

"Perhaps," 2025 would reply. "But suppose participation is asymmetric. Suppose states enter the same system with different intentions—and different definitions of success."

Consider a dictatorship that joins the global order not to improve the lives of its citizens, but to accumulate wealth for a long-term military build-up. What would such a regime do? It would cooperate smoothly, attend every meeting, say the expected things, and avoid provoking suspicion—precisely to delay countermeasures. Stability would not be a shared goal, but a tactical instrument.

"But this is 2005," someone might object. "Great-power conflict is behind us."

"Is it?" the visitor from the future would ask. "Political grievances do not disappear simply because markets expand. Are you certain that no authoritarian regime harbors resentment—and the patience to act on it?"

That is the worst case. And the essential question is simple: if it began to unfold, would you recognise it in time—and know what to do?

We will stop the thought experiment here. A good way of approaching the UN's Millennium Development Goals is to consider the UN's current 17 Sustainable Development Goals, which were adopted in 2015.

If one is to be honest, a decisive part of the success of the Millennium Development Goals was not created by the UN. The fact that the number of people living in extreme poverty worldwide was more than halved over a period of 25 years—while the world's population grew by more than two billion people—was primarily the result of globalisation, for which the UN cannot claim credit. What made the decisive positive difference, in particular, was the integration of China and India into the global economy. This generated unprecedented economic growth in both countries, where sizeable middle classes now exist (although it is difficult to measure precisely how large they are). Contrary to what was commonly assumed in the 1990s, however, this development did not lead to overwhelming demands for democracy in China. Instead, India and China have become two of the world's largest emitters of CO_2 when measured in absolute terms.

In short: the future is difficult to predict. And one often ends up underestimating the side effects of the developments one observes.

That said, between 2000 and 2015 the UN underwent a transformation that deserves mention, even if it is uncomfortable to contemplate.

In 2015, the UN was just as effective at managing humanitarian disaster situations around the world as it has always been. Likewise, in 2015 (and still today), the UN was just as effective as it was in 2000 at establishing peacekeeping missions in those places where the Security Council can reach agreement.

However, the Security Council in 2015 was far more dysfunctional than it had been in 2000. By this I mean that Russia and China in particular had begun to block the Security Council from expressing criticism in situations where one of those two countries was itself violating the UN Charter. A clear example from precisely this period is the Chinese and Russian vetoes against UN statements critical of Russian involvement in the Syrian civil war.

It was not only the Security Council that had become more dysfunctional over the course of those fifteen years. By around 2015, the UN Human Rights Council had definitively been captured by countries that do not themselves respect human rights.

Added to this is the fact that the UN in 2015 was far more anti-Israeli than the UN in 2000. The tendency toward disproportionate criticism of Israel that flourishes in full bloom today was already pronounced in 2015.

The long and the short of it is that the Security Council today is paralysed by raw great-power politics to such an extent that it is legitimate to question whether it fulfils its most basic purpose at all. Likewise, significant parts of the UN have been captured by agendas that run directly counter to the intentions that lay behind the creation of the organisation in the immediate aftermath of the Second World War.

And with that, we arrive at the core of my criticism of the Western elites in this book.

There is nothing wrong with setting the goal of lasting peace. On the contrary, it is a noble ambition. Nor is there anything wrong, at a given moment in time, with imagining that the UN might be an appropriate means of achieving this goal.

My critique throughout the book is more specific: one must—especially when at the head of a government or a major multilateral organisation—constantly remain alert to signs that the assumptions underpinning the chosen policy are beginning to erode. And one must—especially when holding a position of trust—always be ready to act and revise one's plans if those assumptions are breaking down. Everyone has the right to become wiser. One might wish that more people exercised that right.

What went particularly wrong for the Western countries after the year 2000 was that, for a variety of reasons that I will attempt to uncover in the remainder of the book, they continued to trust their map of the world. This was despite the fact that the terrain the map purported to represent was quite evidently undergoing dramatic change.

If the map does not match the terrain, the terrain prevails. Anyone who has used GPS understands this. If the screen shows you in the middle of nowhere while you are plainly driving on a new motorway, the reasonable conclusion is not that the landscape has disguised itself. It is that your navigation system needs updating.

Yet this is precisely where most Western decision-makers increasingly failed in the years between 2000 and the second Russian invasion of Ukraine in 2022.

The brief vignette placed above the text of this interlude illustrates my critique. It is taken from a report on Danish foreign policy commissioned by the newly appointed government in 2015 and delivered the following year.

Read with the knowledge one possesses in 2025, it is illusory to imagine that the world towards 2030 will be shaped by a constructive UN in which countries jointly work their way towards the UN's Sustainable Development Goals.

Basing one's criticism on hindsight is, however, not fair. I will therefore refrain from doing so. The problem with the quotation is something else: it was already illusory to imagine this in 2016.

At that point, nine years had passed since Vladimir Putin had thrown down the gauntlet to the Western countries in Munich. Four years had passed since Xi Jinping came to power in China, and three years since he announced the Belt and Road Initiative. The Security Council had long since demonstrated its dysfunctionality, as confirmed by Russia's involvement in the Syrian civil war. The resemblance between, in particular, China's instrumental use of multilateral organisations and the Trojan horse had become increasingly evident. And last, but not least, there were clearly rising internal tensions within Europe, stemming both from the mismanagement of the financial crisis and from the consequences of migration from the Middle East.

Against the background of such developments—which were not secret, but reported in all news media—there was no reason to recommend that the Danish government place its trust in a constructive UN in which large and small countries alike pulled on the same humanistic rope towards the year 2030.

A better piece of advice, for which there was already ample justification in 2016, would have been to set the geo-economic paradigm against the geo-strategic one and, on that basis, to point out the major risks embedded in geo-economic thinking.

Who wins in a confrontation between geo-economics and geo-strategy? This Socratic question ought to have been posed by an experienced adviser not only to the Danish government, but to any Western government.

From both a political and a humanistic perspective, it would have been better for all parties if the world on which the government's advice was based in 2016 had actually existed. But it did not—and policy should have been shaped accordingly.

Chapter 3

CRUSADES AND ILLUSIONS

One can wage a war alone; it is far more difficult to create peace alone.

—Jacques Chirac, 2003[25]

In this chapter, I examine the West's strategic misjudgments in the period following the terrorist attacks of September 11, 2001. As is well known, the response to the attacks took the form of a series of failed interventions that ultimately contributed to a weakening of the West on a global scale.

In the aftermath of September 11, the United States and the coalition against terror first launched the war in Afghanistan and later the invasion of Iraq. Both wars were initially regarded as necessary and legitimate attempts to combat global terrorism and to spread democratic values.

What I will argue is that the optimism and idealism of the Western countries were, in both cases, quickly confronted by realities for which they were wholly unprepared. While the missions were initially perceived as military successes, they therefore developed into protracted conflicts characterised by chaos, anarchy, and a profound lack of understanding of local cultural, social, and political structures.

The decisions to go to war were based on faulty assumptions, inadequate analyses, and an exaggerated belief that democratic institutions could be exported and embedded by military means. The invasion of Iraq in particular caused deep divisions within the West and seriously undermined Western legitimacy. This was further compounded by the revelations that weapons of mass destruction did not exist and by the subsequent destabilisation of the region.

Finally, the chapter highlights how the wars in Afghanistan and Iraq radicalised parts of the Islamic world and contributed to strengthening the West's geopolitical rivals, especially Iran. The result was a dramatic weakening of the West's position in the Middle East and globally, clearly illustrating the consequences of unrealistic political decisions and a lack of strategic insight.

The short century

Eric Hobsbawm, whom we encountered in the previous chapter, famously held the view that the twentieth century lasted only from the dissolution of "the Europe of the Congress of Vienna" in 1914 until the collapse of the Soviet Union in 1991—that is, a century of just seventy-seven years.

But when—if one accepts Hobsbawm's line of reasoning—did the twenty-first century begin? Many would probably be inclined to answer: September 11, 2001.

On that day, the terrorist movement al-Qaeda attacked the United States using four hijacked passenger aircraft. Two struck Towers One and Two of the World Trade Center. A third hit the

U.S. Department of Defense, the Pentagon. The fourth crashed into a field in Pennsylvania after passengers overpowered the terrorists. Nearly three thousand people lost their lives—the greatest loss of American lives in a single day since the Second World War.

It subsequently became clear that the American state of preparedness had been both inadequate and chaotic. Part of the explanation can be found in *Against All Enemies*[26] by Richard A. Clarke, who advised both the Clinton and Bush administrations on terrorism.

Among specialists such as Clarke, al-Qaeda had already attracted attention in the mid-1990s. This concern intensified on October 12, 2000, when the organisation attacked the American destroyer USS *Cole* in the port of Aden in Yemen, killing seventeen and wounding thirty-nine. Yet for a variety of reasons, no one had really sat down and devised a comprehensive plan to counter the threat.

The fundamental problem up to and including September 11, 2001, was that the American counterterrorism effort was fragmented. Fragmentation will always hinder decision-making. According to a simple management principle that many are taught at the very beginning of their leadership careers: if everyone is responsible, then no one is responsible.

In addition, Clarke argues that Clinton was the only president who took counterterrorism seriously, and that the FBI and CIA not only struggled to take the threats seriously, but also struggled to cooperate with one another.

Finally, the effectiveness of the intelligence services and the establishment of a coherent preparedness system were hardly helped by the relatively chaotic presidential transition at the turn of 2000–2001.

One might say that Clarke's book is the expanded and consolidated version of the testimony he gave to the 9/11 Commission in March 2004. It is therefore in that testimony that one finds his critique in its most condensed form:

> *Although there were people in the FBI, CIA, Defense Department, State Department, and White House who worked very hard to destroy al Qida before it did catastrophic damage to the US, there were many others who found the prospect of significant al Qida attacks remote. In both CIA and the military there was reluctance at senior career levels to fully utilize all of the capabilities available. There was risk aversion. FBI was, througthout much of this period, organized, staffed, and equipped in such a way that it was ineffective in dealing with the domestic terrorist threat from al Qida. At the senior policy levels in the Clinton Administration, there was an acute understanding of the terrorist threat, particularly al Qida.*[27]

In accordance with the security doctrines developed during the 1990s, the United States and the United Kingdom attacked Afghanistan as early as October 2001, where al-Qaeda, with the acquiescence of the Taliban regime, maintained its most important bases. Within about a month, the coalition succeeded in defeating the Taliban, and in December 2001 a new transitional government was established under the leadership of Hamid Karzai. According to the plan, this government was to form the foundation of a democratic Afghanistan. Osama bin Laden, however, was not captured; nearly ten years would pass before he was neutralized in a special operation in Pakistan.

The war in Afghanistan ultimately lasted around twenty years, making it the longest war in U.S. history. At the same time, it is difficult to identify any criteria that would justify describing it as a success.

Did the war weaken international terrorism? One cannot say

that it did. Did it weaken international jihadism? Nor can that be credibly claimed. Did Afghanistan become an example of how democratic reforms can be imposed in a country outside the political West? Absolutely not. The war ended with the Taliban's return to power in 2021, resuming where they had left off twenty years earlier.

Finally, the war—together with the invasion of Iraq and the civil war in Syria—led to a decisive strengthening of Iran's position in the Middle East, while Western influence was reduced to a corresponding degree.

However one turns the matter, the attack on the World Trade Center in 2001 thus ended up inflicting on the Western countries one of the greatest—if not the single greatest—strategic defeats of the first thirty years after victory in the Cold War.

There is a straight and unbroken line from the poorly conceived and inadequately analyzed counterattack against al-Qaeda in 2001 to the present situation, in which Western influence throughout the Middle East is at a historic low. I suspect we would have to go back to the heyday of the Ottoman Empire to find a time when the West had as little capacity to assert itself in the Middle East as it does today.

The savage wars of peace

The conclusion drawn in Western capitals in the aftermath of the Cold War throughout the 1990s was, first, that the Western countries had no peers as adversaries, and second, that they possessed both a moral right and a moral duty to spread democracy to all parts of the world—primarily through free trade, but, if necessary, also by means of armed force.

It is in this light that one must view the first years after the invasion of Afghanistan. Following the fall of the Taliban regime in 2001, the doctrine held that a well-functioning democracy should be established in the country—both by building the fundamental state institutions of a parliamentary democracy (such as a parliament, a judiciary, and a central administration) and by developing softer social institutions such as schools and secondary education.

But was this a carefully considered and realistic strategy? I have taken a line from Rudyard Kipling's 1899 poem "The White Man's Burden"[28] as the heading for this section to suggest an answer: *the savage wars of peace.*

Even more than a hundred years after Kipling wrote his poem, the Western countries were still more naïve and unreflective than the British imperialists had been. There is nothing to suggest that, in the early 2000s, Western countries doubted that it was possible to impose democratisation on a non-Western country operating on entirely different premises from, for example, the former Warsaw Pact states.

Unlike the Western elites of the 2000s, Kipling understood very well that the imperial project was fragile. The populations of the areas subjected to Western control had by no means been waiting for Westerners to arrive. On the contrary, they were often fierce opponents of foreign intervention—even in cases where they benefited from Western technology or Western medicine. This "ingratitude," as Kipling saw it, was inseparable from imperialism and therefore a fact that should have been taken into account from the very beginning.

The reasons for this resistance should either have been obvious to the Western elites by virtue of their education, or they should have asked experts to explain them.

First, local elites in a given non-Western country have no interest in relinquishing or sharing power with external actors. They will almost always ask themselves the very relevant question: why should we?

Second, Western thinking challenges the "micro-power" exercised within families and local communities—power that cannot simply be ignored, regardless of one's moral judgment of it. Of course, there were people in a country like Afghanistan who sincerely supported Western values. But we must also be honest: such people do not constitute a majority in Afghanistan. They are relatively isolated small groups, and moreover must be considered highly vulnerable precisely because they are minorities.

What incentive would typically patriarchal men have to give up power over their family or local community? Again, not because their exercise of power should be morally praised, but in order to remain entirely sober and realistic about the exercise and relinquishment of power. The answer is that patriarchally minded men in, for example, Afghanistan have absolutely no incentive to surrender their power to an abstract legal order with impersonal institutions. It makes no sense to them—regardless of the narratives that can be constructed from a Western perspective about what they ought to believe.

Since the Western countries in the 2000s did not see themselves as imperialists—and since few among the various elites were likely reading Kipling—only very few people in the middle of the decade foresaw that the mission in Afghanistan would end in total failure fifteen years down the line.

My home country was no exception as far as Western optimism is concerned. In June 2005, for example, the Danish government submitted Report R 12 to the Danish Parliament, entitled "On the Effort Against Terrorism." It stated:

> *A positive and democratic development in Iraq and Afghanistan will be an important contribution to combating terrorism in the longer term. The government will therefore strengthen the effort in Afghanistan and continue the effort in Iraq with increased focus on training Iraqi security forces and supporting civilian reconstruction.*[29]

The same line of thinking appeared two years later, when the Danish government, in Report R 16, reused the wording from 2005 and wrote: *A positive and democratic development in Iraq and Afghanistan will be important contributions to limiting terrorism in the longer term.*[30]

The foreign minister who presented both reports was Per Stig Møller—an extremely competent and conscientious politician. How he could lend his name to these formulations is, however, puzzling. Even in 2005 and 2007, it should not have been difficult for a figure of his calibre to realise that the opposite was true: the cause of the wave of terrorism that swept through Europe was the Western countries' attempts at forced democratisation and forced Westernisation of Afghanistan and Iraq.

Turning to Per Stig Møller's memoirs[31], written a full decade later, one finds something resembling the explanation that ought to have been offered in the mid-2000s. The truth—now clearly visible—is that the democratisation of Afghanistan was a far more fragile project than the reports suggested. In the section "To Helmand" (pp. 47–54), for example, a recurring theme is Møller's inability to determine whether Afghanistan's president, Hamid Karzai, could be trusted at all. At that time, a case had arisen in Afghanistan that cast doubt on Karzai's genuine willingness to introduce freedom of expression (p. 52).

The case concerned a journalist who had been sentenced to death. After intense international pressure, he was eventually released. But Denmark's foreign minister found himself privately doubting whether Afghanistan's president was in fact part of the country's political progress—or whether, on the contrary, he represented the preservation of the old order.

This episode, brought to light almost ten years after it occurred, is a good example of something we have discussed earlier. There will always be more intermediate calculations and arguments for and against than can be discerned from what ultimately becomes a government's official line.

Nevertheless, the Danish government's official line in the second half of the 2000s was the same as in most of the rest of the West: the prerequisite for limiting terrorism was the establishment of peace and democracy in Afghanistan and Iraq.

Nothing could have been more wrong. One of the most important causes of terrorism in the second half of the 2000s was precisely the Western countries' attempt—if not by sheer brute force, then at least by heavy-handed means—to impose democracy on Afghanistan and Iraq.

Western unity put to the test

Already in the days following September 11, 2001, a notion took hold among President George W. Bush and his inner circle that Iraq's dictator, Saddam Hussein, was the true mastermind behind the attacks. Richard A. Clarke explained—both during the question-and-answer session of his testimony before the 9/11 Commission and in his memoirs—that he unsuccessfully attempted to refute this misconception.

Here is an exchange from the Commission's eighth hearing:

Mr. ROEMER: *Mr. Clarke, is it accurate that on September 12th, 2001, senior officials—up to and including the President—asked you*

> *to find evidence that Iraq was behind the attacks?*
> ***Mr. CLARKE:*** *Yes, sir. The President asked me to "check whether Saddam was involved." I looked again at all the intelligence from CIA, FBI, NSA. There was absolutely no evidence of Iraqi involvement. I drafted a memo stating, "There is no evidence whatsoever linking Iraq to 9/11." The memo came back from the White House with a note that read, "Please update and resubmit." I resubmitted the same conclusion—and I continued to warn that pursuing Iraq would divert resources from the fight against al-Qaeda.*[32]

The inner circle around president Bush was strongly influenced by so-called neoconservatism. Among other things, it held the view that the United States possessed a moral right to intervene in conflicts anywhere in the world—particularly for the purpose of removing dictators and introducing democracy. The doctrine reflected a deeper belief that U.S. foreign policy should be driven not merely by *Realpolitik* but also by higher ideals aimed at promoting American values (which were regarded as universal).

With regard to Saddam Hussein, the gravest (but erroneous) accusation was that the regime under his leadership had developed weapons of mass destruction and was therefore a constant source of regional instability. In addition, the U.S. government—as noted—also held the equally erroneous belief that Saddam Hussein had been behind the attacks of September 11, 2001, and was in general the mastermind of global terrorism. By removing Saddam Hussein, one could thus both eliminate a major regional problem and promote the spread of democracy in the Middle East.

In the run-up to the war, the U.S. administration attempted to assemble a coalition as broad as the one behind the invasion of Afghanistan. That effort failed. France and Germany refused to take part in an attack on Iraq. The United Kingdom joined the coalition, a decision that ultimately created deep divisions within the country.

On the surface, the invasion of Iraq looked like a success. In March 2003 the operation began. The following month the capital, Baghdad, fell. And on May 1, president Bush could declare that the Iraq mission had been accomplished.

It soon became clear, however, that the experienced French president Chirac had been right: peace is the problem—not starting a war.

One of the factors that made withdrawal from Iraq most difficult was the catastrophic decision, in practice, to dissolve the entire Iraqi state apparatus. No decision of such sweeping scope had been taken even with regard to Germany in 1945. There, the state retained its basic structure at the local and regional levels, because the primary focus was on purging Nazis from the very top of the state apparatus.

The dissolution of the Iraqi state apparatus quickly led to anarchy. Local militias formed—both on the basis of clan structures and along religious lines (Sunni versus Shia). Moreover, Iran seized the obvious opportunity to infiltrate Iraqi society and shape it according to its own agendas.

From mid-2003, Iraq was therefore gripped by a chaos that the United States and the coalition of the willing, on the one hand, could not ignore and, on the other, could not defeat.

Matters were not improved by the rapid realisation that there were no weapons of mass destruction in Iraq. That fact—together with the revelations of torture at Abu Ghraib prison—stripped the war of any legitimacy in Western countries over the course of 2004.

In the West, the invasion of Iraq ultimately became extremely controversial. Yet it did not put an end to the ideology that the West had a moral duty to uphold the politically liberal order everywhere in the world. Accordingly, albeit far more cautiously, heavily armed peacekeeping forces continued to be deployed to global hotspots. *The savage wars of peace.*

I have always been of the view that opposition to the invasion of Iraq was not always driven by the highest principles. That view was confirmed when I read Angela Merkel's memoirs[33].

As Merkel presents Gerhard Schröder's opposition to the Iraq war (pp. 272–274), it essentially stemmed from an attempt to win the 2002 Bundestag election. Whereas Schröder's foreign minister, the Green Party's Joschka Fischer, was not averse to a war backed by a UN mandate, Schröder quickly realised that in fundamentally pacifist Germany there were votes—and thus an electoral victory—to be gained by rejecting any participation in war outright.

Angela Merkel opposed such a categorical stance. In her view, it risked creating the impression—particularly in Moscow—that divisions had opened up within NATO and the EU. She later acknowledged that she made a mistake in publishing an article in *The Washington Post* distancing herself from Schröder and his attempt to draw a sharper transatlantic line.

In her memoirs, Merkel concludes that the Iraq War was ultimately a mistake. Yet she also suggests—indirectly—that Schröder's opposition proved justified, even if his underlying rationale was open to question.

This passage in Merkel's memoirs underscores that individuals matter. If we assume counterfactually that Merkel had been chancellor in 2002–03, her own statements suggest that there is considerable reason to believe she would, albeit reluctantly, have joined the Iraq war.

The Western self-conception—that it had a duty to make peace and introduce democracy everywhere in the world—persisted for many years after the invasion of Iraq had, to all but the most obstinate observers, plainly failed. This was followed by missions to, among other places, Libya, Iraq (again), and Mali.

The war—though obviously far less tragic than the loss of life it caused—ultimately destroyed the political legacies of two men: Colin Powell and Tony Blair. Powell expressed regret until his death that he had presented false claims about Iraqi weapons of mass destruction. Blair, who had come to office in 1997 on a wave of enthusiasm more often associated with rock stars than politicians, saw the last of his political aura dissipate.

One might reasonably argue that "New Labour" began to unravel with the invasion of Iraq—and that the defeat by the Conservatives in 2010 was merely the final act in a decline set in motion seven years earlier.

The Muhammad Cartoon Crisis

The repercussions of Middle East policy in the 2000s extended well beyond the immediate theatre of war. They reshaped political climates, public discourse, and relations between states. The Muhammad Cartoon Crisis stands as a particularly telling example.

In 2005 it emerged that no Danish cartoonists wished to illustrate a book about the life of Muhammad planned by the author Kåre Bluitgen. That information provoked the newspaper *Jyllands-Posten* to commission twelve drawings of the Prophet (who, according to many interpretations of Islam, is forbidden to depict).

The publication of the drawings immediately attracted international attention. Yet a request from the Egyptian ambassador for a meeting with the prime minister was flatly rejected. The Danish government was unyielding.

Initially, the scandal subsided. But half a year later—in early 2006—it flared up again. A group of Islamic clerics from Denmark had travelled around the Middle East spreading misinformation about what had actually occurred. As a result, among other things, the Danish embassy in Damascus was attacked by demonstrators.

The wars in Afghanistan and Iraq, together with the publication of the Muhammad cartoons, contributed to triggering a radicalisation throughout the Middle East. In many places in the region, the narrative became that Western countries harbored a hatred of Islam and did not hesitate to back it with military force. This, in turn, ignited a perceived righteous anger among jihadists worldwide, who in the years that followed infiltrated Western countries and carried out one terrorist attack after another.

What was—and remains—striking is that refined Western arguments about principles and values bounced entirely off Middle Eastern publics.

In fact, during the 1990s—as already noted—the Western countries had used military force to prevent Christian Serbs from attacking Muslim Bosniaks and Kosovo Albanians in the former Yugoslavia. The reasons were noble and humanitarian: innocent civilians whom one had a civilisational and constitutional duty to protect. Likewise, also in the 1990s, Western countries reinstated the lawful authority in Kuwait on the basis of purely constitutional considerations—namely respect for the territorial integrity of sovereign states.

That Western countries thus acted on abstract principles without regard to the standing of individuals has always been a completely wasted insight if one followed the news flow in Middle Eastern media. There, it is always about "us" versus "them" along religious lines. The wars of the 2000s led to a massive militarisation of the Western world's relationship with the Middle East—and a corresponding dismantling of Western soft power in the region.

Finally, they led to a growth in global jihadism and terrorism that is impossible to ignore. It was dynamics unleashed by the Muhammad cartoons that in 2015 led to the attack on *Charlie Hebdo* in Paris. Likewise, it was directly the issue of the cartoons and the right to free expression that led to the murder of the French teacher Samuel Paty in 2020.

Russia

Because most Western countries throughout the 2000s were preoccupied with wars in the Middle East that increasingly went off the rails, many capitals failed to notice that Russia, over the course of the decade, veered away from the path toward democracy and moved onto another—one leading toward autocracy. In broad terms, it unfolded as follows.

On the last day of the 1990s—31 December 1999—Boris Yeltsin stepped down. He pointed to Vladimir Putin as his successor. Putin was formally elected President of Russia on 26 March 2000.

In the first years of his presidency, Vladimir Putin's primary focus was on restoring Russia's economy. But he also worked to centralise power. This involved tighter control of the media and a confrontation with those wealthy magnates who did not immediately bow to Putin—for example the oil tycoon Mikhail Khodorkovsky.

Around the middle of the decade, however, something happened that fundamentally changed Russia's perspective on its dealings with Western countries.

In 2003, a revolution broke out in the former Soviet republic of Georgia. It arose from the belief that Eduard Shevardnadze—Gorbachev's former foreign minister, who had in the meantime become president in his home country—had cheated his way to victory in the presidential election.

After large protests—symbolised by a red rose—a new presidential election was held in early 2004. It was won by Mikheil Saakashvili, who wanted Georgia to move closer to the EU and NATO.

The revolution in Georgia was the first of the so-called colour revolutions that involved former Soviet republics. The next took place in Ukraine in 2004.

The cause there was the election fraud that had given the pro-Russian presidential candidate Viktor Yanukovych victory in the presidential election. The protests culminated in Ukraine's Supreme Court annulling the election. In the rerun, closely monitored by international observers, the pro-Western candidate Viktor Yushchenko won. He wanted closer ties both to the EU and to NATO.

In the West, the narrative has always been that the colour revolutions in Georgia and Ukraine were a kind of delayed 1989. After the former Warsaw Pact countries had broken free of Soviet influence, the turn had now come to the former Soviet republics.

In Russia, the colour revolutions are not interpreted in any way resembling the Western interpretation. The Russian narrative in the state-controlled media is that both Shevardnadze and Yanukovych were brought down because the West interfered in the internal affairs of Georgia and Ukraine.

It is important to recall that, in Russian strategic thinking, interference in what Moscow calls its *"near abroad"* is treated as a grave matter. Countries in this region are not regarded as fully external to Russia's security perimeter, but as falling within a privileged sphere of interest.

According to doctrines that shaped Soviet foreign and security policy—and that continue to inform policy under Vladimir Putin—external involvement in the near abroad is perceived as tantamount to interference in Russia's own internal affairs. The underlying premise is clear: within this sphere, Russia claims a special right of influence, and denies that right to others.

The colour revolutions were perceived in the Kremlin as an obvious and direct threat to Russia's status as a regional great power. They therefore became the beginning of the rupture with the West that was consummated in Munich in 2007.

At first, Vladimir Putin began to mourn the dissolution of the Soviet Union in a way the outside world had not heard before. In a public speech in Moscow in 2005[34] he stated directly that the collapse of the Soviet Union had been the greatest geopolitical catastrophe of the twentieth century.

Here Putin broke with the sense of national humiliation that had characterised the first years after the dissolution of the Soviet Union. He pointed directly to Russia's past as a source of pride—and thus indirectly signalled that he would work to carry forward the legacy of the Soviet Union. Finally, the message also contained an appeal to the Russian diaspora around the former Soviet empire: you shall not be forgotten.

I do not think one can blame decision-makers at the time who, in the middle of hectic daily life filled with bad news from the wars in both Afghanistan and Iraq, failed to give the speech the attention that one can see, much later, that it deserved.

But in the offices that house the layer of historical specialists and country specialists, one probably should have drafted a memo about the minority question. When all was said and done, German minorities across Central Europe had, three quarters of a century earlier, been a formidable lever for the Third Reich when it came to intervening in, for example, Czechoslovakia and Poland.

At the security-policy conference in Munich in February 2007[35], Vladimir Putin was even clearer in his speech.

He criticised the unipolar, US-dominated world order and accused the United States—and the rest of the West—of double standards. Normally, Western countries cared deeply about the rules-based international order. But when it suited them—Kosovo, Iraq—they did not care and attacked without a mandate from, for example, the UN.

Very concretely, Vladimir Putin criticised the fact that NATO had expanded way too far eastward, and that, in Russia's eyes, this constituted a provocation. Therefore, he argued, the time had come for a new, multipolar world order. Here one must recall that when the NATO–Russia Council was established in 2002, Vladimir Putin had said the opposite: there was no contradiction between NATO's activities and Russia's interests.

At the NATO summit in Bucharest in April 2008 it was clear that not everyone in the West had grasped the seriousness of the Munich speech the year before. The US government wanted to offer Ukraine and Georgia a Membership Action Plan so that the two countries could become full members of NATO.

France and Germany, however, declared themselves opposed—presumably because they preferred economic engagement and prosperity at home over the security of Ukraine and Georgia. Therefore the final compromise from the summit read as follows:

> *NATO welcomes Ukraine's and Georgia's Euro-Atlantic aspirations for membership in NATO. We agreed today that these countries will become members of NATO.*[36]

With regard to Ukraine, it must be said that by offering NATO membership, the Bush administration sought to honor the commitments undertaken in the 1994 Budapest Memorandum. Under that agreement, Ukraine, in exchange for security guarantees from the United States, the United Kingdom, and Russia, was to relinquish its legacy nuclear weapons from the Soviet era. As is well known, Russia later reneged one hundred percent on its commitments and attacked Ukraine militarily. The United States and the United Kingdom fulfilled theirs only hesitantly and inadequately. In 2008, Ukraine could have been spared the suffering it is enduring today. But shabby compromises prevailed—as so often before, and since—over principles and solemn promises.

After the NATO summit in Bucharest, Russia did not waste time. Over the summer, it contrived an emergency involving Russian minorities in South Ossetia and Abkhazia (the two northernmost Georgian provinces bordering Russia). In Russia's view, this justified an invasion of northern Georgia and the occupation of the two provinces, which continues to this day.

At the latest after the Munich speech in 2007 and the invasion of Georgia in 2008, it should have been clear to all decision-makers that the dream of a peaceful Russia gradually integrating into the rules-based and globalised world order was over.

For example, in 2008 Robert Kagan published *The Return of History and the End of Dreams*. In the book's introduction he wrote:

> *The economic and ideological determinism of the early post-Cold War years produced two broad assumptions that shaped both policies and expectations. One was an abiding belief in the inevitability of human progress, the belief that history moves in only one direction – a faith born in the Enlightenment, dashed by the brutality of the twentieth century, but given new life by the fall of communism. The other was a prescription for patience and restraint. Rather than confront and challenge autocracies, it was better to enmesh them in the global economy, support the rule of law and the creation of stronger state institutions, and let the ineluctable forces of human progress work their magic.*[37]

The author then examined how nationalism was in the process of reshaping the unipolar world order. Russia was rising. China was rising. Japan was rising. India was rising. And Iran was on its way to becoming a regional great power.

One could not imagine an alliance among all these countries (even though many of them shared a pronounced skepticism toward the West), but Kagan warned in particular against one: Russia and China.

Here were two autocracies that were decidedly not on a path toward democracy, and that had a clear incentive to cooperate in breaking the Western monopoly on power—a monopoly Putin had already criticised in Munich in 2007.

Kagan's book was above all an appeal to the United States and the Western countries to face the new realities. Without ideological blinders, but with real-political realism. He also argued, however, that like-minded democratic countries had every advantage in standing together in defence of their values.

Should Western countries have been more skeptical of Russia at the end of the 2000s?

This question cannot be answered in any other way than with a yes. By the end of the 2000s, all the necessary information was available to justify a strategic reorientation by the Western countries. Vladimir Putin had explicitly protested against the world order that emerged after the end of the Cold War and declared his intention to resist it. He had put action behind his words in Munich by invading Georgia. And Robert Kagan—one of the most influential thinkers listened to at the time in the White House—had explained what the deeper problem was.

It is genuinely difficult—even when one tries to leave out of account the knowledge of how history turned out—to understand why there was such confidence, particularly in the EU, that the right doctrine toward Russia had been found by focusing on shared participation in multilateral organisations and on trade and energy.

I myself travelled with the Foreign Policy Committee to Murmansk and Moscow in March 2017. There, the Putin regime showed itself at its worst by detaining and expelling a Norwegian member of our delegation at the border crossing near Kirkenes. Nevertheless, the official Danish position—expressed by Denmark's ambassador—was that when there was so much to cooperate on (illustrated by a wide embrace), one should not focus on disagreements (illustrated by the distance between a thumb and an index finger).

This took place three years after the first invasion of Ukraine. And it does not suggest that there had been any serious revision of Denmark's stance toward Russia within the Danish Ministry of Foreign Affairs since Russia became a member of the G7 in 1998.

As for the United States, the situation was more complicated. As is well known, Barack Obama won the presidential election in 2008 and was inaugurated in January 2009. During his presidency, partisan politics came to exert a significant influence on the U.S. government's approach to Russia.

In the Republican Party there was, in fact, a growing realisation that Russia posed a major problem for the global order and for security in the regions bordering Russia. But thinking was entirely different in the Democratic Party. There, there was firm conviction that globalisation was here to stay and that its underlying economic and political assumptions remained valid. Thus, while Republican politicians such as Mitt Romney and John McCain increasingly warned against Russia throughout the 2010s, Obama and the Democratic Party dismissed this as outdated thinking from before the fall of the Wall.

It is striking how two different ideologies—namely, the Clinton-era faith in globalisation and the Bush-era neoconservatism—guided the United States along roughly the same foreign and security policy trajectory for two decades: history was moving toward ever wider diffusion of both economic and political liberalism, possibly with the United States and the Western countries acting as midwives if the labor proved prolonged.

From Barack Obama onward, one can once again discern a partisan difference between Democrats and Republicans in U.S. foreign and security policy. Unfortunately, power from 2009 to 2017 lay with the party that had the weakest understanding of the new world order implied by the increasingly close alliance between Russia and China—and by the continued advance of jihadism.

China

In his book on the restart of history from 2008, Robert Kagan describes something others have also observed: it is—and remains—a geopolitical problem when new and rising great powers seek to carve out space for themselves among their peers.

One saw this in the nineteenth century, when a unified Germany sought "a place in the sun," as it was called in German political discourse at the time. And one saw it in the twentieth century, when the Soviet Union struggled to be recognised as a great power on a par with the United States after the Second World War.

The problem is banal enough: established great powers never wish to cede any of their power and prestige to others. Consequently, the position of rising powers is always something they must fight for.

In China, those in power often speak of the "century of humiliation"—the roughly hundred years from the First Opium War in 1839 to the revolution in 1949. China's actual rise begins with the Nixon administration's opening in 1971, which, among other things, made China a permanent member of the UN Security Council, and above all with the reforms Deng Xiaoping initiated a few years after Mao Zedong's death in 1976.

In explaining the restart of history, Kagan notes, among other things, how China throughout the 2000s expanded its military—and most strikingly its naval power. For Kagan, this indicated that the country did not accept the geo-economic thinking underpinning globalisation. He saw the proof in the Taiwan question. For a geo-economically minded state, it would be immaterial whether an independent government sat in Taipei or not—as long as trade continued and there was economic growth. But that was manifestly not how the leadership in Beijing viewed matters. Instead, it thought in old-fashioned geopolitical terms: the island is ours; therefore it must be governed from the country's capital.

China's open marriage with the WTO

In keeping with the geo-economic thinking of the era, China was admitted to the World Trade Organisation (WTO) in 2001. The motivation was the widespread belief that, once integrated into the world economy, China would not only contribute to higher global economic growth, but would also gradually converge toward economic and political liberalism.

But China never was—and has never previously been—a good-faith actor. Let us take this from the beginning. Under WTO rules, China is obliged to comply with the same copyright and intellectual-property regulations that apply in the West. It never has.

Instead, the country has engaged in large-scale piracy of software, films, and music, as well as the manufacture of counterfeit branded goods. This has led to multiple cases brought by the United States and the EU against China through the WTO system.

Under WTO rules, China is also required to refrain from export restrictions and price dumping. This, too, has resulted in lawsuits filed by the United States and the EU.

Still under WTO rules, China is obliged to refrain from granting state aid to Chinese companies. This rule has likewise not been observed.

China has discriminated against foreign firms seeking to operate in China by forcing technology transfer.

China has placed obstacles in the way of foreign firms through an opaque regulatory regime that at times appears outright arbitrary—also prohibited under WTO rules.

China has manipulated the value of its currency—again, not permitted under WTO rules—and has denied a number of Western companies access to the Chinese market, which is likewise prohibited.

In short, throughout the 2000s China behaved as anything but a good-faith actor. On the contrary, it acted in a manner that unilaterally abused its WTO privileges without any intention of complying with the rules or honoring the principle of reciprocity that underpins all agreements.

Why, then, did Western countries tolerate China's behaviour throughout that decade? The answer, I suspect, is disarmingly simple: greed. If one happens to make a living—say—by producing chocolate bars, the prospect of selling just one at a profit of ten pence to every Chinese citizen is so enticing that many are tempted to suspend their better judgement.

The South China Sea

As early as 1947, the Republic of China advanced the absurd claim that virtually the entire South China Sea constituted Chinese territorial waters. The claim is absurd because of the sea's vast extent: it stretches from China in the north to Indonesia in the south, and from Vietnam in the west to the Philippines in the east. There are no rational grounds for asserting that China should enjoy a prescriptive monopoly over the exploitation of this enormous body of water.

Nevertheless, China sharpened its claim throughout the 1990s, among other things by occupying the reef known as Mischief Reef. And during the 2000s, Chinese claims appeared to accelerate further.

In 2002, China concluded a treaty with the ASEAN countries concerning the South China Sea, committing the parties to resolve conflicts peacefully and to refrain from aggressive actions or actions that might upset the balance in the maritime area.

Even so, in subsequent years China intensified its military patrols of the area, and in 2007 submitted an official note to the UN reiterating its claim to territorial rights over nearly the entire sea. With regard to the South China Sea, the decade ended in 2009 with China submitting a document to the UN Commission on the Limits of the Continental Shelf in which it reused the old so-called "nine-dash line"—the 1953 replacement for the 1947 "eleven-dash line"—to delineate its territorial claims.

After 2010, China's conduct in the South China Sea has only worsened, despite being in direct contradiction to the UN Convention on the Law of the Sea, which China itself has signed. The Convention stipulates that no country may appropriate the high seas or other countries' exclusive economic zones.

As with the WTO, throughout the 2000s it was evident in the

maritime legal domain that China—like the United States at times—regarded itself as an exceptional country not required to respect agreements it had freely entered into.

Time and again during the decade, China demonstrated that agreements are something to be entered into cynically in order to obtain advantages one has no intention of reciprocating. As a Danish businessman living in Beijing once put it to me: when a Chinese partner says "win-win," it means you get slapped on both sides of the head and lose twice.

The same question as before: why does everyone seemingly tolerate this? Again, I suspect that in most cases it is due to greed—by now also combined with a sense of impotence. China is an enormous country that does not give up and is not haunted by the kinds of criticism, self-criticism, and scruples that invariably characterise public debate in a Western country.

Chinese soft power in Africa

Nevertheless, China exercises considerable soft power in Africa. I experienced this personally during a visit to Mali in 2009.

The week before I arrived in the capital, Bamako, China's then leader Hu Jintao had paid a state visit. Everywhere in Bamako there were still posters celebrating Sino-Malian friendship. And as I delved further into the matter, I discovered that Hu had, of course, brought a host gift to the Malian government: a third permanent crossing over the Niger River.

It should be noted that where the Niger flows through Bamako it is about a kilometre wide during the rainy season, and that the two existing crossings were wholly inadequate for a city with a population of several million.

China is popular in many places in Africa. I experienced this in

2009 and again in 2024, when I visited the headquarters of the African Union (AU) in Addis Ababa. In Ethiopia I also received an explanation for this popularity from an economist working for the AU.

China is popular because it builds physical infrastructure that ordinary citizens experience as lacking in their daily lives: bridges, roads, telecom towers. Many people, the economist told me, do not realise that Western countries spend roughly similar sums on social and political infrastructure—that is, clinics, hospitals, schools, or governmental apparatuses and administrative functions such as fisheries control or environmental regulation. A well-educated person like the economist I spoke with can, of course, see these connections. But the benefits of effective environmental regulation or an efficient tax system are not what preoccupy the ordinary man and woman on the street. I will conclude by noting that our conversation took place in a highly successful city park in central Addis Ababa—also built by the Chinese. One readily understands their popularity across the African continent.

China's path toward building the global dominance that Robert Kagan already perceived as emerging toward the end of the 2000s has had almost nothing to do with the "geo-economic" or globalist principles that guided Western international conduct in the 1990s and 2000s. Instead, it has been shaped by old-fashioned great-power thinking of the kind Europe knew in the nineteenth century. To this day, China complains about the so-called unequal treaties it was forced to sign during the century of humiliation. As a form of revanche, since 2000 it has concluded a multitude of treaties that it subsequently made unequal in the opposite direction—by benefiting from them without ever respecting them.

Energy

In earlier decades, thrillers were if anything more formulaic than they are today.

The pattern was familiar. We are introduced to the hero—usually a man—and to the qualities that define him: idealism, patriotism, love. His motives are noble; his character is clear.

Then comes the summons. A letter arrives. A meeting is requested. An unexpected visitor appears. Something small, perhaps even trivial, disturbs the surface of ordinary life. The hero hesitates. The matter seems unimportant. Or obscure. Or best left alone.

But he accepts. And once he does, the pace changes. What looked minor reveals itself as dangerous. What seemed manageable turns complex. The task grows teeth.

Soon there are pursuits and narrow escapes. The small circle of allies begins to fray; trust erodes. And somewhere around the midpoint comes the inevitable moment of darkness: the sense that there is no way out.

The Green Transition in the 2000s

In the first decade of the twenty-first century, the green transition developed in much the same way as the hero of a classical thriller.

When we first encounter our protagonist, he is young and naïve. This is in Kyoto in 1997. But then the green transition makes the acquaintance of Al Gore and his inconvenient truth. Idealism grows. Our hero acquires a deeper and more fully formed character.

As the 2000s unfold, it becomes clear that the mission—reducing global CO_2 emissions—is far more daunting than anyone, even Al Gore, had anticipated. What began as a manageable assignment turns into something sprawling and structurally complex. The plot thickens; the stakes rise.

And then comes the inevitable scene familiar from every thriller: the moment when everything converges. The hero and his allies. The rivals and their accomplices. The grave figures of authority and even the comic side characters. All gather in one place for the decisive confrontation. In December 2009, that stage is Copenhagen—COP15—where the accumulated tensions of the decade are meant to be resolved once and for all.

In a James Bond film, this is the point at which Bond is strapped to the table, the laser inching closer, escape uncertain. In climate politics, COP15 played a similar role: the dramatic midpoint where the promise of an orderly solution collided with geopolitical reality.

Looking back, we can now see that the 2000s were the decade in which Western countries—almost inadvertently—placed effective control over the green transition in the hands of their two most serious strategic competitors, Russia and China.

From the Western countries, Russia was given the role of supplying inexpensive fossil energy. This served several purposes. Renewable energy, by its nature, is intermittent and requires backup capacity. Moreover, if nuclear power were to be phased out in Germany—as indeed became conceivable—dependence on fossil fuels would, somewhat paradoxically, increase in the short to medium term, given the time required to expand renewable capacity.

At the same time, China came to supply a significant share of the new technologies underpinning the transition: solar panels and battery storage.

Taken together, these choices shaped the structure of the green transition in ways that warranted a more systematic assessment of their long-term strategic implications.

The Climate Conference in Copenhagen

In Barack Obama's memoirs, there is a relatively long passage about COP15 in Copenhagen. The president initially notes how peculiar a venue the Bella Center really is as the hub of an international conference:

> *It was a dark, Arctic morning when we arrived in Copenhagen, the roads into the city shrouded in fog. The conference venue itself felt like a repurposed shopping mall. We wandered through a maze of elevators and corridors—one of which, for reasons that escaped me, featured a row of mannequins lined up against the wall—before sitting down with Hillary and Todd for a briefing on the latest developments*[38].

And then there is the entire question of political substance. Expectations for COP15 had been sky-high, because it was anticipated that an agreement would be reached to replace the now twelve-year-old Kyoto agreement. Given such lofty expectations, COP15 could hardly avoid disappointing—and it did.

The Danish government had not allocated sufficient time or space to hold meetings and consult with developing countries. As a result, these countries very quickly—and rightly—came to feel poorly treated.

Then we arrive at hard politics. China had come to the conference with a clear plan to obstruct it. Already at the Kyoto conference, China had secured the advantage that it—together with India—was classified as a developing country, and was therefore exempted from binding targets and from financing the green transition.

China's covert plan at the conference was to band together with India, Brazil, and South Africa (that is, 80 percent of the so-called BRICS countries) and prevent any of them from having to commit to binding targets—or to pay for the whole enterprise at all.

In Obama's memoirs, the conference concludes on a note of urgency. A snowstorm is approaching Washington, D.C., and he must leave in haste. Before departing, however, he and Hillary Clinton make an unannounced appearance in the room of the Chinese delegation—who are, at that very moment, coordinating positions with India, Brazil, and South Africa. The interruption is hardly greeted with enthusiasm. Still, chairs are gathered, space is made, and an agreement takes shape. It is diffuse, non-binding, and modestly funded—but it is an agreement.

And so, as the 2000s came to a close, the Green Transition found itself at a moment that was less triumph than reprieve: not a decisive breakthrough, but a fragile understanding reached in the half-light between ambition and geopolitical reality.

The State of the Green Transition at the end of the 2000s

By the end of the decade, the Western countries had taken decisive steps toward making themselves dependent on their worst geostrategic adversaries—both with regard to the old fossil fuels and the new forms of energy, based on electricity generated primarily from solar and wind power.

As in the old films, it had already become apparent that the task was very different from—and far greater than—what our hero thought he had agreed to.

Both solar and wind were immature technologies, which moreover presupposed an infrastructure that did not exist.

Almost no one had allocated resources to researching a Plan B or C, in case solar and wind should prove incapable of powering a complex industrial and computer-based society. Such alternative plans might, for example, have included a new generation of nuclear power plants, carbon capture and storage, or hydrogen.

Nor had the economic and social costs been properly understood. There is a substantial risk that green energy can never function without massive subsidies. And there is an equally substantial risk of social unrest when wind turbines are erected in scenic areas, or when the price of essential transport and heating rises dramatically, or when entire regions are threatened by mass unemployment due to the closure of, for example, mines or the automotive industry.

Finally, the almost all-encompassing naïveté and idealism blocked the banal insight that the green transition was, above all, something Europe desired.

None of the truly major emitters seriously embraced the green transition—at least not if they were expected to pay for it, or if it would inconvenience large segments of their populations.

The decade of shattered illusions

The first decade of the twenty-first century began with great ideals, but it ended in terror and domestic crisis, as well as deep disappointment with developments outside the West.

At the beginning of the decade, belief in Western superiority and in the ability to shape the world in its own image prevailed. Optimistic visions of global democratisation and peace through intervention culminated in the dramatic responses to the terrorist attacks of September 11, 2001.

But optimism was quickly replaced by the realisation that the world could not be molded as easily as expected. Both the Clinton era's and the Bush era's faith—in very different ways—in military power as a means of establishing stability and democracy rested on flawed and naïve assumptions. The interventions resulted in protracted, insoluble conflicts that left deep divisions and widespread mistrust of Western intentions, both internationally and domestically.

The first steps along the path that has led to the West's globally weakened position were taken during this decade. The conflicts radicalised large parts of the Muslim world and created fertile ground for new forms of terrorism and extremism. At the same time, Western missteps strengthened the West's geopolitical rivals, especially Iran and China, which exploited the emerging weakness to expand their own strategic positions.

Within the West itself, disillusionment with political leaders and institutions grew—both because of failures abroad (the hopeless wars in Afghanistan and Iraq) and failures at home (the financial crisis). Consequently, the lofty ideals and promises of a safer world were, over the course of the decade, replaced by a sense of insecurity, political division, and skepticism toward political and military solutions.

Thus, the 2000s ended as a decade in which Western ambitions and self-understanding suffered defeat. Fundamental assumptions about the West's role in the world were challenged in a way that continues to trouble many, leaving behind doubt and mistrust that still shape political reality today.

Chapter 4

WITH EYES WIDE SHUT

Governor Romney, I'm glad that you recognize that al-Qaida is a threat, because a few months ago when you were asked what's the biggest geopolitical threat facing America, you said Russia, not al-Qaida; you said Russia. And the 1980s are now calling to ask for their foreign policy back because, you know, the Cold War's been over for 20 years. But Governor, when it comes to our foreign policy, you seem to want to import the foreign policies of the 1980s, just like the social policies of the 1950s and the economic policies of the 1920s.

– Barack Obama, October 22, 2012. In a televised debate against Mitt Romney.[39]

This chapter deals with the second decade of the twenty-first century: the 2010s. It became a decade marked by growing tensions with Russia, a rising Chinese global influence, and a turbulent Middle East that triggered both refugee flows to Europe and terrorism on the continent—developments that in turn contributed to internal Western crises which further weakened the West's position.

The decade began with the West's continued faith in the positive effects of globalisation, but optimism was soon replaced by concern. Russia's aggressive behavior—most notably the annexation of Crimea in 2014 and its involvement in the conflicts in eastern Ukraine—made it clear that Russian foreign policy had turned against Western interests. In particular, criticism arose from Poland and the Baltic states, directed at Western allies for their naïveté regarding Russia's intentions and their dependence on Russian energy. One place where this became especially visible was in the controversies surrounding the Nord Stream 2 gas pipeline, which my own country also struggled to handle. In this way, Western countries were confronted with their own vulnerability and their limited ability to address Russia's strategic challenges effectively.

China's growing power became a similarly major challenge over the course of the decade. The country's massive economic expansion through the Belt and Road Initiative demonstrated how China strategically used economic investment to build global influence. At the same time, the West long proved unwilling or unable to recognise and counter China's strategic ambitions, leading to an increasing Western dependence on Chinese technology and infrastructure.

Challenges also grew internally within the West. The aftershocks of the financial crisis created political divisions and populist movements that undermined cohesion and confidence in liberal democracy. At the same time, the refugee and migrant crisis of 2015–16 exposed weaknesses in the European countries' capacity for collective action, further strengthening nationalist movements and weakening internal EU cohesion. Neither Brexit nor Donald Trump emerged out of the blue. Both were—seen from the perspective of Western elites—what one might call self-inflicted afflictions.

Taken together, the 2010s became a decade in which the West's strategic weaknesses and internal divisions were laid bare and exploited by rivals such as Russia and China. It was a decade marked by a lack of realism and delayed recognition of the scale of the challenges, which—following the also not particularly successful 2000s—further weakened the West's global position and made its geopolitical adversaries stronger than ever.

The new Prince of Darkness

If I may allow myself a pedagogical device, the political situation in the West after Vladimir Putin's Munich speech bears more than a passing resemblance to the Harry Potter saga.

After 2007, a group of countries—like Harry Potter and his friends—began warning the Western great powers that evil had returned. In the saga, evil is embodied by Lord Voldemort. In the real world, it is embodied by Russian imperialism.

In reality, however, things unfold much as they do in the Harry Potter saga: "the adults" are reluctant to hear about problems—and indeed become mildly irritated when someone tries to warn them. Just as Harry Potter and his friends see the growing danger from Voldemort long before the adults do, a small group of European countries perceive the signs of a threat that becomes ever clearer: invasions of neighboring countries, economic pressure, and dangerous dependence on Russian energy.

In this context, Poland behaves much like Harry Potter himself—brave, outspoken, and clear-spoken, but often dismissed as somewhat hysterical. The Baltic states resemble Hermione Granger: meticulous, attentive to every detail, and deeply serious in their approach, yet rejected as overly anxious. The Czech Republic plays the role of Ron Weasley—fully aware of the dangers but frustrated at not being taken seriously by the authorities. Finland corresponds to Neville Longbottom: quietly vigilant, yet with a historically grounded awareness of the seriousness of the threat. Finally, Sweden functions as Luna Lovegood: alert to the dangers early on, but often regarded as a bit too eccentric for its warnings to be taken seriously.

Opposed to this vigilant group stand "the adults"—represented by the larger, agenda-setting European countries such as Germany, France, and Italy—acting as a kind of Ministry of Magic. They prefer to avoid any unpleasant realisations and deliberately choose to see only favourable trade opportunities, economic rationality, and common sense, while ignoring warnings about the growing danger.

In the mid-2010s, however, the responsible adults in capitals around the world were forced— in light of the invasion and annexation of Crimea—reluctantly to admit that there might be something to what the young had been saying for many years. Accordingly, governments in countries such as the United States, the United Kingdom, Germany, and France informed their respective parliaments that Russia had gradually developed into a strategic threat to the rules-based international order.

Actual action, however, was hard to find. It came only after the Russian invasion of Ukraine on 24 February 2022.

In the mid-2010s, the adults—the Western governments—were compelled to acknowledge, albeit unwillingly, that the warnings from countries such as Poland and the Baltic states had been correct all along. But like Dumbledore in Harry Potter, who knew the truth perfectly well, Western leaders had to balance that realisation against economic and political interests.

How a bright consulting idea turns into a sordid reality

In 2001, an employee at Goldman Sachs had the bright idea that Brazil, Russia, India, and China should be viewed as a group. He even coined a catchy acronym for them: BRIC. The idea was that here was a set of developing countries that were on the rise economically and socially. They were worth watching, because future business opportunities would be almost limitless.

In 2006, the BRIC countries met for the first time. From 2010 onward, South Africa joined. And thus the group acquired the name by which it has become known: BRICS.

There is something almost parodically typical of its time about the idea that Western countries should set about cultivating BRICS because this would generate unprecedented economic growth for all parties—while simultaneously strengthening world peace, on the assumption that countries that trade with one another do not fight one another.

Between the conception of the idea and the birth of BRICS nine years later, Vladimir Putin had delivered his Munich speech. In it, as is well known, he rejected the unipolar world order and set out a strategy: that the countries wishing to oppose it should work more closely together.

As a result, the BRICS that actually emerged became a forum for opposing the West across multiple dimensions. Russia and China have coordinated their use of veto power in the UN Security Council to prevent mandates for peacekeeping operations—most notably in Syria during the 2010s. Mechanisms such as the New Development Bank have been established as alternatives to the World Bank for financing infrastructure. Another mechanism, the Contingent Reserve Arrangement, has been created to provide financial security for member states instead of the IMF. And there are ongoing discussions about how to weaken the influence of the U.S. dollar as an international trade and reserve currency.

BRICS cannot act as overtly anti-Western as Russia and China might wish to do on their own. This is primarily prevented by India and Brazil. For many years, these two countries have sought to balance considerations toward Western countries with their commitments to BRICS. Nonetheless, the very existence of BRICS has undoubtedly given leaders such as India's Narendra Modi and Brazil's Jair Bolsonaro as well as Lula da Silva the backing to behave more anti-Western and anti-American than they would have dared on their own.

There are several examples of this. But the most striking has always been the cohesion of the BRICS countries when it came to refusing to commit to binding CO_2 reduction targets—and, above all, to refusing to pay for whatever promises they might be pressured into making. In recent years, the justifications for doing as little as possible on climate policy have been wrapped in precisely the anti-Western rhetoric that BRICS has specialised in cultivating.

Another area in which the BRICS countries have in recent years acted quite bluntly anti-Western has been the Israel–Palestine issue. In the UN, there has been no hesitation in engaging in one-sided condemnation of Israel. This has undoubtedly contributed to both anti-Zionism and antisemitism in Europe—the last place in the world where, given our historical experience, these phenomena should be accepted.

In connection with the Israel–Palestine conflict, South Africa has even taken the extreme step of accusing Israel of genocide. The accusation has been categorically rejected by Germany in the political arena and is regarded by many other observers as controversial. Nevertheless, it has acquired the character of an established truth in pro-Palestinian circles around the world.

One of the arenas in which the BRICS countries Russia and China very clearly rehearsed their future cooperation throughout the 2010s was the Middle East.

The Arab Spring

Around the turn of 2010/11, social unrest erupted in a large number of countries in the Middle East. Initially, this was triggered by poor governance, which contributed to widespread social deprivation.

In the spring of 2011, unrest in Egypt became so intense that Hosni Mubarak—who had ruled the country as a dictator since 1981—was forced to step down. Owing to the Syrian government's brutal treatment of demonstrators—who were protesting both repression and social conditions—an uprising developed. In the religiously and culturally diverse country, it quickly escalated into a full-scale civil war.

Across the Western world, many optimists imagined that the Arab Spring—as the events were quickly dubbed—would become a kind of Middle Eastern 1989.

In Denmark, for example, the Folketing debated the Arab Spring in a parliamentary inquiry debate in January 2012. The resolution text adopted by a large majority read as follows:[40]

> *The Folketing welcomes the Arab Spring and the beginning democratisation of the Arab world as a watershed, historic event, but expresses concern about the violent developments particularly in Syria, and about whether Islamist electoral victories will harm efforts toward gender equality, minority rights, and the peace process.*
>
> *The Folketing calls on the government to work for broad international*

> *support for the difficult transition processes, including by ensuring that the government:*
>
> *– intensifies dialogue with the newly democratically elected authorities in North Africa and other actors in order to support progress for democracy and human rights. Denmark will assess new governments on their respect for democratic rules of the game, universal human rights, freedom of religion, labor rights, and efforts to combat nepotism and corruption;*
>
> *– prioritizes Danish support for democratisation, reforms, and civil society, and builds on existing initiatives for economic development and job creation under the Arab Initiative and the Arab Investment Fund;*
>
> *– actively supports the Israeli-Palestinian peace process;*
>
> *– actively supports the implementation of the EU's new neighborhood policy in the Middle East.*

Without being unkind, one might well describe the majority's resolution text as naïve. First, because of the implicit assumption that Islamism might *possibly* be harmful to gender equality, the position of minorities, and reconciliation with political opponents. Islamism cannot "possibly" be harmful to these things. It is definitionally and categorically opposed to them and prepared to use violent means to prevent them.

Second, the resolution text lacks any consideration of outcomes other than democracy and human rights. In this way, it remains enveloped in the Fukuyama-inspired thinking that these outcomes represent a form of historical necessity. The resolution does not even hint at the political dynamics that had governed developments in the region at least since the Middle Eastern "year of destiny" in 1979 (with the Iranian Revolution, the Soviet invasion of Afghanistan, and the attack on the Grand Mosque in Mecca).

From my generally disillusioned view of great-power politics, I myself wrote the following about the Middle East in an article in *RÆSON* in 2011:

> *Shall we not guess that they [the countries of the Middle East] will sink into chaos, and that the most well-organized—whoever that may be—will at some point put an end to it? That is, after all, how revolutions usually develop.*[41]

Despite the large majority in the Folketing, this was not a view I held alone. It was the Danish People's Party that had called for the debate. But because the majority supporting the government's resolution text was so large, parliamentary practice dictated that this text be voted on first, after which the Danish People's Party's proposal lapsed.

Nevertheless, the party's spokesperson, Søren Espersen, expressed views not far from my own:

> *We know that here at home [that after winter comes spring] when we struggle free from winter's oppressive darkness, and we want it to be the same with the Arab Spring, because we sincerely wish the Arabs that experience. Is it any wonder, then, that today I feel a bit like a killjoy for having taken the initiative to this inquiry— with the strong sense and suspicion that the Arab Spring is a misnomer, and that what the Arab world is in reality heading toward is not a fresh, life-giving, and free spring, but rather the wretched, unfree, and clammy darkness of Islamism?*[42]

On the international stage, similar warnings were voiced—for example by the internationally renowned expert on Islam and the Middle East, Bernard Lewis. Speaking to *The Jerusalem Post*, he said:

> *I don't know how one could get the impression that the Muslim Brotherhood is relatively benign unless you mean relatively as compared with the Nazi party. In genuinely fair and free elections, [the Muslim parties] are very likely to win, and I think that would be a disaster.*[43]

In the West, many were surprised when the Muslim Brotherhood won the first free election in Egypt after Hosni Mubarak's fall. I found—and still find—that surprise peculiar, because Egypt had for a generation been maintained as a secular country according to the same model as Libya, Iraq, Syria, and Turkey: a regime based in the military. In some cases—Turkey—it allowed elections, but it would always intervene at the prospect of either communism or islamism.

In Syria, opponents of Bashar al-Assad rallied around groups such as the Free Syrian Army. At the same time, Iran began to intervene in the civil war. Iran preferred the Assad regime as a partner in the axis of resistance against Israel. From Iran's perspective, this was preferable to both a Sunni-dominated government and—worst of all—a Western-oriented government.

To make matters worse, the Islamic State began to stir in 2013. The movement originated in al-Qaeda in Iraq, and if there is anything that allows it to thrive, it is power vacuums and the absence of a strong state. In addition to the existing vacuum in Iraq, there was now a growing vacuum in Syria, into which the Islamic State expanded.

By 2014, General al-Sisi had long since shut down the Muslim Brotherhood following his seizure of power in Egypt. This intervention was not consistent with principles of democracy and human rights, but in most Western capitals it was met with a blind eye.

In Syria, the civil war still raged. And in August, the Islamic

State captured the city of Mosul and proclaimed a caliphate. The movement controlled an area the size of Romania and threatened to commit genocide against, among others, the religious minority of the Yazidis.

Under the prevailing political doctrines of the time, Western countries could no longer ignore this state of affairs. Accordingly, the United States carried out air strikes against the Islamic State in Iraq and later also in Syria.

Russia then entered the Syrian civil war actively, and a close cooperation was quickly established between the Russian air force and Iranian ground forces (along with various non-state militias supporting Iran). The goal of both Russian and Iranian intervention was twofold: to save the Assad regime and to defeat the Islamic State.

It was here that the consequences of Iran, Russia, and China having moved closer together began to be felt in earnest.

As a result of the military cooperation between Iran and Russia, the Assad regime experienced battlefield gains for the first time. At the same time, both Russia and China blocked any attempt in the UN Security Council to move the entire issue into the UN framework, where a peace plan might have been formulated.

With China's acquiescence, Iran and Russia sought to avoid a humanitarian ceasefire and a peace and reconciliation process. What the two countries wanted was to crush the opposition as efficiently as possible. Accordingly, between 2010 and 2020, Russia and China vetoed every attempt in the Security Council to impose sanctions on the Assad regime in Damascus.

If one compares this sequence of events with the expectations widely expressed in Western capitals in the early 1990s—and with the ambitious vision articulated by UN Secretary-General Boutros Boutros-Ghali regarding the organisation's role as guardian and preserver of peace in the period 1992–95—the contrast is stark.

What appeared, in the immediate aftermath of the Cold War, to be the beginning of a new era of collective security and rule-based cooperation instead came to mark the high-water point of post-Cold War optimism. Two decades later, little of that confidence remained intact. The institutions endured; the expectations did not.

That the contrast between what was dreamed of in the mid-1990s and the reality lived in the mid-2010s did not give rise to greater reflection and perhaps self-examination is one of the great puzzles that future historians will have to unravel.

Grand words are unnecessary. Yet it is difficult to understand why, in the foreign-policy environment that took shape in the latter half of the 2010s, the widening gap between earlier ambitions and geopolitical realities did not provoke deeper concern or more sustained reflection than it did.

The grounds for a thorough reassessment of European confidence in the United Nations were present. A structured and comprehensive review within the foreign-policy community would have been both timely and justified. Such an initiative, however, was never undertaken.

It is sometimes said that the Spanish Civil War was the dress rehearsal for the Second World War. With due caution, one may draw a parallel and argue that the Arab Spring and the Syrian Civil War, in a similar fashion, served as a dress rehearsal for the political power struggle that in the 2020s has unfolded in full in Ukraine. The political West versus an axis consisting of Russia, China, and Iran—by now also reinforced by North Korea, and with moral backing from a BRICS country such as South Africa.

As I noted at the outset, leading Western powers have, since around 2015, acknowledged that Russia is a geopolitical adversary that must be taken very seriously. That the anti-Western alliance is as tightly knit as the entire sequence surrounding the Arab Spring, the Islamic State, and the civil war in Syria demonstrates is, however, still something studied primarily in think tanks and at universities. It is not something that has filtered through to parliaments or the broader public.

The Arab Spring spreads to Europe

It is possible that I have overlooked it. But to the best of my knowledge, the refugee crisis of 2015 and the wave of terrorism between 2015 and 2018 have never been described as an extension of the Arab Spring to Europe. Yet that is precisely what happened.

In 2015, large numbers of civilians fled from Syria to Turkey and onward to Europe—primarily via Greece. This prompted the German chancellor to commit what I regard as one of her three greatest unforced errors (the other two being the shutdown of nuclear power in 2011 and the passivity with regard to digitising Germany's public sector). The chancellor declared that Germany would manage this crisis: *"Wir schaffen das."*

However nobly and humanistically the statement was intended, it had, from the perspective of Realpolitik, a range of negative consequences for both Germany and Europe—and it has significantly affected Merkel's legacy in a negative direction.

First, it became apparent that it was often an oversimplification to say that the many refugees were merely seeking safety. Of course they were. But they did not seek safety just anywhere. Consequently, one often saw them travel through one safe country after another in order to reach a destination they had already chosen in advance—and only there wait for asylum processing and subsequently family reunification.

This led to a very understandable delegitimisation of the very notion that refugees were simply persecuted people in distress. Most of them were, and that should be remembered. But the full truth was far more complex.

What initially appeared to be a refugee crisis was therefore, in a broader sense, a migration crisis—one in which much of Western Europe, in a very short period of time, was overwhelmed by an enormous number of people, a substantial proportion of whom had planned to emigrate to the continent together with their families. These families could later be reunited thanks to the European Convention on Human Rights.

This mechanism—the right to family reunification—has caused considerable damage to public trust in, and popular acceptance of, both the European Convention on Human Rights and the European Court of Human Rights.

When the right to family reunification undermines confidence in the Convention and the Court, it is because populations in many European countries experience the rule as being abused. Citizens perceive it as a method for circumventing national immigration and asylum rules, which creates frustration and a sense that European institutions stand in the way of democratically taken national decisions. As a result, support erodes and mistrust arises toward both the Convention and the Court.

Second, it became clear that people from many countries other than Syria took advantage of the situation by passing themselves off as Syrians directly affected by war. Whether or not this would be uncovered during the asylum process was uncertain. But that mattered little. The reality was that it was more or less impossible to deport rejected asylum seekers once they were in Europe.

Third, it emerged that the Islamic State, in particular, exploited the situation to smuggle terrorists into Europe disguised as refugees. Many experts initially denied that this could happen. When it happened nonetheless, it led to a sharp decline in trust in the ability of authorities and experts to analyse critical events such as the refugee crisis at all.

Finally, in retrospect, it must be said that the refugee crisis of 2015 is one of the most significant factors in explaining the explosive rise in support for system-critical right-wing parties. These parties mobilise supporters on the implicit or explicit claim that the power or legacy parties are, in reality, indifferent to the problems created in Western Europe by a large contingent of poorly integrated migrants—problems such as crime in many forms, antisocial behaviour directed at women and sexual minorities, Islamisation, pressure on welfare systems, and the importation of Middle Eastern conflicts.

Angela Merkel has always enjoyed a reputation as a great European. But that reputation pales when one considers the actual consequences of her refugee policy in 2015.

In effect, Merkel unilaterally and without consultation with the other EU countries suspended the existing asylum rules—most notably the Dublin Regulation, which stipulated that asylum seekers were to be registered in the first EU country they entered.

By opening Germany's borders to Syrian refugees who had already travelled through other EU countries, she effectively rendered this rule inoperative. This created a precedent, undermined the principles of the Dublin system, and placed immense political pressure on the EU's common asylum and migration policy.

As a result, the financial and political consequences of the decision were not borne by Germany alone but were shared across the European Union.

At the same time as refugee flows surged dramatically in 2015, a wave of terrorism swept across Europe. It began with the attack on the editorial offices of the satirical magazine *Charlie Hebdo* in Paris in January 2015. This was followed by several attacks in France, but also in Germany, the United Kingdom, Spain, and normally peaceful countries such as Finland and Denmark. The wave of terror only subsided in 2018.

I was elected to the Danish parliament for the first time in 2015, and there are few things I remember more vividly from that period than the many cases in the field of asylum and refugees that parliament had to deal with, and the legislation that had to be enacted.

For me personally, it began when, due to illness, I had to take over the second and third readings of one of the first major packages of restrictive asylum measures adopted at the end of 2015, replacing our usual spokesperson.

The left wing—not least the Red–Green Alliance—had turned out in force and did not spare the strong language. The government's measures (which, incidentally, enjoyed a large parliamentary majority) were not merely on the edge of, but a violation of, both the constitution and the European Convention on Human Rights—so one was led to understand.

By the time the allotted period for questioning the spokesperson finally expired, I was utterly exhausted from answering questions that for the most part insinuated that my party and I had now sold out the constitution and human rights in order to satisfy the basest populist instincts.

As the wave of terrorism rolled on, a series of very hard debates took place—both in parliament and in the public sphere—about how militantly a liberal democracy may permit itself to defend against terrorism and Islamist totalitarianism. The dilemma is well known: a democracy should, of course, not sink to the level of anti-democrats in order to defeat them. But pacifism has always been a naïve position. Because, to put it as a wordplay, the last word in non-violence is violence.

Neither Denmark nor Europe has fully recovered politically from these dilemmas. As a Member of the European Parliament today, I can see that Denmark made a number of fortunate choices when compared with the rest of Europe.

The major centrist parties in Denmark have always listened to the domestic variants of the popular concerns that drive immigration-critical parties across Europe. As a result, most people in Denmark do not feel alienated or dismissed by the traditional parties of power when they express concern about immigration—unlike the situation, for example, in Germany.

Denmark took a number of tough decisions with regard to both migration and terrorism. On migration, these included border controls (from 2016), reductions in a range of social benefits for refugees, and the so-called paradigm shift of 2019, which was intended to prevent refugees from more or less automatically becoming permanent migrants. In combating terrorism, measures included stricter rules for religious preachers and increased oversight of the spread of anti-democratic views in Islamic free schools.

Initially, Denmark was criticised for this approach—for example within the EU. But the tone has changed in recent years. The country is now often praised in various EU forums. And when, in 2024, at a hearing with the incoming EU Commissioner for Migration, the Austrian Magnus Brunner, I argued that his mandate would also make him responsible for preventing further growth in support for right-wing populist parties, he agreed.

The Arab Spring, and the way in which it spread to Europe, demonstrated how far the continent had moved away from the optimism of the 1990s. Events in the Middle East in the 2010s ended up significantly destabilising Europe and proved extremely difficult for the traditional parties of power in many countries to manage. In several cases, Europe's political elites understood neither the political logics and rationales that prevail in the Middle East nor the anti-Western coalition of Russia, Iran, and China that was in the making—and that was consciously working to make matters worse for the Western countries.

These difficulties persist today, when it is obvious to everyone that the conflict between Israel and Hamas has spread to the whole of Europe—while it remains unclear what, in fact, can be done about it.

Russia

One rubs one's eyes in disbelief when reading that the last NATO exercise with Russian participation took place as late as 2011—three years after the invasion of Georgia and the annexation of Abkhazia and South Ossetia. Yet that is indeed the case, and here is the story.

In the 1990s it was a widespread aspiration among Western elites that Russia should be integrated into the Western economic and security architecture. This resulted, in 1994, in the so-called Partnership for Peace.

During the 1990s, Russia participated in NATO-led peacekeeping missions in the Balkans, even though cooperation was soured by NATO's intervention in Kosovo.

NATO's cooperation with Russia reached a high point in 2002, when the so-called NATO–Russia Council was established. On that occasion, Vladimir Putin stated, as mentioned earlier, that in his view there were no contradictions between Russia and NATO.

As NATO expanded to include a number of Eastern European

countries, as Ukraine and Georgia oriented themselves increasingly toward the West, and as Western countries criticised the Russian invasion of Georgia, tensions between Russia and NATO grew.

In 2009, under Barack Obama, the United States attempted a "reset" of relations between Russia and the West. This seems odd, given that Russia had invaded and occupied an independent country the year before—and yet less odd when one recalls the Obama quotation that serves as the motto for this chapter.

How sincerely Russia entered into this process can be debated. But in any case, this is why we have to move so astonishingly close to our own time before cooperation between Russia and NATO finally collapses.

If one were to summarize the 2010s, it was the decade in which Western countries clung convulsively to the belief that their world map was an accurate representation of reality—even as information appeared almost constantly showing that the map no longer depicted the world as it actually was.

In 2013, unrest once again erupted in Ukraine. This was due to the fact that since 2004 political power in the country had reverted to pro-Russian forces in the person of Viktor Yanukovych. Opposition to him grew, however, because he refused to sign an association agreement with the EU, and this opposition culminated in an extremely violent confrontation on Kyiv's Maidan Square. In the end, Yanukovych was forced to flee, and a Western-oriented interim government took office.

In response to Ukraine once again turning toward the West and aspiring to membership in both the EU and NATO, Russia in 2014 first invaded the Crimean Peninsula and subsequently the Donbas region in eastern Ukraine.

The invasion of Crimea was striking because it was not carried out by regular troops but by "green men" who did not wear standard uniforms. In that sense, the invasion occupied the upper end of the hybrid-warfare spectrum—just short of outright war.

Both the invasion of Crimea and that of Donbas took place with Russian minorities as the pretext and leverage, even though there had been an overwhelming Ukrainian majority in favour of an independent Ukraine in Donbas in the 1991 referendum, and a clear majority on Crimea as well.

In the first weeks after the occupation of Crimea's parliament and government buildings in Simferopol, Russia officially claimed to know nothing about the invasion of Crimea and asserted that in Donbas it was merely coming to the aid of distressed ethnic Russians. Nevertheless—already at the time—it was clear that events were being directed by Russia. A "referendum" on Crimea's future was swiftly arranged, which to no one's surprise showed a large majority in favour of the peninsula becoming part of Russia. Later in 2014, self-proclaimed, Russian-nationalist governments were declared in both the Donetsk and Luhansk provinces. They have never been recognised by anyone other than Russia and its most compliant vassals.

As 2014 drew to a close, the front line between Ukraine and the Russian-backed separatists had frozen. The conflict entered what Western countries regarded as a diplomatic phase.

The result of this diplomatic phase is known as the Minsk I and Minsk II agreements. What these agreements have in common—formally concluded between Ukraine, Russia, the breakaway regions of Donetsk and Luhansk, and the OSCE—is that they represented a European attempt at appeasement vis-à-vis Russia.

Germany and France favoured a policy of accommodation rather than military confrontation with Russia and therefore pressured Ukraine to accept the two Minsk agreements, even though they were deeply unpopular with the Ukrainian public.

It is difficult to identify a noble motive to justify the conduct of Germany and France. One might say that lives were saved. One might also say that Germany and France were militarily so weak that threatening Russia with hard power would have been an empty gesture. But a large part of the truth is that neither Germany nor France wanted Ukraine to stand in the way of their continued business dealings with Russia. My assessment therefore ends with the conclusion that short-term considerations overrode the strategic imperative of both the inviolability of state borders—fundamental to the UN Charter—and an appropriate deterrence of Russia.

Viewed from a "consequences-based" pedagogical perspective, the period between 2014 and 2022 can be summed up as follows: Western countries did indeed make a note in Russia's contact book that the country had not behaved nicely—but beyond that, they gave Russia every reason to learn that its behavior would not be met with any form of resistance from the West.

One example: in the summer of 2014, Russian separatists shot down a Malaysian passenger aircraft flying in accordance with regulations over Ukraine, using a Russian missile. Although nearly 300 people were killed, there were no consequences for Russia.

Encouraged by the absence of consequences for this and similar events, Russia began to intensify its hybrid warfare against Western countries.

In 2016, Russia intervened heavily—there is now a broad consensus—in the Brexit referendum.[44] Likewise in 2016, Russia also intervened—again, there is consensus—in the U.S. presidential election.[45]

In 2017, Russia most likely interfered in the French presidential election.[46] This finally prompted Western countries to wake up. In connection with Denmark's parliamentary election in 2019, the

Danish Security and Intelligence Service and the Defence Intelligence Service made a joint visit to Christiansborg and warned parties one by one that they should be extremely vigilant for any signs of irregularities.

Alongside election interference, Russia intensified its systematic cyberattacks against both public and private organisations in the West. Disinformation was institutionalised through "news services" such as Russia Today and Sputnik, and through countless fake accounts on Facebook and X (Twitter). Russian narratives—about conditions in Ukraine and the background to the conflict between Russia and Ukraine, for example—were disseminated through these channels.

But hybrid warfare did not stop there. During the refugee crisis of 2015–16 and subsequently, Russia used refugee flows as a weapon by deliberately directing refugees toward specific border crossings in order to overwhelm them. The most curious example was the refugees on bicycles who in 2015 attempted to enter Norway via the Storskog crossing in the middle of Finnmark.

In 2018, Russia went so far as to dispatch a death squad to Salisbury in southwest England. The target of the attack was the Russian spy Sergei Skripal and his daughter, who were subjected to an attempted murder using the nerve agent Novichok.

The appeasement of Russia in the 2010s stands out as a political low point for Western countries. For a justified expectation of due diligence is not hindsight. There was ample information and analysis at the time to warrant a fundamental change of course toward Russia.

It is almost incomprehensible that there was any confidence in the Minsk agreements. Putin's Russia has rarely entered into an agreement with the West with a clear intention to respect or comply with it. Agreements are understood differently in Russian foreign policy than in Western policy. In the West, agreements are taken seriously, and numerous precautions are taken to ensure compliance; violations often carry tangible consequences for individuals and institutions. Russia has indeed occasionally complied with agreements, but typically only when it served the country's short-term interests.

In Russian foreign policy, agreements are one of many pieces on a chessboard that the country can move around to maximise its self-interest—not commitments to be honoured. The best example of this mindset is the UN Charter. Under it, violating the sovereignty of other states is strictly prohibited. Yet Russia can shamelessly exploit its veto in the UN Security Council to prevent criticism of—or responses to—its gross violations of, among others, Georgian and Ukrainian sovereignty.

From the Russian perspective, the 2010s can be summed up as follows: by allocating very modest personnel resources to a fundamentally meaningless series of meetings called the "Minsk agreements," Russia prevented the collective West from rearming. A ruble saved is, as the saying goes, a ruble earned. The perverted "peace dividend" Russia extracted from the West in the 2010s could therefore be converted into substantial and rising military expenditures in the Middle East and in West Africa, where Russia became a major player over the course of the decade.

It is impossible to know whether France and Germany, deep down, believed that the Minsk agreements made sense. In a way, I hope they understood that the process was entirely pointless. Why? Because it at least makes a certain kind of sense to allow pecuniary motives to override Ukraine's security, or to acknowledge that one simply lacks the means to threaten Russia. Not a noble sense—but a sense nonetheless. By contrast, it was unrealistic to believe that a diplomatic process alone would bring Russia to its senses and resolve the situation.

I will conclude this section with some reflections on what I call a devilish dialectic in Western strategy. For many years, Western countries have relied on a geo-economic approach. This means attempting to create peace and stability through extensive trade, economic ties, and mutual interdependence between countries. At the same time, great emphasis has been placed on international organisations, where multiple countries cooperate and seek to resolve conflicts through dialogue and compromise. Finally, the strategy has involved restraint in the use of military force, preferring diplomacy, talks, and dialogue over deterrence or direct military threats.

The devilish element—the problem—is that this strategy, however well-intentioned, has had unintended negative consequences. The mutual economic interdependence meant to create peace has also made the West vulnerable and dependent on countries that do not share its values. The diplomacy and military restraint intended to prevent conflict have, in certain situations, been perceived as weakness and have thereby encouraged aggressive adversaries to test Western limits. It is this paradoxical situation that I call a devilish dialectic.

The strategy sounds sensible, with a touch of the noble. But consider the following: Russia has earned billions from selling fossil fuels to Western countries—and saved billions because its Western flank was safe and secure thanks to decades of disarmament in the West.

Were those funds used to turn Russia into a flourishing welfare state? No—certainly not. They were used to spread destruction and human misery across large parts of the world: Syria and the Middle East. Georgia. Ukraine. West Africa.

In the 1990s, Western countries developed a worldview and a set of economic and security doctrines that were naïve, yet understandable. Over the 2000s and 2010s, reality increasingly failed to match the old map from the 1990s. Yet most Western governments clung convulsively to the map rather than the terrain.

This strategy has made us rich and secure in the Western world—that is the story we like to tell ourselves. But it has also, regrettably, provided the economic foundation that enabled Russia to literally devastate large parts of Syria, dissolve the last remnants of law and order in West Africa, and invade twenty percent of Ukraine—while making life more or less unbearable in the rest of the country.

That is more than ill-conceived. It ought almost to be illegal to behave so recklessly for so long.

China

Set against the Western geo-economic and multilateralist approach to international relations stands, among other things, China's geostrategic and geopolitical one.

The 2010s became the decade in which China truly began to reap the benefits of its strategy, for example with regard to the technologies required for the green transition (notably solar panels and batteries).

Where the Western countries merely saw that Chinese production made these products cheaper, China operated on the assumption that a Chinese monopoly would make the West more dependent—and thus more receptive to Chinese viewpoints and perspectives. This development gathered real momentum in the 2010s and has led to the outcomes we are familiar with today. The chief architect of this phase in China's contest of strength with the West is Xi Jinping. At just under sixty years of age, he became General Secretary of the Chinese Communist Party in 2012, and the following year President of the People's Republic of China. His term of office—which, following changes to China's constitution, may continue for as long as Xi himself wishes—has been characterised by a pronounced degree of geostrategic thinking, always with a view to securing China a long-term advantage over the United States and the EU.

Throughout the 2010s, China strengthened its cooperation with Russia through countless agreements. In 2014 the two countries concluded the first in a long series of strategic partnerships.[47] Over time, this has been translated into cooperation on energy, on infrastructure (including satellite navigation), on arms sales, and on enhanced military cooperation in the form of joint exercises. In addition, China and Russia increasingly coordinated their conduct in the UN Security Council during the 2010s to a degree never previously seen.

Xi Jinping's China has been far more self-confident and aggressive than the China he inherited from his predecessor, Hu Jintao.

Already in the previous chapter we saw how China had militarised the South China Sea. That development continued throughout the 2010s. Over the course of the decade, China transformed several reefs and low-lying islands into large military bases, further increasing the country's dominance over the sea.

When I visited the Philippines in 2018 together with the Danish Foreign Policy Committee, we paid a visit to Western Command (WESCOM) on the island of Palawan.

Palawan is the westernmost major island of the Philippines, and WESCOM is a unified command responsible, among other things, for monitoring the Spratly Islands—one of the island groups China has converted into a military base.

After receiving a briefing on the situation—which also included satellite imagery showing conditions before and after the expansion of reefs and small islands into bases—there was an opportunity to put questions to the head of WESCOM.

I took the opportunity to ask whether freedom of navigation in the South China Sea truly existed, as stipulated by the UN Convention on the Law of the Sea. The commander considered the question and appeared to weigh his words. Then he replied: yes—but solely because of the US Navy.

In short, China does not comply with any agreements whatsoever when it comes to the South China Sea, and this tendency only worsened during the 2010s.

In 2016, the Permanent Court of Arbitration in The Hague delivered its ruling in the case brought against China by the Philippines—with the endorsement of a number of other countries.[48] The ruling held that China's so-called nine-dash line had no legal basis that could withstand judicial scrutiny, and that China therefore had no entitlement to operate in the Philippines' exclusive economic zone. Since the arbitration ruling, China has not even attempted to create the impression that it respects it. The country has continued, as if nothing had happened, to violate both the Philippines' and other countries' economic rights.

The 2010s also became the decade in which China began in earnest to demonstrate its presence in the Indian Ocean. This was made possible both by a massive expansion of the navy, by the completion of the naval base in Djibouti in 2017, and by the takeover—due to debt default—of the port of Hambantota in Sri Lanka the same year. Officially, the latter is a commercial port, but Chinese naval vessels can, of course, also call there if necessary.

On the purely commercial front, China announced in 2013 its aforementioned so-called Belt and Road Initiative.

In theory, this is a project intended to create a worldwide transport infrastructure tailored to China's needs and priorities. But when viewed in conjunction with the work carried out within BRICS to dismantle the US dollar's role as the global reserve currency, it points towards a larger objective: the creation of a "Pax Sinica"—that is, a "Chinese peace"—to replace the "Pax Americana" that has prevailed since the end of the Cold War. In other words, a global trading system on Chinese terms, underpinned by global military power.

That China uses its global power to enforce acceptance of its views even in Europe was already evident towards the end of the 2000s, when China forced Denmark officially to accept that there is only one China. This development accelerated throughout the 2010s and has only been reinforced up to the present day.

In 2010, the Norwegian Nobel Committee awarded the Peace Prize to the dissident Liu Xiaobo. China perceived this as a provocation. As a result, diplomatic relations with Norway were frozen, and economic and cultural sanctions were imposed. The conflict lasted six years and ended with Norway yielding in a manner reminiscent of Denmark's concession in the Dalai Lama dispute.

I myself experienced China's aggressive—and highly self-confident—behaviour in 2017, when the Danish Foreign Policy Committee, among other destinations, visited Beijing.

In the period leading up to the visit, there had been talk of representatives of the Dalai Lama meeting members of the Danish Parliament in Copenhagen. This had not been communicated publicly, but nevertheless the Chinese Ministry of Foreign Affairs had become aware of it.

When the committee was to pay a courtesy call on Vice Foreign Minister Wang Chao, the meeting took a very different course from what the members had imagined. One should picture, mentally, a large room in Chinese design. At one end of the room were two deep armchairs intended for the vice foreign minister and the head of the Danish delegation, Søren Espersen. Beside them were two markedly less comfortable chairs intended for the interpreters. As spectators—seated in furniture just as comfortable as that of the two main figures—the Danish delegation sat on one side in two or three rows, and the Chinese delegation on the other.

After only a few superficial courtesies, Wang Chao embarked on what turned out to be a monologue: Danish politicians were not to speak with representatives of the Dalai Lama. Since there was only one China, and it had its capital and official representatives in Beijing.

This message was delivered in a number of variations and with minimal politeness, and after approximately twenty-five minutes the visit was over.

A few moments later, the Foreign Policy Committee found itself, aghast, in the car park in front of the Ministry of Foreign Affairs. Had we really been lectured—without any opportunity for dialogue—for almost half an hour about what we may and may not do at home in Copenhagen, by a Chinese vice minister? It is the most impertinent political meeting I have attended to date. But the conclusion was clear: yes. The Chinese government believed—and believes—that it has the authority to instruct the Danish parliament on what it may do on its own home ground in Denmark and Copenhagen.

It was because of my personal experiences in China, and with Norway's fate in mind, that in 2018 I was convinced of the prudence of the Danish government creating a financing model for the expansion of Greenland's airports that would prevent this being done with Chinese capital. A potential default on the debt could easily have ended as it did with the defaulted debt in

Sri Lanka. And even if the debt were not defaulted, one could still imagine China using co-financing of three planned airports with international specifications to strengthen its influence in the Arctic.

While I was in China with the committee the previous year, it became even clearer to me than it had been before that China's Arctic ambitions must be taken seriously.

At first glance, it may seem strange that China seeks observer status in the Arctic Council. For regardless of the perspective from which one views a world map, China has no connection to the polar regions of the North. But China wants to be a player in the Arctic—both because China is closely allied with Russia, and because, in the long run, China tends to get what it wants. It is a geostrategic chess move when China moves closer to the Arctic, and it should therefore be perceived and treated as such.

The Western countries were exceedingly slow to understand the principles underpinning China's strategic conduct. But the 2010s end with this gradually dawning on them. Consequently, across Europe—much to China's loud and rather aggressive regret—Huawei begins to be excluded from 5G network planning from around 2018.

It was not a moment too soon. Both the experiences Denmark and Norway have had as countries, and the experiences I personally have had in Beijing and on Palawan, confirm for me the correctness of that course.

Energy

In 2011, the German Federal Chancellor Angela Merkel decided that nuclear power should be phased out of Germany's energy supply. The decision was influenced by the accident at the Japanese Fukushima nuclear power plant and was, by all accounts, taken after consultation with a rather narrow circle of people[49].

If the decision deserves praise, it is for its break with path dependency in German energy planning. Infrastructure is always a well-chosen example when one pedagogically wants to explain what path dependency is. Once one has, for example, decided on the technical specifications according to which a country's electrified railway network is to be designed, an almost infinite number of subsequent decisions will follow from that overarching choice: which spare parts must be purchased, which new trains should be acquired, how new rail lines are to be constructed. A decision about the technical design of a railway network is therefore a decision that reaches decades—and perhaps more than a hundred years—into the future.

With the decision to break the path dependency of nuclear power, Angela Merkel, however, cast Germany into another form of path dependency: dependence on Russian natural gas.

When Russia began offering large quantities of natural gas to Western markets in the 1990s, Germany very quickly became a customer. This led to the development of the Nord Stream 1 gas pipelines in the 2000s and to the decision to build the Nord Stream 2 pipelines in the 2010s.

Both projects were subject to international criticism from the outset. Ukraine protested as early as the 2000s over the loss of transit revenues once Nord Stream 1 became operational. But from the moment Nord Stream 2 appeared on the drawing board, the criticism broadened.

From the Polish side, it was argued that Nord Stream 2 was a political project, against which one wished to issue a warning. In 2016, Poland joined forces with, among others, the Baltic states to the extent that they wrote to the European Commission warning against the project. The argument was that one could not— as Germany did—view the project narrowly in economic terms. It also had to be seen geopolitically. And in that light, it had to be said that it would create a dangerous dependence on Russia in Western Europe.

From the mid-2010s, Lithuania invested in liquefied natural gas in order to reduce its dependence on Russian energy. Poland, for its part, invested in the Baltic Pipe project, which was intended to supply the country with natural gas from Norway.

As I have already mentioned, Denmark also came under pressure toward the end of the 2010s because of Nord Stream II. At one point, the plan was for the pipeline to pass through Danish territorial waters southeast of Bornholm. Under the rules in force at the time, this would have required Denmark to approve the connection from Germany—at the same time as the United States forcefully argued that Denmark should refuse approval. From 2016 onwards, the Trump administration had—correctly—joined the chorus of critics of Nord Stream 2.

The problem resolved itself because the route was changed. But the Danish parliament took the opportunity to pass legislation that generally made it possible to intervene in a similar situation in the future. Such legislation had not existed previously.

Nord Stream 2 ultimately ended—quite literally—with a bang in 2022. Without ever having been put into operation. But that is another story, which I will return to later in the book.

At the time, the Paris Agreement of 2015 was seen as a triumph for the green transition. In reality, however, it exposed both the weakness of using the international treaty system as a method for driving the green transition and the alarming gaps in Europe's strategic thinking about its energy policy.

The major weakness of the Paris Agreement was—and remains—that countries are allowed both to define for themselves how they intend to reach the agreement's goal (keeping the increase in global temperature below 2 degrees by the year 2100) and to define how they will enforce compliance with the targets they have set.

To this, a Realpolitik-minded observer would say that if two or more parties agree to reach goal X, but at the same time write into the document that, in practice, it is irrelevant what measures they take to reach the agreed goal, then there is no agreement in the ordinary sense of the word.

If the matter were not so serious, one might say that the Paris Agreement points to the fundamental weakness of everything that goes under the label of the rules-based international order: that it rests on rules and agreements which only the Western countries (and from time to time—as with the Paris Agreement—only the EU) genuinely intend to respect. The United Nations works in the same way. The WTO works in the same way. The human rights conventions and the Law of the Sea Convention (as we have seen in the case of the South China Sea), and numerous other agreements, also work in this way.

The geostrategic weakness in the green transition that emerged from the Paris Agreement is even more serious.

Where Germany, through its gas cooperation, had placed both itself and Europe in a very dangerous position with regard to vulnerability to Russian coercion, the lack of timely geostrategic foresight meant that Europe would become just as dependent on China for new technologies as the continent had been on Russia for the old ones.

There is a saying that is apt to quote here: *Fool me once, shame on you. Fool me twice, shame on me.*

That all these weaknesses were built into the Paris Agreement was not widely discussed when Europe underwent its climate revolution in the years around 2019–2020. Consequently, they were without exception built into the plans for the green transition drawn up by EU Commissioner Frans Timmermans and implemented during Ursula von der Leyen's first term as President of the European Commission.

Dangerous divisions

The 2010s became the decade in which dangerous divisions began to leave their mark on Western societies.

One of the divisions worth highlighting in this context is Brexit.

Whether or not Russia interfered in the referendum, and whether or not the "Leave" side oversold the blessings of leaving the EU, the fuel that drove the opposition was a protest against the consequences of the political elites' geo-economic line. A protest against the idea that "the nation" no longer mattered— in other words, a protest against the elites' lack of care for the national community itself and its symbols and meaning-giving frameworks.

This lack of care manifested itself in many ways: mass immigration, which the political elite expected people simply to accept; the economic and social collapse of the old industrial cities, which people were likewise more or less expected to accept; and the perceived imbalance between the state's concern for newly arrived immigrants and its indifference toward Britons whose fathers, grandfathers, and great-grandfathers had fought and sacrificed their lives in the First and Second World Wars.

In France, those who were hit by rising fuel prices because the green transition was to be implemented—and for whom taking the bus or cycling was not an option because they lived in peripheral France—put on yellow vests and took to the streets in protest.

The Yellow Vests demonstrated that there was also something elitist about the green transition as conceived by ideologues. The type of ideologues who demand a green transition at any price often forget to say out loud that "any price" is also a price to be paid by people who already have very little money to spare—people who cannot simply afford to energy-renovate their homes and who cannot easily dispense with having two cars because their work depends on long commutes through sparsely populated areas.

In Germany, anger at the elite reached a peak after the riots in Cologne on New Year's Eve 2015, when a large number of women were assaulted by men of Middle Eastern background, in some documented cases newly arrived refugees.

The combination of refugees, sexual violence against innocent German women, and Islamist terrorism—which ravaged Europe during that period—was already explosive. The spark that caused it to explode was the political elite's almost complete denial that the three phenomena were connected. How many citizens in Germany were, during this period, disposed to listen to and vote for Alternative für Deutschland is unknown. But it is a reasonable guess that the number was high.

The American sociologist Rob Henderson later coined a term for the phenomenon that ignited the anger in Britain, France, and Germany alike: *luxury beliefs*.[50] That is, beliefs which the political elite enjoys expressing on social media and on late-night television talk shows, but which share the characteristic that it is not the elite itself that has to bear their consequences.

In this way, the 2010s end in a very dangerous place for the Western world.

The political elites still fail to see that their geo-economic strategy is inflicting a massive defeat on the West at the hands of opponents who think geostrategically and geopolitically.

At the same time, the part of the population that does not belong to the elite in many countries is becoming increasingly angry at having to bear the domestic political consequences of the geo-economic approach.

The decade in which resistance grew

As noted, the 2010s were a decade marked by growing resistance to the policies that Western elites wished to pursue.

At the same time, it was a period in which earlier assumptions about the inevitable triumph of globalisation and liberalisation were fundamentally challenged. Much against their will, Western elites were forced to confront the uncomfortable truth that not all countries shared Western values—and that many actively opposed them.

The decade was marked by increasing confrontation with Russia, particularly evident in the annexation of Crimea in 2014 and the support for separatists in eastern Ukraine. This was not merely a geopolitical challenge but also a clear manifestation of the West's failed policy toward Russia.

At the same time, China emerged as an even more complex challenge. Over the course of the decade, it gradually dawned on Western foreign ministries that what China was in fact working toward was, as previously explained, a "Pax Sinica" to replace the old "Pax Americana."

But this realisation was slow in coming and difficult to sell to the respective governments. As a result, Western countries continued to develop a dependence on Chinese investment and technology, undermining their ability to act freely and independently.

Internally, the West experienced a weakening of political cohesion and faith in its own institutions, creating space for successful populist movements—helped along by the slow recovery from the financial crisis and the poor handling of the refugee crisis in 2015–16.

Taken together, the 2010s became a decisive turning point, where earlier strategic mistakes and a lack of realism became evident. It was the decade in which the West lost momentum and confidence, both internally and externally, and in which the challenges from geopolitical rivals became more pressing than ever. The optimism that had previously defined the West's self-perception was replaced by a new, more anxious awareness of its own weaknesses and limitations.

Chapter 5

THE SHACKLES OF ENERGY

When I was a relatively young man, I was deeply influenced by two books. One of them was The End of History and the Last Man, *by Francis Fukuyama, and the second was* The Clash of Civilizations and the Remaking of World Order, *by Samuel Huntington. Fukuyama's book was a description of a brave new world, a new utopia where every country has the same political system based on a liberal parliamentary democracy — a nice dream, but nothing more. As for Huntington, he was realistic and cynical. He simply predicted the gradual emergence of conflicts among various types of civilisations.*

– President of the Czech Republic Miloš Zeman
At the UN General Assembly, 19 September 2017

Neglect always has a price. The debt that the Western countries had accumulated by ignoring geostrategy and geopolitics in favour of geoeconomics fell due for payment in the 2020s.

It was (probably) not a hostile political act in the traditional sense that revealed how costly it had been for the West to disregard its own security and focus on short-term interests. It was the COVID-19 pandemic.

It brutally demonstrated that the West had made itself vulnerable to global supply chains controlled by China and susceptible to exploitation for that country's economic or political benefit. In addition to being a global health crisis, the pandemic thus became an eye-opener for Western countries. Their economies and security rested on a foundation that had always been fragile and dangerous—above all because it had been extraordinarily naïve. And no one had listened to the warnings that had been continuously sounded since the 1990s.

As if the pandemic were not enough, Russia's invasion of Ukraine revealed that Europe had made itself far too dependent on Russian energy. A whole series of misjudgments—particularly German ones—collided at the beginning of the decade: the rejection of security guarantees for Ukraine; dependence on Russian gas; the abandonment of nuclear power; a failed migration policy and a failed handling of the criticism of that policy.

With the growing cooperation between Russia and China to counter Western interests, the first half of the 2020s became a "perfect storm" over the Western countries.

The Western countries now stand weakened. For that reason, there is cause for concern about their ability to solve these problems.

The weakening is due to a combination of many factors: declining trust in the EU; declining confidence that national politicians will resolve the most pressing problems, such as immigration; growing dissatisfaction with the cost of the green transition; and increasing polarisation, as many years of immigration from the Middle East now manifest themselves in the spread of conflicts from the region into Europe.

For the first time in decades, the Western countries find themselves engaged in a struggle they cannot be sure of winning.

An unlikely alliance becomes reality

At the parliamentary election in 2019, my party suffered a poor result. We lost nine seats and ended up with four—one of which quickly disappeared due to internal disagreement. There is little good to be said about this period in the party's history. But one bright spot deserves mention: we had rapid and effective decision-making processes within the parliamentary group.

We divided the many tasks that must be handled in a parliamentary group—so far as possible according to our individual interests—into three roughly equal piles. That is how I ended up becoming the party's spokesperson on health.

In 2020, the entire world was struck by COVID-19. It was a bewildering time, in which many major, serious, and not least controversial decisions had to be taken. Unsurprisingly, it was also an extremely demanding period. Against that background, I asked my two colleagues in the parliamentary group whether it would be acceptable for me, at the end of 2021, to say thank you for this round and hand over the position as health spokesperson. They were, of course, agreeable. So when the year 2022 dawned, I was no longer health spokesperson, but defence spokesperson.

How long was Adam in paradise? In my case: eight weeks. Then came 24 February 2022. Russia invaded Ukraine—first and foremost a catastrophe for the country's population. For my part, I was back where I had been before the New Year: holding a spokespersonship that required many long meetings almost around the clock, necessitated major decisions, and placed far-reaching demands on constantly mastering new material. One can never hide in politics. And one can never know where the next major crisis will strike.

With Russia's war against Ukraine—and let us be honest: against the Western world—the threads of action in this book converge. The war has shown that Russia, China, and Iran are allied with one another down to the practical level. Russia sells energy to China and thereby keeps its war machine running. Iran supplies drones and other weapons to Russia. In short: the war would not be possible for Russia without China and Iran.

As early as 1997, Zbigniew Brzezinski imagined that an anti-Western alliance between Russia, China, and Iran might one day emerge. Today it is a reality, even though Brzezinski also wrote that such an alliance was unlikely.

The motive for entering such an alliance, he said, would be a shared sense of grievance over Western dominance. That this shared grievance exists is beyond any doubt. Whether there also exists a positive shared vision is more doubtful.

There is a historical irony in the fact that both the predecessor state of modern Russia, the Soviet Union, and modern Iran were created through a "double revolution": first a common front against the old rulers; then a reckoning among the partners of the first revolution. In the Soviet Union's case, the Bolsheviks prevailed; in Iran's case, the religious fundamentalists under Khomeini.

If I stretch my imagination, I can envisage a kind of "February Revolution" against the Western countries—a revolution that in itself has no constructive program, but merely seeks to dismantle the existing order, led by the Russia–China–Iran alliance. But I cannot envisage how the three countries would thereafter lead the world into a new phase characterised by stability. As dreadful as it is to contemplate, a "February Revolution" against the West would undoubtedly end in an "October Revolution," in which the partners turn on one another.

Although the 2020s have become a decade in which the questions of Russia, China, the Middle East, and energy have flowed together, I will preserve the book's systematics and address them one at a time.

Russia

The Russian invasion of Ukraine in 2022 had been foreseeable since 2014, even though many media experts maintained until the very end that a Russian attack on Ukraine was unlikely. The Russian government does not recognise Ukraine as an independent country or an independent culture. It therefore seeks, at any price and under any pretext, to carry out an "Anschluss."

The pretext is that power in Ukraine has been seized by Nazis and that the Russian minority population is suffering.

The issue of Russian and Ukrainian language is delicate. Across Ukraine, Russian is often the language of everyday communication, and it is even Volodymyr Zelenskyy's mother tongue. But this means nothing in relation to Ukrainian patriotism. That clearly resides elsewhere than in language. I experienced this in November 2023, when I was travelling by car from the border between Moldova and Ukraine to Mykolaiv in southwestern Ukraine. At one point, our delegation needed to stop at a gas station. Everyone got out, and I was among those who wanted a cup of coffee in the cafeteria. Before I could order, however, the waitress had to dispose of two cups of coffee for a pair of truck drivers who had lost interest in their coffee and thrown themselves into a discussion about something or other. She caught their attention by shouting "maltjiki!" across the room. That is Russian and can loosely be translated as: "Hey, guys!" That people speak like this in the area around Odesa and Mykolaiv has nothing to do with patriotic sentiment. It is simply a tradition that does not change overnight because of the war.

That "true Russia" and "true Ukraine" belong together is a lie one is immediately reminded of when speaking with representatives of the Ukrainian government. When the Foreign Policy Committee met with Prime Minister Denys Shmyhal in Kyiv in

March 2023, one item on his agenda was a request that Denmark officially recognise the Russian genocide against Ukrainians in 1933–1934, known as the Holodomor. Unfortunately, this is a sensitive issue, because Denmark does not, as a rule, maintain a list of officially recognised political truths.

When later in 2023 I had the opportunity in Copenhagen to exchange a few words with Zelenskyy, I therefore took the opportunity to say that in Denmark we were aware of the desire for some form of recognition and hoped to be able to find a way forward. Zelenskyy responded by saying that this was particularly important because it was something that could not be spoken about in Soviet times and that, for the sake of the younger generations, it needed to be brought into the open.

Zelenskyy's visit to Copenhagen was prompted by the agreement to deliver F-16 fighter jets to Ukraine. It marked a kind of provisional conclusion to the by now long history of Western hesitation vis-à-vis Ukraine. For many years—going all the way back to Russia's first aggressions against the country in 2014—the Western countries had repeatedly been slow or reluctant to assist Ukraine with anything beyond symbolic means. In particular, they avoided sending heavy weapons such as tanks, advanced artillery, and combat aircraft, for fear of provoking Russia. But when Russia launched its full-scale invasion of Ukraine in February 2022, this picture gradually changed. Although many Western countries were still cautious and often hesitant at the outset, the consequence of the invasion was nonetheless that they gradually abandoned their restraint. With each new phase of the war, the boundaries were pushed back, and the Western countries gradually supplied more advanced weapons and more extensive military assistance.

Despite this growing Western effort, the result has nevertheless been a stalemate. As these lines are written, the conflict has therefore ended up as a frozen conflict, in which the front lines move little and Russia continues to control approximately one fifth of Ukraine's territory.

Politically, Russia's war against Ukraine has, in the most paradoxical (and dialectical) way, had a number of beneficial effects in the Western countries. Sweden and Finland have joined NATO. This completely alters the balance of power in the Baltic region. From a Russian perspective, it has tipped in the wrong direction in recent years. It should also be noted that, by joining NATO, Sweden abandoned a security doctrine introduced in the aftermath of the Napoleonic Wars. That says everything about the seriousness of the Russian threat to the West.

The greatly increased deterrence in the Baltic region has not, however, prevented Russia from escalating its hybrid warfare in the area. With sabotage against critical infrastructure, cyberattacks, jamming of GPS signals, and constant provocations by the Russian air force, it is incorrect to say that Russia is threatening the Western countries with hybrid war. The hybrid war is already under way. It is a fact we must relate to—and initially learn to live with.

Russia interferes in elections in a manner that can only be described as disturbing.

A couple of Russia's—and previously the Soviet Union's—overarching goals have always been to divide the Western countries and to weaken European cooperation.

In recent years, Russia has sought to promote division by interfering in elections wherever it can. Both Georgia and Moldova felt this during their respective elections in 2024.

In both countries, independent election observers expressed serious concern that the elections had not been conducted properly, and in both cases there was highly credible testimony of Russian interference.

When the Foreign Policy Committee paid a visit to Moldova at the end of 2023, the country's president, Maia Sandu, had set aside time for a meeting. She made a strong impression by responding thoughtfully and candidly to every question posed. With regard to Russian interference, she said that it was a problem and something that made her view the (at that time) upcoming election with concern. But the reality, she said, was that one could not and should not resort to illiberal means such as censorship—even if the aim were to preserve Moldova as a politically liberal and democratic society. Maia Sandu added that, in dealing with disinformation, she was greatly inspired by Estonia and that, as a former minister of education, she placed her trust in good schools as an effective means of countering it.

As for the weakening of the EU, it is a well-known fact that Russia—sometimes, regrettably, with success—has resorted to bribing members of, for example, the European Parliament. But the country also pursues a strategy of infecting countries in Eastern and Central Europe with Russian narratives. As one of my Czech colleagues in the European Parliament remarked, there appears to be a Habsburg problem: for reasons unknown, countries that were once part of Austria-Hungary seem particularly susceptible to listening to, and in some cases yielding to, Russian propaganda.

It is debated how hard Russia has been hit by Western sanctions. A good indicator is the interest rate, which has been sky-high for most of the war against Ukraine. An economist would say that interest rates at such levels are probably the result of a reduced supply of the most sought-after goods (for example, foreign spare parts for machinery and the like), combined with capital flight due to rising general uncertainty. And they are an attractive choice for the central bank only because the alternative to the declining economic activity caused by high interest rates is worse: inflation spiraling completely out of control.

Because Russia is not a democracy, however, the government finds itself in the—for itself—fortunate position of not having to take into account the popular discontent that, in a Western country, would be the inevitable consequence of the explosive price increases experienced in the country. The government's position vis-à-vis the population is also strengthened by the fact that a quite substantial share of the Russian population presumably supports the war.

No one can say how the Russian–Western relationship will develop over the next five to ten years. But I can say this much: at a Nordic-Baltic evening in Brussels in the spring of 2025, where the Finnish prime minister and most of the center-right EU commissioners were speakers, no one suggested anything other than that one must, regrettably, expect the worst—and therefore rearm and have a fully credible deterrence in place by 2030 at the latest.

As compensation for the completely frozen relationship with the Western countries, Russia has thrown its energy into BRICS cooperation. This was evident not least at the BRICS summit in Kazan in 2024.

The summit was the first since Egypt, Ethiopia, Iran, and the United Arab Emirates formally became members of BRICS on 1 January 2024.

It was carefully staged to demonstrate how the Global South stands united in combating Western influence—among other things by introducing the concept of "partner countries," which at the Kazan meeting included Algeria, Belarus, Bolivia, Cuba, Indonesia, Kazakhstan, Malaysia, Nigeria, Thailand, Turkey, Uganda, Uzbekistan, and Vietnam.

The meeting continued to focus on undermining American

and Western dominance over the global economy, among other things by strengthening trade in local currencies between BRICS and partner countries and by continuing the development of a BRICS-controlled replacement for the Western system of international payments known as SWIFT.

From a Western perspective, perhaps the most worrying aspect was that the Kazan meeting also provided the setting for a summit between Xi Jinping and Narendra Modi. In the West, India has always been seen as a strategically important country attempting to balance between the West and the anti-Western axis. Consequently, no one in the West fundamentally wishes for India to move away from its carefully cultivated neutral position.

In a certain sense, there is nothing new about anti-Western countries cooperating to weaken Western influence. They have done so since the Bandung Conference in Indonesia in 1955, to which we shall return. Even so, in the context of how anti-Western sentiment has developed over the past twenty years, it is deeply worrying that today it is as formalised as it is.

China

With respect to China, the 2020s in many ways continued along the trajectory on which the 2010s had ended. Aggressive behavior in the South China Sea, for example, manifested itself in an escalation of the conflict with the Philippines over the grounded ship *Sierra Madre*. Since 1999, it has functioned as a Philippine base at the reef known as Second Thomas Shoal. In 2023, however, the Chinese Coast Guard used water cannons to prevent supply vessels from reaching the site, and floating barriers were also deployed. This behavior on China's part was met with sharp international protests.

In 2021, it was Lithuania's turn to experience that China does not tolerate countries holding views that diverge from those of the government in Beijing.

In Vilnius, a representative office was opened under the name "Taiwanese Representative Office." This prompted protests from China, which regarded it as a challenge to the principle that there is only one China.

The government in Vilnius refused to fall into line. As a result, China recalled its ambassador from Lithuania and declared the Lithuanian ambassador in Beijing persona non grata. In addition, Chinese trade restrictions were imposed, disrupting supply chains not only in Lithuania itself but across Europe.

The EU's response has been significantly tougher than it had previously been accustomed to. In 2023, the EU introduced its so-called Anti-Coercion Instrument (ACI). This is an economic tool designed to prevent a single country from being economically targeted by a non-EU country. There is no doubt that the instrument was designed with China in mind. Paradoxically, however, after Donald Trump came to power in the United States in 2025, it became necessary to consider whether it might also have to be used if the U.S. were to punish an individual EU member state.

The activation of the ACI can be decided by a majority vote and operates by allowing the EU to impose both tariffs and trade restrictions on a non-EU country that threatens an EU member state. In addition, the EU can restrict that country's access to public procurement and conduct controls on investments and services.

One can say that, in this way, the EU has become far more conscious of its sovereignty and how it is protected than the organisation was previously. After the pressure exerted on Denmark in 2009 and on Lithuania in 2021, the next conflict between China and an EU member state will, in all likelihood, follow a very different course.

A pandemic begins in China

The single most significant event to affect China's relationship with the rest of the world in the 2020s, however, has been the COVID-19 pandemic.

At the end of 2019, news emerged from Wuhan, China, of a previously unknown type of virus. This was the so-called SARS-CoV-2, which causes acute problems with the lungs and thus with respiration. The new virus quickly became known as COVID-19.

Although China informed the World Health Organisation (WHO) relatively quickly, the country was nevertheless criticised internationally. Information about the severity of the disease was initially suppressed, critics claimed, and China also displayed considerable sluggishness toward the international community when it came to getting to the bottom—medically speaking—of what kind of disease it actually was.

However, it was the consequences for global supply chains that truly alarmed economists and other observers around the world.

The outbreak of the pandemic revealed that global supply chains were far more fragile than had been assumed—above all because many countries had put all their eggs in one basket and were unable to find alternatives when supplies from China stopped. The pandemic also exposed how dangerous it was for Western countries to outsource critical supplies such as medicines and pharmaceuticals.

Although the origin of the COVID-19 virus remains contested, it makes more sense to compare the pandemic to a natural disaster than to a deliberate hostile act. But this natural disaster nonetheless turned into a severe shock for Western countries.

It did so because, despite the advances in medical science that had occurred over the preceding hundred years, it became the deadliest epidemic since the Spanish flu, which ravaged the world in the years immediately following the First World War.

It also became an economic and political shock because it exposed a fragility that had been built systemically into globalisation and was therefore not easily remedied. Prior to COVID-19, very few people had considered that outsourcing could be downright dangerous and cost human lives—just as very few had reflected on the risks of relying on a single country as a supplier of critical components.

As a result, the COVID-19 pandemic triggered more discussions about societal security, strategic autonomy, and the reshoring of production than at any other point in the history of globalisation since 1990.

Although it was rarely stated openly, all of these discussions shared a tacit heading: that the world had inflicted upon itself a very serious problem in its relationship with China.

Where the financial crisis around 2008 had been a warning about the risks associated with the fact that virtually the entire world was interconnected financially, the COVID-19 pandemic—just over a decade later—became a warning about the dangers inherent in the global integration of the production economy itself.

Cooperation with Russia intensifies

The 2020s have also witnessed a sharp intensification of Russian-Chinese cooperation. Given the differences between the two countries' economies and their global influence more generally, there is no doubt that China is the senior partner in the Russian-Chinese relationship.

Russia's extensive war effort against Ukraine since 2022 has been possible solely because China has backed it with money and weapons.[51]

As already noted, Russia and China have for many years cooperated on energy matters. This has, for example, been expressed through the *Power of Siberia* gas pipeline, which opened in 2019.

In order to compensate for sanctions, China has significantly increased its purchases of natural gas, oil, coal, and electricity. This is, of course, advantageous for China, which has been able to exploit Russia's export crisis to push prices down. But it is an even greater advantage for Russia, because it ensures that money continues to flow into the state coffers at a time when Western markets are largely closed.

As part of its efforts to counter the West and strengthen itself, China has also pushed through the settlement of Russian-Chinese energy transactions in yuan rather than in U.S. dollars.

Officially, China denies exporting weapons and dual-use products to Russia. Nevertheless, there is reliable evidence that China has at least exported drones, small arms, body armor, rare metals, processors, and similar items, as well as chemicals necessary for the production of artillery shells. There is also reliable evidence that China provides satellite intelligence to Russia.

All in all, the situation is therefore that China has become actively involved in the largest war in Europe since the Second World War. It is impermissibly naïve to believe that the country remains a neutral manufacturing hub that has simply found its place in the geo-economic order. Every day, Europeans die who would not have lost their lives had China stayed out of the Russia–Ukraine war.

That China is actively contributing to the deterioration of Europe's security environment and forcing the continent into massive rearmament is, however, difficult to discuss during official visits.

I travelled to China with the Danish Foreign Policy Committee in 2023. It was my first visit to the country since 2017, and the difference was noticeable. This time we were received with considerably greater coldness (perhaps also because we began the visit with a few days in Hong Kong). And the list of topics that could not be discussed had grown longer.

It is an old joke among Western diplomats that, on official visits to China, one should avoid "the three Ts": Tibet, Tiananmen, and Taiwan. The list has clearly had been expanded to include Russia and Ukraine. If one—as the delegation attempted several times—steers a conversation toward the fact that China is approaching a kind of tolerance threshold by involving itself in an armed conflict in Europe, the typical reaction is that it is ignored, after which the Chinese interlocutor moves on to another topic.

At a dinner at the Chinese embassy in Copenhagen shortly after the official visit, I was seated next to the ambassador. He was a congenial elderly gentleman, and the atmosphere was good. I therefore tried—without being confrontational—to explain to him why Russians were unpopular in Europe. "They helped start the Second World War," I told him (because the Soviet Union, as a consequence of the Molotov–Ribbentrop Pact of 1939, attacked Poland a few weeks after Germany). Whether the ambassador was an excellent actor or genuinely believed the old Soviet narrative of being Hitler's victim, I do not know. But he appeared genuinely surprised by my remarks—after which, as usual, we got no further.

At the same time as China has become actively involved in a proxy war against Western countries, it has, throughout the 2020s as already noted, continued to recruit countries in Africa and

South America to its anti-Western project, not least under the auspices of BRICS.

It is well known that discretion can take one far—even in relations between states. But it is my personal view that, in the long run, the West does not act wisely by pretending that nothing is happening when it comes to China. In my view, it would be salutary if Western countries were to officially declare geo-economics dead and formally acknowledge that relations with countries hostile to the West are now entering a new phase.

This need not be a phase characterised by overt hostility. But it should be a phase in which interaction takes place on the premise that interests do not coincide, and on the premise that Western countries will no longer tolerate being exploited in the same way as before when it comes to violations of agreements—agreements that, for example, China has voluntarily entered into. That presupposes a credible military deterrent. But so be it.

Energy

When Russia invaded Ukraine on 24 February 2022, Germany's energy strategy collapsed overnight. On that day it became clear to everyone that Germany's dependence on Russian natural gas had led to an accommodation of Russia that was not only dangerous for Germany, but for all of Europe.

But the invasion also revealed that the entire European strategy for both growth and security—one in which Germany had taken the lead—was a dangerous illusion that had now fallen apart.

Put bluntly, the European strategy consisted of outsourcing energy to Russia, production to China, and security to the United States. Russia's attack on Ukraine now challenged the entire world order that had prevailed since the Second World War. China, by accepting in the UN Security Council that Russia was violating the UN Charter, helped undermine the multilateral system and Europe's security. And since Donald Trump's first term in office, the United States had threatened and stated explicitly that NATO's Article 5 on collective defence was not a given if Europe continued to underinvest in its own security.

What could Europe do about this? In the short term: not much. Without a replacement for Russian energy before the heating season began in the autumn of 2022, the population of Germany would have had to freeze through the winter of 2022/23. Long before that, serious difficulties would have arisen for the energy-intensive parts of German industry, which are substantial. Democratically elected politicians could not afford to ignore either of these realities.

Without a solution to the China question, economic activity in Europe would quickly grind to a halt, as shortages would emerge of components and critical raw materials that had been outsourced to China.

And without credible deterrence, Europe could adopt as many strongly worded resolutions as its politicians had the stamina to vote for. It would make no impression on the two dictatorship states, Russia and China. They could calmly afford to disregard what a paralysed and defenceless continent thought about the course of world affairs.

In September 2022, the Nord Stream 2 gas pipelines were blown up. To this day, no one knows who was responsible. But the sabotage triggered an acute energy crisis in Germany and across Europe.

The crisis was averted through a combination of measures. Energy supplies were diversified by building terminals for liquefied natural gas (LNG) and purchasing LNG from various countries such as Qatar, Norway, and the United States. Fortunately, Poland had shown foresight and taken the initiative on the Baltic Pipe project, which connects Norway with Poland and was from the outset intended as an instrument to reduce dependence on Russian gas. It now proved to be more than useful.

Germany also had to resort temporarily to coal-fired power generation, which hardly brings the country any closer to achieving its green objectives.

In the longer term, Europe will benefit from the more strategic initiatives triggered by the gas crisis. These include the RePowerEU plan, which focuses both on expanding renewable energy and on improving energy efficiency, as well as Germany's national plans to expand hydrogen infrastructure.

As far as the latter is concerned, there is reason to warn against excessive optimism. At a seminar in Brussels in the spring of 2025, I heard the chief executive of a steel plant explain the energy consumption of the steel industry. It emerged that, at that point, a single hydrogen-powered production facility was consuming as much hydrogen as was produced in the EU over an entire year.

This does not, of course, mean that a sharp increase in hydrogen production in the coming years is impossible. But it does point to the fundamental problem that many of the energy solutions proposed in connection with the green transition require astronomical investments in new infrastructure. The financing of hydrogen infrastructure and new electrical infrastructure has not even been specified. When that eventually happens, projects must be developed and environmentally approved before they can be built. There is therefore good reason to caution against the belief that the green transition can be completed in the near future.

The uncomfortable truth about Russia and energy has so far been that Europe, regrettably, continues to transfer significant sums to the Russian state treasury each year and thus, paradoxically, helps finance the very Russian war effort it most vehemently opposes.

Europe's energy problems are structural in nature. They stem from the success of scare campaigns against the use of nuclear power in so many countries—above all Germany. Had there been serious resistance to the exaggerations and distortions advanced for decades by green movements across the continent, CO_2 emissions would be significantly lower today. At the same time, Europe would not be forced to rely on unstable energy sources and on energy technologies whose most critical components are outsourced to the geostrategic rival China.

But again: the geostrategic perspective has for decades been displaced in Europe and the West by a geo-economic one. As a result, Western countries are chronically vulnerable to blackmail by all manner of regimes they dislike when it comes to energy: Islamist regimes in the Gulf and autocratic adversaries such as Russia and China.

It is impossible to say when the weakness of the green transition—its structural dependence on supplies from geostrategic adversaries—will produce tangible consequences. But given that developments in recent years point only towards sharper antagonisms, there is ample reason for concern. The green transition could very well become the next prominent victim of the intensifying rivalry between the West and the Russia–China–Iran axis.

In connection with all these failings, it is impossible to avoid discussing Germany's role.

Germany was among those who rejected Ukraine and Georgia as candidates for NATO membership in 2008. Ultimately, this contributed to both countries being invaded by Russia. In Georgia's case, the invasion occurred before the country could realistically have become a NATO member. In Ukraine's case, accession could quite plausibly have been completed before Russia was militarily capable of attempting an invasion.

For many years, Germany pursued an energy policy that was extremely risky and rested on a premise that was demonstrably false from at least 2007 onwards: that Russia was a credible and reliable partner. Poland and the Baltic states warned against this on numerous occasions, as did Donald Trump during his first presidential term. All to no avail, regrettably. Germany knew better, and the arguments against German energy policy made no impression in Berlin.

Taken together, one therefore cannot escape the unfortunate conclusion that few countries in Europe have done more than Germany to strengthen Russia and to make the former Soviet republics insecure.

Germany has not been alone in underestimating the risks of outsourcing critical production to China, nor in underinvesting in credible military deterrence. The problem lies in the fact that Germany has assumed a leading role in the EU and has been asked by most other countries to do so.

Unfortunately, geostrategic thinking has been even more underdeveloped in Germany than in the rest of the EU. The risk of trusting one's map rather than reality grows when one begins to believe in ideologised narratives about this or that. It is therefore especially regrettable that faith in the civilising effects of trade was stronger in Europe's most important country than anywhere else. But it is also a mark of poor leadership not to make it an integral part of one's practice to ask a group of trusted experts and officials to stress-test the premises of day-to-day policy. Any leaders who wish to be equal to the task must build this into their way of working. Clearly, this did not happen.

One final area in which Germany most regrettably failed both itself and Europe from the 2010s to the present is immigration policy.

Because of its historical experience, Germany has a particular reluctance to rejecting asylum seekers. This is something the political elite is deeply uncomfortable with, even though the German constitution actually allows for it, and the Constitutional Court has ruled that the right to asylum is limited to cases of political persecution.

In Germany, however, there has been less awareness than in Denmark that rulings by the European Court of Human Rights mean that asylum seekers usually become migrants, and that migrants usually obtain family reunification. One consequence has been that the demographic composition of major cities such as Berlin has changed noticeably over recent decades.

Another issue that has received less attention in Germany than in Denmark is that culture has consequences.

As a group, immigrants from the Greater Middle East tend to stand out, both in relation to serious crime and to the milder forms of criminality that can be categorised as antisocial behaviour. They also tend to stand out in terms of patriarchal violence in the home, mediocre performance in schools, and high levels of unemployment and dependence on social benefits.

This does not mean that there are no exceptions at the individual level. But as a statistical aggregate, the data confirm my description. We know this in Denmark because it is not taboo to collect statistics on such matters.

In Germany, however—and here historical experience again plays a role—it is taboo to speak in general terms about ethnic groups. This is understandable, given that one particular group paid a terrible price for such generalisations under the Third

Reich. But it has resulted, seen from a Danish perspective, in a highly inflamed and distorted debate on immigration in Germany. Positions that are considered entirely banal in a Danish political debate can often be extremely controversial when expressed in German debates.

The heavy taboos surrounding the discussion of immigration in Germany have unfortunately contributed to significant radicalisation of political life. On the one hand, Alternative für Deutschland has undoubtedly become more radical in its political expression as a result of being ostracised from normal political life. On the other hand, the opponents of Alternative für Deutschland have undoubtedly become more radicalised in their denial and rejection of the real problems associated with immigration from the Greater Middle East, because this often forms part of an almost identity-political rejection of the immigration-critical position.

The result has been a Germany that is extremely difficult to govern. This is because the political elite has decided, at any price, to disregard the voices of 20–25 percent of voters—and thereby also to disregard a large share of the problems that 20–25 percent of voters consider the most important.

This has given disproportionate power to the Greens, who have contributed more than anyone else to Germany's failed energy policy through their opposition to nuclear power. And it has given ordinary voters a sense of powerlessness. CDU/CSU and the SPD confront each other during election campaigns with harsh rhetoric and sharply drawn contrasts, only in many cases to come together afterwards in a governing arrangement. That German citizens are often struck by the disillusioned feeling encapsulated in the line, "Meet the new boss. Same as the old boss," is hardly surprising.

Germany's extremely naïve approach to refugees and immigrants—particularly from the Greater Middle East—spread throughout the 2010s and 2020s to the entire EU. This happened because Germany delayed a revision of the regulatory framework governing the area and obstructed effective control at the external border. In this way, Germany has, over the period in question, helped export its own right-wing radicalisation to other European countries. Regrettably, one must conclude that the leading country in the EU became a leader across a wide range of areas in making the West's problems worse—not in solving them.

The Middle East

On 7 October 2023, Israel was attacked by Hamas. Approximately 1,200 Israelis were killed, and around 250 were taken hostage. The attack constituted the worst massacre of Jews since the Second World War.

The attack is, in any case, worthy of close examination. But the reason it must be addressed in this book is that it illuminates both Western weakness and the strength of the anti-Western axis in a manner that is analytically revealing.

The United Nations has never, in unequivocal terms, condemned Hamas as the party responsible for the massacre—neither in the Security Council nor in the General Assembly. In the Security Council, Russia has been the principal force blocking an unambiguous condemnation. In the General Assembly, large parts of the so-called Global South have been unwilling to condemn Hamas without qualifications.

This is paradoxical, given that the United Nations is a direct product of the Second World War and thus of the Nazi persecution of the Jews.

Yet the UN has, regrettably, developed into an institution that displays a particular zeal in criticising Israel while showing understanding for the Palestinian cause—even when that cause, as is the case today, is fundamentally infiltrated by a terrorist organisation such as Hamas, and thus by Iran, which pulls many of the strings in the struggle against Israel.

What is particularly striking, when one is interested in the West's contemporary defeat at the hands of its anti-Western adversaries, is the aftermath of the attack on Israel on 7 October 2023.

In retaliation, Israel—as expected—launched attacks against Hamas in the days that followed. This triggered a global propaganda war, of which it is difficult to say anything other than that Hamas has won.

In the Western world, news media have generally been uncritical in their reporting of figures and accounts emerging from Gaza, despite the fact that these are entirely controlled and managed by Hamas.

This has, for example, led to a general downplaying of the fact that Egypt also shares a border with Gaza—a border that is just as closed as Israel's, for the same reasons: a desire to avoid infiltration by a terrorist movement devoid of scruples.

It has also led to a general downplaying of the fact that Hamas systematically violates international humanitarian law by conducting military operations from civilian areas, including hospitals. Similarly, it may reasonably be argued that it constitutes a violation of international humanitarian law when what is in effect an army fights without uniforms.

Conversely, Western media have generally relayed Hamas's casualty figures, despite serious doubts having been raised about their reliability. They have likewise repeated Hamas's claim that famine prevailed in Gaza, even though this later proved to be incorrect.

What can now be said to be true is that Israel has primarily killed men of fighting age, although there have also been collateral casualties—and that there has been no famine among the civilian population in Gaza.

Hamas—supported by countries in the Global South—has been remarkably effective in promoting a narrative portraying Palestinians as victims of Israel. The most striking example is the lawsuit alleging Israeli genocide that has been brought before the International Court of Justice.

In 2024, the International Court of Justice ruled that the case was sufficiently plausible to warrant consideration on the merits. Although representatives of the Court have explained that this decision had nothing to do with a determination of guilt, Hamas's propaganda apparatus has since worked around the clock to establish genocide as an accepted fact.

Another international judicial body, the International Criminal Court (ICC), has issued arrest warrants against, among others, Benjamin Netanyahu. This has led to fierce condemnation in the Global South of countries that do not arrest Netanyahu.

This condemnation rings hollow for several reasons. Countries such as China, India, Saudi Arabia, and the United Arab Emirates are not members of the ICC at all. Consequently, they have had no difficulty hosting Vladimir Putin, who is also wanted by the ICC.

Ahead of the BRICS summit in Johannesburg in late 2023, the African National Congress (ANC) went to great lengths to avoid having to arrest Vladimir Putin should he attend. In the end, Putin stayed away, partly because the opposition Democratic Alliance sought to force the ANC to demonstrate greater consistency in its condemnation of war crimes than has actually been the case. That the ANC is hypocritical when it comes to condemning war crimes and war criminals can hardly be subject to reasonable doubt.

The most remarkable aspect of the entire episode surrounding Hamas's massacre of Jews on 7 October 2023 and its aftermath has, however, been the reaction in the West.

In French, one speaks of *islamo-gauchisme*—that is, the alliance between Islamism and the far left in the West. The islamo-leftist alliance is, in itself, so paradoxical that it merits discussion. Hamas is an Islamist movement whose political programme bears more than a passing resemblance to that of the Islamic State. The extreme left, by contrast, consists of militant advocates of, among other things, the rights of sexual minorities—including forms of rights that many in the West consider extreme, such as allowing men who identify as women access to women's changing rooms and participation in women's sports.

That sexual minorities of the kind championed by the extreme left would, after a brief process, be executed by Hamas appears not to trouble the left. Nor does the fact that Islamists occupy a fundamentally different position on women's general equality.

Islamo-leftism has captured a large number of universities in the United States—a development the Trump administration has begun to confront, though that is another matter. It has, however, also captured many universities in Europe.

In conjunction with large-scale immigration from the Middle East, islamo-leftism has thus, overall, imported the Israel–Palestine conflict into Europe as a "hot" conflict and has contributed to a sharp rise in antisemitism across Western Europe.

It is extremely difficult to engage islamo-leftists in ordinary political discourse. This is because they uphold their dogmas at any cost and against any argument. For example, the many structural similarities between the way modern Turkey was created and the way modern Israel was created make no impression whatsoever on the typical islamo-leftist.

Turkey is never criticised for occupying land colonised at the expense of Greeks, Armenians, and Kurds, whereas Israel is consistently criticised for occupying land colonised at the expense of Palestinians—despite the fact that Turkish conduct toward non-Turkish peoples on Turkish territory has often been far more violent than Jewish conduct toward non-Jews on Israeli territory.

Personally, I cannot arrive at any conclusion other than that the difference in islamo-leftist perceptions of Turkey and Israel ultimately rests on antisemitism.

The developments following 7 October 2023 demonstrate, first, what *lawfare* entails. Conducting political and military struggle through litigation is extraordinarily effective from a propaganda perspective.

Second, they show that the battle on social media is global. It is fought with troll factories, manipulated videos, and disinformation of every kind, and it can be extremely difficult for a Western country to win.

Third, they show how a multilateral organisation such as the UN has been hijhacked and instrumentalised by the Global South—a process that has been underway since the Bandung Conference of 1955, to which we shall return.

Fourth, they show that even on home ground in the West, Western agendas now struggle to prevail. Ultimately, there is only one winner of the propaganda triumphs celebrated by islamo-leftists in the West: the Islamists and global jihad.

A Northern realism

Since the Russian invasion of Ukraine, Denmark—historically cautious in its dealings with Germany—has aligned itself firmly with Sweden, Finland, the Baltic states, and Poland in a markedly more hard-edged security posture: it has been among the most generous supporters of Ukraine in military and financial terms, it has committed unprecedented long-term increases in defence spending, and it has abolished its EU defence opt-out with a strikingly strong popular mandate; at the same time, it has not hesitated to criticise those European partners whose policies on Russia, China, energy, and migration it regards as naïve or strategically short-sighted—a message clearly understood in Berlin. Yet Europe does not speak with one voice: threat perceptions diverge sharply across the continent, some governments remain openly pro-Russian, southern member states have contributed only modestly to Ukraine's defence, and the institutional landscapes of the EU and NATO only partially overlap. The likely result is neither grand design nor seamless unity, but a pragmatic adhocracy in which countries sharing a sober assessment of geopolitical realities intensify cooperation within and beyond existing treaty frameworks. In that light, groupings such as the UK-led Joint Expeditionary Force—bringing together the Nordic and Baltic countries, the Netherlands, and the United Kingdom—may evolve into a de facto northern pillar of European security. After decades in which trade was treated as a diplomatic panacea, Western countries are rediscovering that strategic autonomy and credible deterrence require power, alignment, and political will. The first step is recognition; the second is sustained action.

Chapter 6

FAITH IN INSTITUTIONS

With the end of the superpower confrontation, new opportunities for international cooperation have emerged. One of the most prominent examples of this is the cooperation among the permanent members of the UN Security Council.

– Danish minister of foreign affairs
Niels Helveg Petersen, 1993

It is not the case that political elites were seized by collective madness after the fall of the Wall. It made good sense to pursue at least some of the policies that were adopted. At a very basic level, it should be remembered that after defeating the Soviet Union, the Western countries were left without a workable roadmap for what should follow the dissolution of that empire.

There were many good reasons to reject the model from the First World War. The humiliation of Germany played a major role in setting in motion the dynamics that led to the creation of the Third Reich and thus the Second World War. Moreover, that model presupposed the existence of an official document akin to an armistice agreement.

The model from the Second World War, by contrast, presupposed that the defeated party had surrendered unconditionally or almost unconditionally—as was the case with Germany and Japan. In that situation, the victors could move in and de facto occupy the two countries, dismantle the old political elites, and dictate a new constitution and new political institutions. None of these conditions were present when the Soviet Union and the Eastern Bloc dissolved.

Nevertheless, there was—perhaps unconsciously—a considerable degree of inspiration drawn from post–Second World War reconstruction when the Wall fell. It was quickly agreed that the countries that had broken free from the Soviet Union should be offered generous economic assistance to build a standard of living comparable to that of Western Europe. It was also agreed fairly swiftly to offer the countries of Central and Eastern Europe integration into the cooperative organisations that already existed. Taken as a whole, all these measures were sensible and, to a large extent, worked as intended.

Unfortunately, there were early signs of discord. The integration of the GDR and the Federal Republic of Germany was never as successful as contemporary politicians had dreamed. Angela Merkel—who herself comes from the GDR—addresses this at some length in her memoirs and urges her readers to try to view reunification from the East German perspective.

Many East Germans felt that the privatizations handled by the state agency Treuhand were "structurally unjust" toward them. Because of the way the rules were designed, for example, the prices of land that homeowners were legally obliged to purchase rose in ways that were highly unpredictable and varied widely from place to place.

In some areas, West German speculators took over homes that

had previously been intended for permanent residence and converted them into holiday properties. This meant that the original residents were forced to move to new addresses that were far less attractive.

Elsewhere, West German companies acquired East German firms that they initially intended to turn into subsidiaries. But at the first sign of crisis, the East German branches were shut down, leaving people without jobs.

Everywhere, infrastructure was underdeveloped compared with what could be observed in West Germany. Although substantial funds were allocated to remedy this deficiency, it naturally took many years to do so.

And almost worst of all: the criteria for receiving compensation as a victim of the East German Socialist Unity Party (SED) regime were defined very narrowly. This, of course, caused great pain to the victims—especially because, in 1999, the German Federal Constitutional Court decided that former employees of the Stasi and the National People's Army were still entitled to their pensions in the new, reunified Germany.

Unfortunately, when the reckoning is done, the shadow border between the GDR and the Federal Republic became more pronounced rather than softened during Merkel's long tenure. The difference in the relative popularity of Alternative für Deutschland in the two parts of Germany bears this out.

But it was not only the experience of reconstructing Western Europe after the Second World War that spoke in favour of the political course pursued from the 1990s onward.

The economic theories most popular among Western political elites in the 1980s and 1990s emphasised market liberalisation above all else. It was through liberalisation that the economies of both the United States and the United Kingdom had been revitalised during the 1980s. Similarly, it was through market economies that an economic growth miracle had been created in Southeast Asia.

To defend the political elites of the 1980s and 1990s, they had a good case for believing that market liberalisation would lead both to economic growth and to the development of a democratic culture.

Correlation confused with causation

Germany and Japan had developed into democratic societies after the Second World War. And by the late 1980s, democracy had finally arrived in South Korea—not because it had been imposed from outside, but because the majority of the population desired it.

The fact that, in three major countries on two continents, there was a correlation between market liberalisation and entrenched democracy tempted many to assume that there was also a form of causality. The idea that this was not merely a coincidence but also a causal relationship unfortunately evolved rapidly from a hypothesis into something like an ideology.

Without critically examining their own assumptions or stress-testing them sufficiently, political elites came to assume that market liberalisation—especially when combined with the creation of democratic institutions—would causally lead to democracy. This was what the superficial observer might infer from Germany and Japan immediately after the Second World War and from South Korea in the 1980s.

What likely contributed to elites confusing the correlation between market economies and democratic institutions in three war-torn countries with a general causal mechanism was the sense of triumph that also spread after 1989.

As I have already noted, 1989 is in fact an ambiguous year, because it contains both the uplifting news that totalitarianism can be defeated and the depressing news that totalitarianism was advancing in Iran and remained firmly entrenched in China. Yet the narrative quickly took hold that 1989 was a jubilee year for democracy and human rights. Along with it came the narrative—inspired by a superficial reading of Francis Fukuyama—that the market-based and politically liberal society represented a kind of historical necessity, and that trade, interdependence, and integration into the world economy had a civilising effect.

There was some empirical basis for the decision to integrate Russia and China into the world economy. But many of the hopes that this alone would transform the two countries into liberal democracies rested on a banal confusion of correlation with causation (aided by far too few data points). On top of this came a triumphant sense that Western countries were on the right side of history and, in a sense, midwives to historical necessity.

As for the belief that the Islamic world could be democratised, it is harder to discern the good reasons that might justify this delusion. I will address that in detail later.

The integration of the two Germanies as an experimental setup

It is difficult to determine precisely how quickly political elites should have revised their belief in a straightforward causal link between market liberalisation and institution-building, on the one hand, and the organic flourishing of democratic culture and norms, on the other. Yet the troubled integration of the former GDR into the Federal Republic during the 1990s should already have prompted a more systematic re-examination of that assumption. One might view German reunification as a natural sociological experiment—arguably the closest approximation to a laboratory setting that modern European history can offer. Five new federal states were incorporated directly alongside nine old ones; they shared language, geography, and a long common history. If massive economic transfers and intense administrative effort were sufficient conditions for democratic consolidation, the outcome should have been straightforward. The implicit hypothesis would read: inject capital, construct institutions, align legal frameworks—and democratic culture will follow.

It did not. What became evident was that institutional and economic integration, however necessary, were not sufficient. The former GDR carried social patterns, expectations of authority, and civic habits shaped by decades without meaningful democratic experience—apart from the brief and fragile interlude of the Weimar Republic. Cultural legacies proved more resilient than anticipated. As Angela Merkel's memoirs indirectly illustrate, everyday life in the GDR, despite its official ideology, often remained more socially conservative and norm-bound than the Federal Republic that had undergone the cultural liberalisation, individualisation, americanisation, and permissiveness of the 1960s and 1970s. At reunification, the two Germanies were aligned constitutionally but not culturally; the gap could not be closed by fiscal transfers alone. Moreover, the response from parts of West German society—marked at times by condescension rather than curiosity—hardly eased the process of mutual adaptation.

The broader lesson, available even without the benefit of hindsight, is that economic resources and institutional design create the framework for democracy, but not its substance. Cultural dispositions—trust, habits of compromise, expectations of the state, informal norms of responsibility—evolve slowly and unevenly. Had this insight been more fully internalised in the 1990s, Western policymakers might have approached subsequent engagements with Russia, China, and parts of the Middle East with greater caution about assuming that markets and formal institutions alone would generate democratic convergence.

A template mistaken for a law of history

In the early 1990s, many Western governments interpreted the end of the Cold War as confirmation that market economy, sustainability, democracy, and human rights constituted the natural template for political development. Denmark serves here merely as a well-documented example of a broader Western mindset. In 1993, the Danish government articulated foreign-policy priorities that would have sounded familiar in numerous European capitals: promoting common security, safeguarding democracy and human rights, fostering global economic and social development, and ensuring ecological sustainability. The institutional anchor for this worldview was equally typical of the era. With superpower confrontation over, the United Nations—and especially the Security Council—was expected to evolve into the central arena of cooperative global governance. "An Agenda for Peace," presented by the UN Secretary-General, was embraced as a blueprint for more assertive conflict prevention, crisis management, and even humanitarian intervention. Denmark, like several other Western states, declared itself willing to commit forces to genuine UN-led operations. The expectation was clear: the old predatory logic of power politics had receded, and multilateral institutions would increasingly domesticate international conflict.

This framework proved remarkably durable. In Denmark's case, it shaped foreign and security policy for nearly a quarter of a century. Yet its longevity was not the product of individual incompetence; it reflected a structural mode of thought shared across much of the West. Once strategic guidelines were institutionalised in foreign ministries and endorsed by parliamentary majorities, they acquired the inertia of orthodoxy. Path dependence and confirmation bias did the rest. Signals that should have prompted reassessment—Russia's increasingly overt imperial ambitions after 2007, China's assertive diplomacy and economic coercion in the late 2000s, and the growing paralysis and instrumentalization of the UN system—were interpreted within the existing paradigm rather than as reasons to abandon it. Continuity, normally a strength in statecraft, became a liability when the underlying geopolitical environment shifted.

Intellectually, this posture aligned with what might be called a Fukuyamian reading of 1989: the belief that liberal democracy represented not merely a Western achievement but the endpoint of ideological evolution. A counterfactual narrative inspired by Samuel Huntington would have sounded very different. It would have suggested that civilisational patterns and historical trajectories are more resilient than regime changes; that Russia's imperial reflexes were unlikely to dissolve; that China's ruling elite would not relinquish centralised control simply because it embraced markets; and that cultural and religious fault lines in the Middle East would not disappear under the influence of Western-oriented governments. Such a narrative would have been darker, less comforting, and politically inconvenient. Yet, judged against developments from the 1990s to the present, it would have provided a more reliable guide.

Faith in the civilising power of globalisation

The second cross-cutting error among Western political elites was their belief in the civilising power of globalisation.

It is true that globalisation (which some prefer to call the second globalisation, since the world was also globalised from roughly 1870 until the outbreak of the First World War) generates economic growth in all countries that are integrated into the world economy—setting aside those countries that contribute only raw materials. It is therefore also true that globalisation has reduced the proportion of poor people worldwide to the lowest level ever recorded in human history. From time immemorial and up until globalisation, the statistically most common condition globally was to be very poor. That changed with globalisation. Poor people continued to exist. But as I have documented in my review of the UN's Millennium Development Goals in the Interlude section, the extremely poor today constitute a modest minority.

From the 1990s onward, however, something normative crept into the most prominent descriptions of globalisation—something for which the authors themselves can scarcely be blamed.

In 1991, Robert Reich published *The Work of Nations*.[52] In that book, he portrays a world characterised by a global division of labor and the waning significance of nation-states and borders. What replaces relatively autonomous national economies is an economy shaped by networks and global supply chains. In the globalised economy, Reich defined three types of work: symbolic analysis, services, and routine production. In the Western world, he foresaw a positive future for symbolic analysts, with high wages and high job satisfaction. Conversely, Reich predicted that those engaged in routine service tasks and mass production would fare poorly. He argued that their real wages would come under severe pressure—that is, even if their nominal wages did not fall outright, their purchasing power would be eroded over time. In particular, for those working in routine production—jobs involving repetitive tasks—Reich predicted a marked decline in job opportunities. Many of these jobs would either disappear entirely due to automation or be relocated to countries with lower wages. Reich therefore believed that, in the long run, this type of work would almost vanish from Western countries, and that the people holding such jobs would face increasing economic hardship.

Reich is not an unwavering optimist in his book. He anticipates rising inequality and, from a social-liberal standpoint, discusses what might be done to mitigate it.

Reich was widely regarded as Bill Clinton's "court economist," a perception reinforced by the fact that he became Secretary of Labor in Clinton's first administration. Unfortunately, as with Francis Fukuyama, a kind of "Reichism" emerged—far more primitive than Robert Reich himself and, regrettably, far more normative.

According to Reichism, first, it was more or less inevitable that a global division of labor structured around symbolic analysis, routine services, and routine production would emerge. Second, this was something to be welcomed. Most people would become richer through globalisation. And there was no reason to lament the offshoring of production from, for example, the United States to China. According to Reichism, the people who had worked in factories in the Midwest would quickly find new employment that was at least as good.

As usual, Bob Dylan captured the spirit of the age with seismographic sensitivity. In 2006, he wrote in *Workingman's Blues #2*:[53]

There's an evenin' haze settlin' over the town
Starlight by the edge of the creek

The buyin' power of the proletariat's gone down
Money's gettin' shallow and weak

Where the place I love best is a sweet memory
It's a new path that we trod
They say low wages are reality
If we want to compete abroad

From the vantage point of the weary narrator, declining purchasing power appears less as a political choice than as a law of nature. That, at least, is what "they" say—the symbolic analysts clustered along the American East Coast, in New York and Washington, who explain structural change with fluent assurance and statistical composure. Their language has been internalized. The worker speaks as if the verdict has already been delivered and cannot be appealed. What remains are memories: the blue hour settling over the city, when factories generated not only wages but sound, rhythm, and a sense of belonging. In *Workingman's Blues #2*, the protest is muted, almost metaphysical. The revenge, when it came a decade later, was not lyrical but electoral. That chapter belongs to history rather than to Dylan's song.

Parallel to the emergence of a Reichism in the United States, a "Giddensism" arose in the United Kingdom, named after Anthony Giddens, who was widely regarded as Tony Blair's "court sociologist" in the 1990s.

On the substantive level, there are only minor disagreements between Robert Reich and Anthony Giddens about what globalisation actually is. And Giddensism shares the same weakness as Reichism: it treats globalisation in a normative fashion—even though, strictly speaking, this was not endorsed by the originator of the "-ism." In this way, the two most prominent symbols of Western self-confidence in the 1990s—Bill Clinton and Tony Blair—came to represent a normative misinterpretation of globalisation that had very serious consequences, both domestically in their respective countries and internationally.

Strategic autonomy

When Emmanuel Macron, in a 2017 speech at the Sorbonne[54], emphasised the importance of Europe achieving strategic autonomy, many dismissed the idea. Around Western capitals, it was probably thought to be "typically French" or "Gaullism in disguise."

As time has passed and further experience has accumulated, it has become clear that Macron was farsighted and visionary in this regard.

Europe's outsourcing of the production of so many critical products and technologies to China has created very dangerous dependencies and opportunities for coercion. As things stand, Europe cannot manage on its own—and it will take many years before it can.

The most dangerous aspect of outsourcing is not even narrowly economic. What is truly dangerous is that when the production of a given technology disappears from a country, the fundamental competence to produce that technology will also, over time, disappear.

If a country that has outsourced the manufacture of this or that product over many years decides to bring production home again, it often turns out that one cannot simply pick up where one once left off. It takes far longer than most people imagine to regain the same level of competence in producing medicines, computers, advanced fighter aircraft, or whatever it may be, as one once possessed. I will delve into these problems in Chapter 8.

That is why it was so visionary of Macron to speak of strategic autonomy. It is about much more than economics—namely, the very ability of a country or a continent to rely on itself and to cope in a world of adversaries who have goals quite different from one's own.

In the many years when globalisation was also a normative "-ism," it was almost impossible to present such arguments—especially if one wished to remain a member of polite society.

Russia

The arguments in favour of the Russia policy pursued by the Western countries after the dissolution of the Soviet Union rest, first and foremost, on the idea that it made sense to try to prevent Russia from developing into an isolated and hostile state. That was a laudable objective of the policy that was pursued, and one that certainly deserves recognition.

The method chosen to prevent Russia from isolating itself was to offer membership in a number of multilateral cooperative organisations: the G7, which with Russia's accession became the G8; the Council of Europe; and the WTO. In addition, the NATO–Russia Council was established in order to build confidence and avoid dangerous misunderstandings.

This policy made a great deal of sense under Boris Yeltsin. Both he himself and his most centrally placed ministers appeared sincere in their commitment to market liberalisation and the development of democracy.

Finally, one should not forget the pragmatic argument: Russia is where Russia is. The country cannot be wished away and is too large to ignore. A pragmatic assessment of Russia will always suggest that one should try to make the best possible use of any given situation.

The great failure in the Western countries' handling of Russia lies in their inability to deal with the situation when the assumptions underpinning the policy adopted in the 1990s collapsed toward the end of the 2000s.

It is—and remains, even without the benefit of hindsight—very difficult to understand why the view that Vladimir Putin actually meant what he said from 2005 onward was so relatively rare in Western Europe and the United States.

In this regard, it is interesting to reflect on the split that emerged between the majority of capitals in the Western world and a minority consisting primarily of the Baltic states and Poland.

The dangerous illusions about Russia that have characterised the majority of Western countries have never taken hold in countries that share a border with Russia. No European country bordering Russia ever abandoned its territorial defence—even at the height of naivety regarding Russia. From the outset, the Baltic states and Poland also warned against the dependence on Russian energy that began to loom on the distant horizon in the 2000s.

The Baltic states and Poland have been almost saintly in refraining from gloating and saying, "We told you so." If they were to do so, it would be more than difficult to blame them. The unwillingness of the majority of Western countries to listen properly and constructively to a minority presenting well-founded and well-argued warnings does not do this majority any credit.

Nor does it do Barack Obama any credit that he virtually mocked Mitt Romney when, during the 2012 presidential campaign, Romney argued that Russia was a geostrategic enemy of the United States and the West. To dismiss this by saying that the 1980s were calling because they wanted their foreign policy back was not merely cheeky and (uncharacteristically) rude. It was also foolish and dangerous.

There are many things for which it is slightly hindsight-driven to claim that they could and should have been avoided. By contrast, I believe it is entirely reasonable to say that Ukraine's tragic situation today could and should have been avoided by admitting the country to NATO in 2008. First, because this would have followed logically from the 1994 Budapest Memorandum, under which Ukraine surrendered its nuclear weapons in exchange for security guarantees. Second, because Vladimir Putin had already announced that he intended, in practice, to resume the foreign policy of the Soviet Union.

The United States and the other Western countries should have realised that the weaponisation of the United Nations was a fait accompli by the mid-2010s, when Russia's and China's systematic use of the veto in the Security Council made it possible for Russia to reinstall Bashar al-Assad as dictator in Syria.

The United States and the other Western countries should also have recognised that Russia was moving into West Africa when Mali began to destabilise from 2012 onward.

Here I will be honest and say that I, too, belong among the politicians who misjudged the geostrategic situation in the mid-2010s.

After visiting Mali in 2009, I had reached the conclusion—shared the Danish Ministry of Foreign Affairs—that the country was a fragile but stable democracy. I had not reflected on how dangerous it was to exclude the two tribes, the Fulani and the Tuareg, entirely from power-sharing—until it was too late.

It is common to equate Islam with an Arab way of life. But that is a misconception. When I visited Mali in 2009, it struck me that street life in Bamako was visually almost entirely secular, even though the majority of the population is Muslim. It also struck me that Mali has a highly developed musical culture, with bands that perform at music festivals across Europe.

On that basis, I believed that Mali's citizens possessed a greater resilience to an Arabised and puritanical form of religious expression than they in fact turned out to have. My impression was that most people in Mali—or at least in Bamako—were quite strongly opposed to an Arab religious expression, among other reasons because it would strike at the music they hold in such high esteem.

For that reason, in 2016 I voted in favour of Denmark contributing troops to the French-led stabilisation operation in Mali. I had seen the television images from 2013 of people in Bamako waving the Tricolore and shouting "Vive la France!", and I thought that here, for once, was a stabilisation operation that made sense.

What I underestimated, first, was how fragile the state in Mali actually was (and thus how dependent it was on the personal authority and political skill of the "father of the nation," Amadou Toumani Touré). And second, I underestimated the decisiveness with which Russia, through the Wagner Group, had long planned to take over the dominant influence in Mali and West Africa. In 2016 I did not see the game Russia was playing in West Africa. I therefore mistakenly believed that the Western countries could stabilise the situation in Mali and restore the order that had prevailed before 2012. And for that reason I voted to send Danish troops to the country.

An uncomfortable—and costly—truth

The most pressing question when one looks at the Western countries' Russia policy after 2007–08 is why the countries that actually issued warnings were not listened to.

There is probably no definitive explanation. But it most likely had to do with the fact that the truth about Russia was too uncomfortable for the large majority of Western countries to want to hear it. If Poland and the Baltic states were right, large parts of Germany's and Europe's energy policy would have had to be reconsidered—and massive sums invested to change it. The same applied to defence and security policy: it would have been staggeringly expensive to heed the Polish and Baltic warnings. For many years, therefore, this was avoided, and the money was spent on other purposes that were politically difficult to ignore.

When the economic costs associated with taking this or that viewpoint seriously become too high, path dependency truly sets in. Unfortunately, this is often obscured by confirmation bias and cognitive dissonance. These two mechanisms make it all too easy to convince oneself—and one another—that there is no basis for the warnings.

As a result of their almost endless patience with Russia between 2008 and 2022—including in relation to hybrid warfare—the Western countries bear a significant responsibility for encouraging Vladimir Putin and his regime to believe that they could get away with anything. It would be an exaggeration to claim that today's Russia is a scourge entirely of the West's own making. But it is a tempting thought.

China

The rational argument underpinning the West's China policy resembles the rational argument behind the Russia policy that was pursued. If the Western countries integrated China into the global economy, this in itself would reduce the risk of conflict. The experience with Japan after the Second World War, among others, seemed to demonstrate this.

According to the doctrines prevailing in the 1990s, one also had to expect that economic progress in China would lead to increased democratisation. The calculation ran roughly as follows: if China prospered over a prolonged period, it would develop a large middle class, and this middle class would undoubtedly demand to be heard and taken seriously—if nothing else, in local elections. At the same time, many were also captivated by the fact that China constituted the world's largest market. If it opened up, only imagination would set the limits for the new business opportunities on offer.

Accordingly, the strategy became to offer China membership of the WTO. If the plan held, this would be the prerequisite for the economic integration that, in due course, would pull all the other benefits along with it.

China has undoubtedly benefited from being located very far from the Western countries. Few in the West speak the language, and even fewer can read it, since the script is not phonetic. Few have travelled in China and formed an impression of the culture that has shaped the country over centuries.

When solid knowledge about a subject is limited, myths often creep in and come to dominate thinking. In China's case, this took the form of fantasies about mysterious and inscrutable Chinese people obstructing a cool-headed assessment of reality: that China is a dictatorship ruled by the Chinese Communist Party, and that the Party has one overriding objective—to expand and consolidate its power indefinitely.

Samuel Huntington formulated this insight brilliantly as early as the mid-1990s. China does not regard human rights as universal; they are seen as Western and will never be embraced. In the West, the willingness to ignore what was actually happening in China has been remarkable. We looked away in 1989 when the uprising in Tiananmen Square was crushed. We looked away in

1997 when Hong Kong was incorporated into China on the basis of implausible promises of "one country, two systems." We have looked away every time WTO rules were violated. We have looked away as the South China Sea was increasingly militarised, or when human rights—even by Chinese standards—were trampled in Xinjiang. We hurried on when Denmark, Norway, or Lithuania were bullied.

The only party in the Danish parliament that has consistently drawn attention to these issues is the Danish People's Party. The party has therefore repeatedly raised the criticism in parliamentary debates. Each time, however, successive governments have said the same thing: we are certainly very concerned about human rights, but this is something that must be handled within an EU framework. I do not claim to be better than I am. While my own party held the post of foreign minister, I too stood at the parliamentary rostrum and spoke in accordance with the very line I have just outlined.

From a narrowly economic perspective, the Western countries' China policy has been an extraordinary success. It has produced a market full of products with an almost unprecedentedly attractive quality-to-price ratio.

Conversely, the fundamental lack of knowledge about what was actually happening in China has led most people to cling to the myth that China is a country that mindlessly copies Western products. That is nowhere near the truth.

Not least since the 19th Party Congress in 2017, the Chinese Communist Party has focused on the "Made in China" strategy launched between two congresses in 2015.[55]

The strategy, which outlines China's development up to 2025, aims to ensure that China no longer copies but becomes a leader in product development and design. Since the strategy was launched, China has invested massively in achieving a technological lead over the West. Today, China is world-leading in high-speed rail and solar panels. The country is also at the forefront in batteries, quantum communication, robotics, and artificial intelligence—though not yet with a decisive lead over the West. In addition, China currently operates one of the world's most successful space programs, with missions to both the Moon—including its far side—and Mars.

China is a rising superpower that does not itself believe it has significant overlapping interests with the West. For many years, the question of who is exploiting whom has been an open one. My personal view is that the question has long since been settled—and not in the West's favour. When China's militarisation of the South China Sea and the Belt and Road Initiative are seen in their proper context, it becomes clear that the objective is not merely economic growth or increased international cooperation. Rather, as has been emphasised repeatedly, the goal is the establishment of a Chinese world order—"Pax Sinica"—in which China sets the terms and defines the norms for global trade, security, and political relations. This is also why China invests so heavily in BRICS cooperation and in undermining the U.S. dollar as the international reserve currency.

Taiwan's situation in particular clearly illustrates how far China is willing to go in pursuit of "Pax Sinica." The question of the island's status is the most obvious potential source of conflict between China and the West and demonstrates that China's ambitions are not limited to economic dominance, but extend to geopolitical control.

The Chinese peace will reflect the Communist Party's own logic of power and worldview rather than Western principles of freedom and democracy. China's ambitions are therefore far more far-reaching and challenging than many Western politicians were willing to acknowledge when they embarked on cooperation with the country.

Energy

The rational argument in favour of Germany's energy policy after 2000 rests primarily on the role of energy prices—especially in a country characterised by strength in highly energy-intensive industries such as steel production. In a world that, already in the immediate aftermath of the turn of the millennium, was marked by intense competition, it was not possible to rely on energy that cost more than absolutely necessary.

As the new century progressed, the idea took hold among the German elite that the country should—and ought to—serve as a pioneer of the green transition. Many therefore welcomed the 2011 decision to phase out nuclear power. Over time, according to the strategy, Germany would rely on solar and wind energy. The energy source best suited to the transition phase, however, was natural gas.

All in all, at the dawn of the twenty-first century there were many good arguments for Germany purchasing large quantities of natural gas from Russia.

What the German elite neither could nor would acknowledge before 2022 were the consequences of the fact that, after Vladimir Putin's speech at the Munich Security Conference in 2007, Russia had in practice resumed the foreign policy of the Soviet Union. I experienced this myself in Berlin in 2018 during the delegation visit I have already mentioned.

One should not indulge in personal attacks on civil servants.

But it is difficult to refrain when revisiting a famous television clip from the UN General Assembly in 2018. In it, Donald Trump warns—entirely timely and correctly—that Germany, because of its energy policy, is heading toward a dangerous dependence on Russia. The camera then captures a group of German officials in the audience who are unable to conceal their contempt for Trump and their laughter at his claim. This does not do the German civil service any credit, and the clip has certainly not aged gracefully. Germany could have pursued a different energy policy than the one it ultimately adopted—particularly in light of the many warnings from Poland and the Baltic states. But two factors militated against this.

The first was purely economic: it would have been extremely expensive to rebuild the infrastructure for, for example, liquefied natural gas (LNG). Infrastructure is one of the most powerful drivers of path dependency, and this is understandable. Even though, in hindsight, we can see the necessity of—partially—abandoning rail infrastructure in favour of motorway infrastructure, we must also honestly admit that, for the politicians tasked with making the decision at the time, the costs were daunting.

The second factor was political: even though it would, on balance, have resulted in lower CO_2 emissions and reduced political risk, it was impossible in the political climate of Germany in the 2010s to reverse the decision to phase out nuclear power.

To add insult to injury, irresponsible energy policy toward Russia has led a number of European countries indirectly to help finance Russia's war against Ukraine. By mid-2025, however, the EU had finally corrected this mistake.

A plan has now been adopted to completely phase out imports of Russian oil and gas as a decisive step toward reducing Europe's energy vulnerability. From the turn of the year 2025/2026, it will be prohibited to conclude new agreements and spot contracts with Russian suppliers, while existing long-term contracts must be terminated no later than the end of 2027. From 2028 onward, all imports of Russian energy are to cease. This decision marks an important recognition of earlier strategic errors and will entail a fundamental reorientation of Europe's energy policy.

In politics, as elsewhere, it is better late than never—although "late" in this case was at least ten years too late.

The enigmatic understanding of Russia

The pro-Russian sentiment in Germany and in the core countries of the Habsburg Empire—Austria, Hungary, the Czech Republic, and Slovakia—is a difficult puzzle to solve.

None of these countries has, historically speaking, had positive experiences with Russia. The Soviet "liberation" of Germany involved mass rapes that were suppressed for many years, and it culminated in an occupation of eastern Germany that lasted until 1989.

Both Hungary—in 1956—and Czechoslovakia—in 1968—were invaded by the Soviet Union because their populations dreamed of more freedom than Moscow was willing to grant them. What followed was further repression and persecution of the opposition.

And yet, in the German-speaking world, a specific term emerged to describe those who habitually rationalise or relativise the Kremlin's conduct: *ein Putin-Versteher*. Literally translated, it means "a Putin understander," but the connotation is more pointed. It refers not to someone who merely seeks analytical insight into Russia, but to a person who, under the guise of nuance or contextualisation, ends up excusing or justifying Vladimir Putin's domestic repression and foreign aggression. The label is typically used critically, implying a posture that blurs the line between explanation and exculpation.

Part of the explanation may be historical. The power realist Otto von Bismarck regarded close relations with Russia as an important ingredient in balancing the power of Britain and France. This may have lingered as a kind of historical memory.

Another part of the explanation may lie in the logic that the enemy of your enemy is your friend. After the Second World War, a pronounced pacifism and anti-Americanism emerged on the German left (including the left wing of the SPD). This allowed the "peace movement"—which we now know functioned as a fig leaf for the Soviet Union—to gain significant strength in Germany. Protests followed against American troops stationed in Germany, against the deployment of Pershing II missiles in the 1980s, and against similar measures that in fact guaranteed democracy and personal freedom in Germany.

It is supposedly a myth that Lenin explicitly spoke of "useful idiots" who could serve the Soviet cause—although the idea itself was probably not alien to him.

That Lenin may never have used the term does not mean that useful idiots are fictional. On the contrary, they very much exist, and there is reason to believe that the concentration of useful idiots serving the Soviet—and later Russian—cause has always been conspicuously high in Germany and the broader German cultural sphere. Many of these useful idiots eventually came to occupy important and trusted positions in the country.

It is, in a sense, a poor explanation to say that an entire country can place itself in a collective delusion about the risks it chooses to take—even for seemingly rational reasons. Yet I can reach no other conclusion than that Europe's largest and most important country was, unfortunately, for many years gripped by illusions when it came to energy policy.

All's well that ends well, as the saying goes. The consequences of Germany's illusions about Russia could have been far worse—although the actual consequences were bad enough.

The Middle East

It is entirely understandable—and politically legitimate—that the American government after September 11, 2001, wanted to go after al-Qaeda and Osama bin Laden. That said, nothing in terms of ignorance and naivety surpasses the West's relationship with the Middle East in the part of the 21st century that has already passed.

To understand the current situation in the Middle East, one must identify the region's pivotal year. It is not 1989, but 1979.

That year, the Shah of Iran was overthrown by a coalition of opponents, after which Ayatollah Khomeini defeated his former allies and established a theocracy in the country. Iran's theocracy altered the dynamics of the Middle East in so many ways that the scale of its impact is almost overwhelming.

It decisively shifted the balance between Shi'a and Sunni Islam, and between Arab and non-Arab Islam. It shifted the struggle between a secular developmental vision for the region and a theocratic one decisively in favour of the latter. And it made global jihad a reality, as illustrated, among other things, by the fatwa against Salman Rushdie.

But this was not the only major event in the Middle East in 1979.

That year, the Soviet Union decided to invade Afghanistan. The British had long referred to Afghanistan as the graveyard of empires. Over the course of ten years, the Soviet Union was now allowed to learn that British lesson through a bloody and exhausting pedagogy of experience.

It is one of history's greater ironies that Western countries—displaying their habitual ignorance of what they were actually doing—set about arming the Taliban to harass the Soviet Union. There exist rather priceless photographs of the later Danish prime minister Lars Løkke Rasmussen in Afghanistan dressed in mujahideen attire—images he would probably wish could disappear by some benevolent magic trick. But they underscore the almost youth-political naivety that characterised the Western approach to Afghanistan in the 1980s.

Western governments, especially the United States, supported the mujahideen with weapons and training in order to inflict heavy losses on the Soviet Union, while consistently ignoring the risk that they were thereby creating a far greater threat to themselves in the long term.

The war in Afghanistan led to radicalisation across large parts of the Islamic world and to a pilgrimage of jihadists to the country, where they were further radicalised and trained in the use of many types of weapons. This radicalisation process in Afghanistan had fatal consequences decades later, when veterans of the Afghan war became leading figures in al-Qaeda and were responsible for the terrorist attacks against the United States on September 11, 2001.

The final Middle Eastern event of 1979 is the least well known. That year, a conspiracy of 400–500 Salafists attacked the Grand Mosque in Mecca. It is difficult to imagine how transgressive such an act appeared within the Islamic world. One might attempt a comparison by imagining how an armed occupation of St. Peter's Basilica would be perceived in the Catholic world.

What the Salafists sought to expose was that the Saudi royal family was weak and incapable of protecting Islam's holiest site. They also sought to expose the reason for this weakness: that the Saudi royal family had, in reality, surrendered to the West and accepted Western dominance over the Middle East.

Initially, Saudi security forces were unable to dislodge the insurgents from the mosque. This only occurred weeks later—with substantial assistance from French special forces. This reinforced the narrative among radicalised Sunnis that the Saudi royal family was weak: without help from infidel Frenchmen, they could not even keep order in their own house.

As a reaction to the occupation of the Grand Mosque, the Saudi royal family decided to veer sharply to the right—both politically and religiously. This decision also appeared correct to the monarchy itself, as it wished to act as a counterweight to Iran.

Religious rules were enforced far more strictly in Saudi Arabia after the attack than before, and religious institutions received greater support. At the same time, the Saudi royal family invested substantial resources in strengthening Wahhabism—the official and highly puritanical version of Islam in Saudi Arabia—globally. In effect, it embarked on a direct and global confrontation with Iran over who would be number one in the Islamic world.

However, the Saudi royal family did not succeed in eliminating the insurgent movement. The ideology that the West corrupts the Middle East and its rulers survived and became the driving force behind both al-Qaeda and Islamic State. How potent this ideology is became evident as early as 1981, when a group of ideological heirs to the 1979 insurgents succeeded in assassinating Egypt's secular and Western-oriented president Anwar Sadat (along with a significant portion of the Egyptian elite).

It is a striking paradox that, after 1979, Western countries—

most notably the United States—deepened their political and military cooperation with Saudi Arabia. From a short-term strategic perspective, this made sense: revolutionary Iran had become the primary destabilising force in the region, and Riyadh was seen as a necessary counterweight. Yet this alignment also had unintended consequences. Saudi Arabia used its oil wealth to promote Wahhabism far beyond its borders, helping to disseminate a rigid and exclusionary interpretation of Islam worldwide. In seeking to contain one revolutionary ideology, the West indirectly facilitated the global expansion of another.

Yet almost no members of the Western elites grasp just how decisive the events of 1979 were for the political dynamics that dominate the Middle East. As a result, in the decades that followed, Western actors repeatedly wandered into the lion's den, only to be surprised by the fundamental conditions that apply there.

If the Middle East in the 21st century has seemed like an enchanted place where Western plans invariably failed, this is due in no small part to the events that unfolded in 1979.

It would go too far to return all the way to the dissolution of the Ottoman Empire after the First World War. I will therefore limit myself to saying that from the creation of modern Turkey in 1923 until the Iranian Revolution in 1979, the Middle Eastern agenda was set by (often brutal) regimes that sought rapprochement with the West and a sharply reduced role for Islam. From 1979 to the present day, the Middle Eastern agenda has been set first by fundamentalist states such as Iran and Saudi Arabia, and second by non-state actors such as al-Qaeda and Islamic State.

This has not only meant that the Middle East as a region has been shaped by agendas originating from these sources; it has also meant that jihadism has become a factor to be reckoned with everywhere in the world—even in the Western core countries.

It is popular to claim that Western interventions such as those carried out in Afghanistan, Iraq, and Libya in the 21st century created a Middle Eastern "us versus them" narrative.

I fundamentally believe this to be wrong. The idea that the entire world should be divided into "us versus them" is not a Christian one. Throughout the New Testament, it is emphasised that God loves all His creations. Already in the New Testament, this view planted the seeds of later humanism and democracy. It is the Qur'an that divides the world into believers and infidels—into halal and haram.

The radical division between believers and infidels certainly does not originate in the Christian West. It originates in the Islamic Middle East—and to believe otherwise is an expression of Western self-hatred.

There is no place where Fukuyamaism has failed more conspicuously than in the Middle East, just as there is no region where Samuel Huntington's analyses were more accurate and more appropriate. A very large share of the geopolitical delusions the West has indulged in since the fall of the Wall could have been avoided had Huntington been taken as a premise for concrete policy—especially in the Middle East.

Faith in institutions

One of the most pervasive errors in the West's geopolitical and geostrategic approach since the fall of the Wall has been faith in multilateral organisations and in the belief that democratic institutions in themselves produce genuine democracy. A good example is the thoroughly naïve and unrealistic notions about the United Nations held by the Poul Nyrup Rasmussen government in 1993, which I have discussed earlier in this chapter.

Today, the UN appears as an impotent organisation, incapable either of calling out member states for violating the UN Charter or of engaging substantively with international crises. The latter is due to the fact that a veto in the Security Council guarantees that the UN will refrain from seriously addressing a crisis—even in cases where the cause, consequences, and a possible solution are entirely obvious.

One such example is the war in Ukraine. Russia has absolutely no right to violate Ukraine's borders and territorial integrity. There is nothing in the UN Charter that opens even the smallest or most theoretical possibility that such behavior could be acceptable. The solution is therefore entirely obvious: Russia must cease hostilities and withdraw its troops behind the internationally recognised border.

Even a problem this simple to analyze and resolve is something the UN today proves incapable of addressing.

I trace the UN's complete derailment and inability to fulfill its core mission back to the Bandung Conference of 1955.

Bandung is a city on the island of Java, part of Indonesia. In 1955, a major conference was held there, attended by 28 countries. Most were newly decolonised, and most were authoritarian states or outright dictatorships. A minority—Japan, India, Sri Lanka, the Philippines, and Lebanon—could reasonably be described as democracies at the time.

I visited Bandung in 2023 and observed how the large convention center where the conference took place now functions as a museum dedicated to the event. The official narrative presented there is that the Global South was born in 1955—that former colonial countries became aware of their political agency and their right to shape their own future without interference from former colonial powers. The means, according to the Bandung narrative, was to act with confidence and assertiveness within the UN. To this I would add, on my own account, that the means also included the creation of the Non-Aligned Movement, formalised at a major conference in Belgrade in 1961.

It quickly became clear that the Non-Aligned Movement was somewhat less non-aligned with the Soviet Union than it was with the United States and the West. And it also quickly became clear that the main conclusion of the Bandung Conference was rather more sinister than the exhibition suggests.

Put very briefly, the main conclusion of Bandung was that participating countries would not tolerate interference by former colonial powers in their internal affairs.

This sounds progressive and anti-imperialist. In reality, however, it meant that any authoritarian country could, armed with the conclusions of Bandung:

- reject criticism of its human rights record and external monitoring thereof;
- legitimise itself by claiming that criticism from democratic countries amounted to neo-imperialism;
- claim to be non-aligned, even when it was far less non-aligned with the Soviet Union than with the United States and the West;
- assert that demands for democracy and human rights lay outside the domain in which the UN, by virtue of its Charter, had any right to intervene.

It is possible that Poul Nyrup Rasmussen personally, and Niels Helveg Petersen personally, were unaware of these connections. But it is astonishing that their civil service did not inform them that the confidence in the UN expressed in the 1993 foreign policy report was completely misguided.

Already at the Bandung Conference, authoritarian countries

and outright dictatorships learned that there were significant advantages to employing anti-colonial and anti-imperialist rhetoric. It served as a perfect camouflage for dictatorship—especially because it activated Western guilt over colonialism and its very real oppression, injustice, and unfairness.

With willing assistance from left-wing scholars in the West, authoritarian and dictatorial regimes around the world have since perfected the art of speaking a woke language about imperialism, racism, colonialism, and other evils allegedly attributable to Western countries—thereby obscuring their own role in domestic repression and human rights abuses.

The ever-growing weaponisation of the UN since Bandung has had significant consequences. When I served as a delegate to the UN General Assembly in 2017, I witnessed firsthand how the Danish government at the time—and behind it, the foreign service—poured enormous energy into securing Denmark a seat on the UN Human Rights Council. This succeeded in 2018, when Denmark was elected for the 2019–2021 term.

What Denmark is meant to do in this meaningless forum, dominated by countries that trample human rights daily, is impossible to understand. Why civil servants should waste their valuable time and taxpayers their hard-earned money on such nonsense is beyond me. We are badly in need of a government that will put an end to this kind of folly.

What finally caused me to abandon any belief that Denmark benefits from its UN membership was the campaign to secure a temporary seat on the UN Security Council.

To secure support from countries organised in the Organisation of Islamic Cooperation, Denmark agreed in 2023 to restrict freedom of expression and tighten its blasphemy laws. In light of the enormous costs the Muhammad Cartoon Crisis imposed on

Denmark—and in light of the necessity of insisting that Islamic rules cannot, of course, apply to non-Muslims—this capitulation by the Danish government was both embarrassing and humiliating to witness, not least because I was still a member of parliament when the law was passed in December 2023.

That Denmark was in fact elected in 2024 to serve temporarily on the Security Council in 2025–2026 merely adds insult to injury. It will have absolutely no impact on world affairs and was paid for with a restriction of citizens' rights at the behest of Islamic countries.

The weaponisation of the UN by authoritarian and non-democratic states—so that the organisation today resembles a fig leaf for Islamism and antisemitism more than an effective mechanism for conflict resolution and the promotion of democracy and human rights—has led me to abandon any faith in the UN.

Unfortunately, this is not how Western thinking has evolved. Throughout the 21st century, Western leaders have repeatedly spoken of the rules-based international order and the blessings of multilateral organisations without recognising that it was only European countries that actually respected this so-called rules-based order. This is one of the most important foundations of the illusions that have shaped the West's approach to Russia, China, and the Middle East.

Institutionalism and its limits

One final issue worth mentioning with regard to Western delusions—especially in the Middle East—is the belief that democracy is created by institutions. Let me illustrate this.

In the summer of 2018, I was summoned to a routine meeting between Denmark's foreign minister and the foreign policy spokespersons of the three governing parties at the time.

While we were waiting for the last spokesperson to arrive, and because we had jointly visited al-Asad Air Base in Western Iraq in the autumn of 2017, I shared with the foreign minister the thought that democracy would never come to an Islamic country.

"You shouldn't say that," replied the foreign minister—who was also my party leader. "There have just been elections in Iraq. It will all work out."

It is difficult to maintain civility when confronted with such naivety. I will therefore limit myself to saying that it is something one should take careful note of. It is typical of how not only the Danish foreign ministry, but Western elites in general, have thought about nation-building in large parts of the world outside Europe and North America.

As is evident, among other things, from former Danish minister of foreign affairs Per Stig Møller's memoirs, Western countries invested colossal energy in building state apparatuses, institutions, and administrative procedures in both Afghanistan and Iraq. Møller writes with pride and appreciation about the Danish contribution to creating a new police force in Afghanistan.

It later emerged that the picture he paints was largely a glossy one. Many of the police officers trained became the subject of credible accusations of criminality, corruption, and abuse of power. That things went so badly was due in part to sloppy recruitment and inadequate training.

When the Taliban launched their decisive assault on Kabul in 2021, it also became clear that the so-called Afghan army was essentially worthless. In reality, it was an administrative construct that existed in ring binders scattered around offices, but bore little relation to conditions on the ground.

The roots of faith in institutions

In Europe, there exists a deeply rooted belief that if one creates the institutions, democracy will follow. This belief even has a name: institutionalism. One cannot even argue that the theory is wrong—at least not in a European context. The modern European Union is, to a large extent, built on the assumption that once institutions are established, a democratic political culture will gradually emerge alongside them.

Why the institutionalist approach so rarely holds outside Europe is a difficult question to answer.

As a sociologist, I am inclined to think that this is because Europeans have internalised Weberian bureaucracy as a normative ideal. We believe—almost as a guiding principle—that whom God grants office, He also grants reason. Consequently, it is a widely shared norm in Europe to comply with instructions issued by the lawful authorities.

But the fact that things work this way in Europe does not mean that they work the same way elsewhere in the world. If a society is held together by the type of authority that Max Weber described as "charismatic," formal institutions do not carry the same weight. Charismatic authority draws on different sources, such as physical strength, personal networks, and the distribution of reciprocal favours.

If my assumptions are correct, the introduction of formal democratic institutions has limited impact in places where the actual exercise of power rests on charismatic authority.

I have previously argued that the British in the nineteenth century were far more effective imperialists than Western countries have been in the twenty-first century. This was also evident in their approach to the exercise of power—particularly in India.

The British rarely exercised power directly. Without openly using the term "vassal," they instead made it advantageous for local power holders—whose authority was charismatic in nature—to align themselves with British interests. As a result, the British could govern by discreetly signalling to their vassals what was desirable, after which those vassals ensured that outcomes were delivered in their own way within local communities.

When we look back at Western foreign and security policy after the Cold War, one pattern emerges with troubling clarity: competent and well-intentioned decision-makers repeatedly committed the same mistakes because their understanding of the world was systemically and structurally flawed. Faith in the inevitability of democracy, in the civilising force of globalisation, and in the capacity of institutions to generate democracy automatically prevented the West from seeing reality clearly.

The economic integration of Russia and China was driven more by wishful thinking than by realism. A failure to grasp the deep significance of culture meant that economic and institutional integration never amounted to more than necessary—but insufficient—conditions for democratisation. The unwillingness to acknowledge this proved costly, both politically and economically.

Worst of all was perhaps the misjudgement of the Middle East, where the decisive events of 1979 were ignored and the region's fundamental cultural dynamics were consistently underestimated. Here, faith in institutions and military solutions proved particularly catastrophic.

The evolution of the United Nations from an organisation of hope into a tool exploited by authoritarian regimes demonstrates all too clearly the fatal consequences that arise when wishful thinking is allowed to dictate policy. At the same time, the afterlife of the Bandung Conference illustrates how anti-colonial rhetoric can be weaponised to legitimise repression.

The central lesson of the lost peace must be the recognition that there are limits to what economic integration and institutions can achieve. Democracy cannot be exported. It must grow organically from local cultures. And globalisation does not always create peace—it can also intensify conflicts, create dangerous dependencies, and make democracies more vulnerable.

Only by accepting this insight—uncomfortable though it may be—can we prevent future generations from repeating the mistakes of the past. The first step is to admit that even the most capable elite can be wrong when its analytical starting point is shaped more by hope than by an honest recognition of reality's harsh constraints.

Chapter 7

WHAT IF?

In this chapter I will undertake a number of counterfactual excursions into roughly the last thirty years of history: What might the world look like today if a relatively small number of events had turned out differently from how they actually did?

The purpose of this exercise is to show that human beings do in fact make a difference in politics. It is not irrelevant who occupies an important office. Nor is it irrelevant which decisions are taken by people in positions of power. History is not inevitable. It is shaped by the will and judgment that concrete individuals bring to bear in concrete situations.

It is not possible to express mathematically how likely it was, for example, that Al Gore would have won the U.S. presidential election in 2000. But one can state as a matter of fact that if he had received fewer than six hundred additional votes than he actually did in Florida, he would have won the election. The alternative outcome is realistic in the sense that it would have required only a few small changes in the actual course of events—none of them structural—for the election to have produced a different winner.

At the very low end of the "how-farfetched-is-this" scale we find events such as Lee Harvey Oswald missing his target in 1963, or roughly six hundred Democratic couch voters in Florida deciding to get up from the sofa in 2000.

At the very high end of the same scale we find alternative outcomes that presuppose an entire set of conditions, each of which is itself improbable. It is pure fantasy to imagine that Denmark could have held out against Germany from the invasion on 9 April 1940 until the end of the Second World War. That would have required either that Denmark possessed a military larger than its population could realistically sustain, or that it had entered into an alliance with a well-prepared superpower long before 1940. Both scenarios are entirely implausible.

Behind this first chain of improbabilities lie further ones: differences in national economic capacity, political will, and geographical position, each of which would be wholly unrealistic to compensate for.

To illustrate the middle ground on my scale—from a highly realistic alternative course of events to pure fantasy—one can think of something that is neither impossible nor wholly implausible, but that would nonetheless have required major changes compared to how the world was actually structured at the time.

The example I will give of a counterfactual scenario in this middle range is that Denmark had reconquered Scania, Halland, and Blekinge within the first 50–60 years after the Treaty of Roskilde in 1658 (which was Denmark's political objective until and including the Great Northern War from 1700 to 1721).

From a military point of view this would not have been impossible. But it would have been intolerable, particularly for England and the Netherlands, that the same country controlled both sides of the narrowest point on the maritime route between the North Sea and the Baltic Sea. We are therefore dealing with a relatively high degree of conjecture.

A reconquest in the second half of the seventeenth century or the beginning of the eighteenth would have triggered immediate international intervention by stronger naval powers such as England and the Netherlands. Such an intervention would undoubtedly have ended with England and the Netherlands getting their way. Such were the balance of power and the hard realities of the period.

The counterfactual scenarios I have chosen to include in this chapter all lie at the end of the spectrum where either chance or a marginal change in a single factor could have made a difference. Likewise, none of the scenarios presuppose that things would have been structurally different from how they actually were. Structural changes here mean deep, long-term, and fundamental shifts in political, economic, or social conditions that are difficult or impossible to alter quickly or by chance.

Nor do any of the scenarios presuppose that a long series of factors would each have had to unfold in a significantly different way.

Counterfactual event no. 1: Bill Clinton appoints Samuel Huntington as national security adviser after his 1996 re-election

After Bill Clinton won the election in 1996, the time had come to assemble a new team. He therefore appointed Samuel Huntington—professor of international politics at Harvard—as his new national security adviser.

Huntington was not a man who flaunted his partisan views. But during the Carter administration he had for a period been a member of the National Security Council, and he was therefore already familiar with the rules of the game in Washington, D.C.

With Huntington as national security adviser, Bill Clinton began during his second term to make a clear shift in U.S. foreign policy.

The most profound change was that Huntington succeeded in convincing the president that the unipolar world was a fiction. The United States therefore had to pursue a policy based on the reality that Russia still possessed its nuclear weapons; that China was plainly not on its way to becoming a liberal democracy but was instead a nuclear-armed communist dictatorship; and that international jihadism—often sponsored by Iran—was a power factor that had to be taken seriously.

At Huntington's urging, Bill Clinton began discreetly warning, for example, Tony Blair that the world was not structured in such a way that it made sense for Western countries to imagine themselves on a civilising mission—let alone that such a mission had any real prospect of success.

Instead, what the United States and the West ought to do was, first, to consolidate themselves as a politically and economically liberal part of the world; second, to act with such authority—and with such deterrence behind it—that neither Russia nor China would dare challenge the existing balance of power; and third, to understand that security was a broad concept. It encompassed both domestic cohesion and strategic independence from external powers that might seek to exert pressure if given the opportunity.

Instructed by the United Nations' major failures in Rwanda in 1994 and throughout the Yugoslav civil war, Huntington succeeded in persuading the rest of the U.S. administration that the UN could not be expected to play any significant role as a power factor in the cause of peace and human rights. The organisation was simply too weak and too divided.

It would be in the long-term interest of the United States to see the UN reformed through a very deep and far-reaching process. But in the meantime, U.S. policy should be not to take the UN too seriously.

During his tenure as national security adviser, Huntington also argued that the U.S. State Department should be reorganised.

The correct division of labor within the department—according to Huntington—would be to divide it into sections corresponding to the cultures the United States faced. That is, a Europe department closely coordinating its work with departments for the Western diasporas of Australia and New Zealand and for the liberal democracies of Southeast Asia; a Russia department; a China department; a department for the Islamic world; a department for South America; and a department for Africa.

Within each of these departments, work should be conducted on an interdisciplinary basis, so that economic arguments did not always override historical or sociological-anthropological ones.

With regard to the Islamic world, Clinton—during his second term and inspired by his national security adviser—formulated the doctrine that states were always preferable to power vacuums. States were predictable. States responded to incentives. States could, so to speak, be called on the phone and asked for a conversation. None of this applied to non-state actors operating in a power vacuum.

On this basis, U.S. policy became that Kemalism should not be dismantled in Turkey. Both the country and the region were—compared to the alternatives—best served by a regime that cracked down on both communism and Islamism. Likewise, it became U.S. policy that secular governments in power by virtue of their control over the military should not be challenged beyond the point where they could remain in office, nor ever criticised to such an extent that they lost face. With regard to Israel, the United States sought to create incentives for more countries to follow Egypt's lead and normalise their relations.

With respect to terrorism, the attack on the World Trade Center in 1993 led, during Clinton's second term, to the creation of a unit within the CIA tasked with penetrating deeply into non-state jihadism. In 1999 it ultimately recommended that special precautions be taken in the future to protect against jihadist attacks on sites and symbols representing America's soft power and global dominance: Disneyland and Disney World; Hollywood; the Statue of Liberty; Manhattan.

The counterfactual legacy of Samuel Huntington's tenure as Bill Clinton's national security adviser was a United States that did not focus on exporting democracy to the farthest corners of the globe; a United States that placed strong emphasis on the negative aspects of immigration and the need for cultural integration; a United States that very carefully—and skeptically—considered calls for humanitarian intervention, approving them only if they were short-lived and accompanied by a very clear exit strategy; and finally, a United States that was always attentive to the dangers posed by great powers whose strategic interests were irreconcilably opposed to its own.

In retrospect, Clinton's choice of Huntington appears not merely as a wise political decision, but as a decisive turning point in Western foreign policy. By insisting on a sober analysis of the state of the world and by grounding decisions in cultural understanding and realistic power balances, Huntington ensured that the West retained both its strength and its credibility. The world order he helped to shape was perhaps never perfect—but it was far more stable than many had imagined possible at the end of the Cold War.

Counterfactual event no. 2: Bjørn Lomborg beecomes an internationally recognised authority in climate research

In the real world, the Danish assistant professor Bjørn Lomborg broke through in the national public sphere in 1998. In the newspaper *Politiken* he argued that the state of the world's environment was improving in many areas rather than deteriorating.

Warning against alarmism was not new at the time. And it was, in fact, an important agenda.

In 1980, the optimistic economist Julian Simon made a bet with the pessimistic demographer (and environmental activist) Paul Ehrlich over the price of raw materials. If copper, chromium, nickel, tin, and tungsten in 1990 were cheaper than they had been in 1980 (adjusted for inflation), Ehrlich would pay Simon the difference. If, conversely, they were more expensive on the same terms, Simon would pay Ehrlich the difference.

In 1990, all five commodities had fallen in price, by a combined total of nearly 600 dollars, which Ehrlich then paid to Simon as the winnings of the bet. The example is curious, but it shows that there is good reason to warn against excessive pessimism. Humanity's ability to invent new things and processes and to improve existing ones should not be underestimated. It often prevents crises from developing and escalating.

The effect of Lomborg's critique, however, was that the public became deeply divided between a group that embraced his claims with enthusiasm and a group that rejected them with equal hostility.

In 2001, the pattern repeated itself when he published his Danish op-eds in revised form in English as *The Skeptical Environmentalist*. The international audience likewise split into two factions—one enthusiastic, the other furious.

In Denmark, the affair took on a "lawfare" character, as Lomborg's opponents accused him of scientific misconduct. This seems a rather bizarre accusation. For while Lomborg was employed at a university at the time, he never claimed that his op-eds and books were scientific research, nor that they had been subjected to peer review.

From 2004 onward, Lomborg significantly toned down his controversial statements. He succeeded in raising funds to establish the Copenhagen Consensus Center (CCC). This was not an institution that saw it as important to dispute established positions, such as the idea that humans can damage the environment or that emitting large quantities of CO_2 into the atmosphere is problematic.

Instead, the center focused more quietly on conducting cost–benefit analyses of the various policy proposals that existed, particularly in the fields of environmental and climate policy.

The way CCC operated closely resembled the approach of the Bill & Melinda Gates Foundation.

In both cases there was a strong focus on how cost-effectively one could alleviate evils such as malnutrition or infectious diseases that affect large populations in developing countries.

Because both organisations worked in a data-driven manner, they sometimes arrived at the same conclusions—for example, that investing in nutritional supplements was an effective way to combat malnutrition.

In our counterfactual world, we assume that during the first five or six years of his career, Bjørn Lomborg devoted his unquestionable talent, creativity, and energy to writing peer-reviewed articles on cost–benefit analyses of climate and environmental policy. He also used his growing prestige to publicly warn against betting on technologies that were not fully developed or not ready to be scaled up. As a result, by around 2005 he is a lecturer on the cusp of a professorship, on his way to international recognition for presenting thorough and well-documented cost–benefit analyses in the climate field.

One factor that greatly strengthened the counterfactual Lomborg's recognition was that he allied himself with influential individuals and organisations that thought along similar lines—for example, the Bill & Melinda Gates Foundation and Robert C. Hornik's research group at the Annenberg School for Communication, which studies evidence-based strategies for improving public health.

In my counterfactual scenario, political elites after the Kyoto Agreement and Lomborg's breakthrough as a serious climate realist begin to ask themselves some difficult questions.

If only Europeans and left-wing Americans favour a climate policy that presupposes deep and tangible societal transformations, then the world should pursue a different strategy.

If the fight to protect the climate is truly to gain traction, its ideological imprint—which can superficially be read into the political struggle between left and right—must be removed.

Even if it may be unfair or mistaken criticism, the climate cause is weakened by its susceptibility to misinterpretation. The policies pushed by activists in Europe and the United States are too easily perceived as a pretext for introducing socialist reforms involving more state control, and culturally radical reforms involving a more austere, back-to-nature lifestyle.

To build broader support for the climate cause beyond Europe and the United States, and to avoid the suspicion that climate action is in reality either an attack on capitalism or a privilege-blind attack on growth to the detriment of broad populations in the poorer parts of the world, the entire approach must be radically rethought.

In this way, the fight to reduce CO_2 emissions becomes— in my counterfactual scenario—primarily a fight to introduce better technology, not a fight against economic growth and modern conveniences.

The very fact that the struggle to reduce CO_2 emissions ceases to be ideological makes it far more popular worldwide. A large part of the American controversy surrounding climate protection therefore never materialises. The pro-growth approach to climate protection also makes India and China far more constructive participants in the many Conferences of the Parties (COPs) that are held.

Thanks to the broad acceptance of Lomborg's cost–benefit analyses, climate policy in the twenty-first century avoids developing into a struggle to introduce measures based on technologies that are still underdeveloped (for example, aircraft powered by climate-neutral fuels) or not yet scaled up beyond laboratory models (for example, facilities for producing hydrogen via catalysis).

Moreover, climate policy avoids evolving in such a way that astronomical sums are sometimes spent to achieve marginal gains. As the real Bjørn Lomborg has pointed out, there is nothing wrong with protecting against rising sea levels by building dikes—something that has in fact been done for centuries in regions along the Wadden Sea.

In his capacity as a widely recognised scientist, Bjørn Lomborg also highlights an important point: one should not be afraid to incur costs if doing so breaks a dangerous path dependency.

If thorough analyses, for example, show that vehicles powered by electric motors are preferable to those with internal combustion engines, one should not neglect to build a properly dimensioned electrical infrastructure merely because of path dependency. Calculations show that in the long run it is far more expensive to allow path dependency to prevail for decades and then finally change course far too late.

Because Bjørn Lomborg—counterfactually—became a respected scientist, leading countries removed ideology—particularly growth skepticism—and speculative technological gambles from the climate struggle. This made the climate cause far more popular in the United States, China, and India than it actually is today, and thus contributed—still counterfactually—to the world emitting far less CO_2 up to 2030 than it has in reality.

In historical perspective, it proved decisive that Lomborg early on chose the path of rationality and evidence. The analytical clarity he brought to the climate debate enabled both politicians and the public to navigate by the compass rather than by fear. As a result, the climate struggle became not only more realistic, but also far more effective. Lomborg's greatest contribution may in fact have been that he made it possible for the world to act collectively—not because everyone agreed on the same worldview, but because they could agree on the same reality.

Counterfactual event no. 3: Al Gore wins the 2000 presidential election

If Al Gore had received 538 more votes in Florida than he actually did, he would have won the state's 25 electoral votes by a margin of one vote over George W. Bush. Gore—not Bush—would therefore have been sworn in as the 43rd president of the United States in January 2001. "President Gore" is thus the least implausible counterfactual event in this chapter.

It is one hundred percent certain that the counterfactual president Gore would have pursued a different climate policy than president Bush. Climate policy was Gore's particular passion as a politician. With the power of the American presidency behind him, Gore would undoubtedly have accelerated the green transition in the United States. One can imagine him investing heavily in the development of new green technologies, and likewise adapting the tax system to reward green investments and improvements to the existing housing stock.

Whether Gore could have avoided pursuing a green policy that created division is more uncertain. It was the issue of fuel prices that sparked the Yellow Vests movement in France—and that issue is even more politically explosive in the United States than in Europe. If one were theoretically inclined to start a revolution in the United States, massive increases in gasoline prices or bans on handguns would undoubtedly be effective means of doing so.

That said, the United States would likely have become a more constructive player at various international conferences and would undoubtedly have used its political influence vis-à-vis other countries in a different way than the Bush administration did.

It is difficult to imagine that Gore would have opposed China's accession to the WTO, as the negotiations took place during the final years of the Clinton administration, when Gore was vice president. Even in a world of counterfactual events, it is hard to envision a president reversing a decision made while he himself was vice president. But Gore would likely have had a different focus than Bush—one centered on human rights, in keeping with the spirit of the time, and on more vigilant enforcement of WTO rules.

The two events that above all define George W. Bush's political legacy are 9/11 and the Iraq War. With regard to both events, there are strong reasons to assume that either they would not have occurred at all, or that they would have unfolded in a markedly different way had Gore been in the Oval Office.

As far as 9/11 is concerned, our assumptions can be divided into two. We can assume that it would not have happened. Or we can assume that the event would have taken a different course.

Clinton and his advisers were highly focused on jihadist terrorism. This is not counterfactual—it is simply the case. Not least because of the first attack on the World Trade Center in 1993. Therefore, we must therefore first and foremost assume that a Gore administration would not have been as chaotic and unprepared on September 11, 2001, as subsequent investigations revealed the Bush administration to have been.

When Gore moved from vice president to president in 2000, we must assume that a large part of the Clinton administration would have continued as part of Gore's administration.

After the attack on the USS *Cole* in Yemen in the autumn of 2000, one can easily imagine that Richard Clarke and others on his staff would have pressed for tighter security more generally against large-scale terrorist attacks on the United States. And it is not particularly exotic to imagine that they would also have demanded improved security around iconic symbols of American power. It therefore makes sense to imagine that several of the twenty terrorists would have been detained at some point before boarding one of the four aircraft involved in the attacks. Likewise, it makes sense to imagine that different rules would have applied to flying close to Manhattan and close to Washington, DC. And, last but not least, that there would have been different procedures for intercepting aircraft that violated those rules.

So let us assume that 9/11 does take place in our counterfactual scenario—but that the terrorists only manage to seize control of two of the four planes, and that these aircraft are only able to approach targets far less spectacular than the World Trade Center and the Pentagon.

What does our counterfactual president Gore do? Much the same as president Bush. The difference is that he primarily deploys special forces in Afghanistan (and secretly in Pakistan). Their task is to eliminate Osama bin Laden and as many senior al-Qaeda figures as possible.

By contrast, it is highly unlikely that president Gore would have pushed for an attack on Iraq. To be sure, many people—also outside Bush's inner circle—were convinced that Saddam Hussein possessed weapons of mass destruction.

But president Gore would not have scoured the landscape for a pretext to invade Iraq, dismantle the country's central administration, and conduct a Nuremberg-like trial against Saddam Hussein.

The consequences of president Gore never invading Iraq would have been profound:

- It would have altered the dynamics of jihadism and radicalisation both in the region and globally.
- The power vacuum in which Islamic State later operated would have been confined to Syria (assuming the Arab Spring still occurred).
- No groundwork would have been laid for a Shiite axis stretching from Tehran westward toward the Mediterranean.
- The Abu Ghraib scandal would never have occurred.

As events actually unfolded, the Iraq War led to massive radicalisation across the Islamic world and significant recruitment to jihadist organisations such as al-Qaeda. Some of this radicalisation manifested itself in large-scale terrorist attacks in Europe, such as those that struck London and Madrid in the mid-2000s. But radicalisation also meant that non-state Islamist actors became an even greater problem in the Middle East than they already were prior to the Iraq War.

The prerequisite for Islamic State's declaration of a caliphate in 2014 was the power vacuum that arose in Iraq after the dismantling of the Baath Party's state apparatus, combined with the collapse of central authority in Syria following the outbreak of civil war.

In the counterfactual scenario in which Gore is president, Iraq remains a centrally governed state. As a result, there is no significant power vacuum in the region before the Syrian state collapses in 2011. This does not mean that the problem of Islamic State would never have emerged—but it would have been far less severe.

The Saddam Hussein regime was Sunni Muslim and pursued a harsh policy of repression against the Shiite population. Iran would therefore never have succeeded in becoming a power broker in Iraq had the Baath Party remained in power.

The revelations of torture and abuse at Abu Ghraib prison in 2004 constituted a scandal that cost the United States dearly in terms of soft power. Together with the wars in Afghanistan and Iraq, the Abu Ghraib scandal destroyed decades of painstaking efforts by Western countries to build credibility and soft power in the Middle East.

The wars in Afghanistan and Iraq represent—without any exaggeration—the greatest American policy failures of the century. I once discussed with a group of professional historians what constituted the worst policy mistake in Danish history. We agreed that it was Denmark's decision to enter the Thirty Years' War in 1625 without good and compelling reasons. That decision weakened Denmark's international position for centuries and constituted a clear historical rupture.

Whether the Afghanistan and Iraq wars will ultimately be regarded as equally monumental errors in American history we cannot yet say. But there is no doubt that they have led to a tangible and lasting weakening of Western influence and reputation throughout the Islamic world.

One final area where Al Gore's victory in the 2000 presidential election would likely have had major consequences concerns the Democratic Party itself.

As president, Gore would undoubtedly have continued to work with Richard Holbrooke, who had performed well in the Clinton administration. He would probably also have worked closely with John Kerry—and Hillary Clinton would hardly have been avoidable, whatever one's opinion of her.

It is conceivable that under Gore's leadership, the Democrats would have remained the centrist, broadly appealing party they were under Bill Clinton.

One of the party's major weaknesses today is that it no longer attracts ordinary wage earners—what used to be called "workers"—in large numbers. The party has become an academic party and, to some extent (more pronounced under Barack Obama), a minority party. It has also become radicalised to a considerable degree. Figures who even in Europe would be considered left-wing wield far greater influence over the Democrats in the mid-2020s than they did under Bill Clinton—and than they would likely have under Al Gore, even though Gore was more left-leaning than Clinton.

A Gore administration would not have solved all the problems of its time. But by avoiding the catastrophic mistakes made by the Bush administration in the Middle East, and by pursuing a more pragmatic climate policy, it would undoubtedly have left the world a better place. Gore would not have prevented every disaster, but he would at least have averted some of the most serious ones. Our counterfactual history thus serves as a clear reminder of how much a single individual's judgement matters for the course of world events.

Counterfactual event no. 4: Friedrich Merz wins the power struggle with Angela Merkel

In the late 1990s, Germany's CDU/CSU was shaken to its core by a financial scandal. The nation's patriarch, Helmut Kohl—who had governed Germany for sixteen years and led the country through a reunification of enormous emotional and real-political significance—turned out to be a common fraudster. In clear violation of the law, he had accepted large donations to his party that he neither disclosed, properly recorded, nor paid taxes on. Short of a violent crime, it could hardly have been worse.

As a result, it was unavoidable that a new leader of the CDU be chosen at the party congress in 2000. The winner was the former junior minister under Kohl and then secretary general, Angela Merkel. To balance power against the market-liberal but otherwise more conservative right wing of the party, Friedrich Merz was appointed parliamentary leader of the CDU/CSU group in the Bundestag.

In the years that followed, Merz and his faction lost the power struggle to Merkel. This became evident in 2002, when Merz was removed as parliamentary leader and replaced by Merkel. But what if the Merz faction had won? I have no doubt that Germany would have taken on a very different character.

At the time, Merkel was regarded as the "Mutti" (mommy) of the nation and one of Europe's greatest stateswomen. That assessment has not survived into our own time.

Merkel did not put her foot down over the Nord Stream 2 project. That was her first major policy failure. She believed wholeheartedly in the doctrine of *Wandel durch Handel*. That was her second major failure. She allowed the Bundeswehr to decay. That was her third. She shut down nuclear power in Germany without thorough impact assessments. That was her fourth. She neglected to digitalise Germany. That was her fifth. She failed to grasp the political, economic, and social risks inherent in uncontrolled immigration. That was her sixth. And finally, she placed her trust in the worthless Minsk agreements with Russia, thereby sacrificing Ukraine. That was her seventh major failure.

When criticising Merkel, one must not forget the extraordinary dilemmas she faced. No European leader in recent history has been under greater pressure to balance economic considerations, political stability, and European cohesion. Merkel navigated a financial crisis, a euro crisis, a refugee crisis, Brexit, the election of Donald Trump, and growing internal political tensions—often without easy or obvious solutions. She succeeded in maintaining a stable and strong Germany at a time when many other European countries descended into chaos and division. That her policies later proved flawed in crucial respects does not change the fact that she appeared at the time as one of Europe's few genuine leaders willing to take responsibility under pressure and safeguard trust in democratic institutions. Criticism of Angela Merkel is justified—but one would do well to read her memoirs. The picture is incomplete unless one understands how difficult the decisions she faced truly were, often with very limited room for manoeuvre.

I assume that Friedrich Merz would have become the CDU/CSU's own Helmut Schmidt. Many within the party, safely out of earshot of journalists, praise Schmidt with the remark that he ran for the wrong party. To be "a Helmut Schmidt" is to be realistic, pragmatic, market-oriented in economic policy—and decisive. One of my favourite political quotations is also his: *Wer Visionen hat, soll zum Arzt gehen* — "Anyone who has visions should see a doctor."

As chancellor throughout the 2000s and 2010s, Friedrich Merz would likely have pursued a market-liberal economic policy. He would have pushed for the digitalisation of Germany at a faster pace than actually occurred (which, admittedly, is not saying much). He would not have been naïve or accommodating toward Russia. As a committed transatlanticist, he would have honoured the 2014 Wales Summit decision to raise defence spending to two percent of GDP. He would likely have advocated a strict immigration policy already in the 2000s. And he would undoubtedly have spent all his political capital crushing the Greens and preserving nuclear power in Germany's energy mix.

How can one know this? Because Friedrich Merz did in fact end up becoming chancellor—just twenty years too late relative to the enormous risks Angela Merkel ultimately exposed both Germany and Europe to.

The policy points listed above are the real—not the counterfactual—Friedrich Merz's positions. The only counterfactual element is my imagining that they could have been implemented twenty years earlier.

Had Friedrich Merz been at the helm from the early 2000s, Germany would likely have avoided many of the serious strategic mistakes that characterised Merkel's years in office. No one is perfect. But both Germany and Europe would have stood far stronger in the face of the crises to come. Angela Merkel's political legacy confirms how difficult it is to judge people and events up close.

After reading Merkel's memoirs, one is left in no doubt that she is a modest, thoroughly honest, and decent human being. I therefore conclude my section on Friedrich Merz with a counterfactual description of Merkel.

After losing the power struggle to Friedrich Merz, Angela

Merkel returned to her original profession: quantum chemistry. There she pursued an outstanding career until retiring as professor and institute director on her 65th birthday in 2019.

Angela Merkel achieved a surprising but well-deserved breakthrough as an author with her book on the GDR, published in 2022. Without defending the communist system, it describes life as it was on the wrong side of the Wall—more conservative, with greater emphasis on local community life than in the Federal Republic. Reading the counterfactual Merkel's fine book on the GDR, one readily understands why psychological and emotional reunification has been so difficult.

Counterfactual event no. 5: Obama becomes president in 2004

In the fifth counterfactual scenario, Al Gore, for personal reasons, chooses to step down after only one presidential term. But who is to succeed him? President Gore hesitates for a long time. In the end, he chooses a young senator from the Illinois state legislature: Barack Obama.

There is some resentment among Democrats born in the 1950s. Both Clinton and Gore were born in the 1940s, and politicians from the next decade felt it was now their turn. But Gore has chosen correctly. Voters like the fresh style of the young man, who has only just turned forty the year before the election. He therefore wins the 2004 election with ease.

In my counterfactual world, the Iraq War never happens. And operations in Afghanistan are primarily carried out by special forces. As a result, Obama's counterfactual presidency from 2005 to 2013 is above all concerned with consolidating the American economy.

The real Barack Obama recounts in his memoirs that, sometime in the mid-2000s—by then a member of the United States Senate in Washington—he began to sense that the American economy was more fragile than most preferred to admit. A friend drew his attention to mounting structural vulnerabilities, above all those linked to Clinton-era legislation designed to expand homeownership by enabling borrowers with limited means to enter the housing market.

Banks and other financial institutions naturally feared that interest rates might rise in ways that would push already overstretched homeowners—who had only received loans because of the Clinton legislation—over the edge. They therefore hedged their risk by bundling bad loans into packages known as mortgage-backed securities (MBS) and trading them on financial markets at fixed, predetermined prices in the future. In financial jargon, these are known as derivatives.

To make matters worse, financial institutions also traded derivatives of derivatives—the so-called credit default swaps (CDS). These were essentially bets on whether the underlying instruments would generate losses or profits. It is no exaggeration to say that if interest rates suddenly rose—or the economy were hit by another shock—the entire edifice could begin to resemble a Ponzi scheme: dependent on ever-rising asset values and continuous inflows of confidence, and liable to unravel the moment those conditions failed.

In the mid-2000s, the Federal Reserve begins raising interest rates because the housing market is overheating. This renders many fragile homeowners insolvent. They default, financial institutions lose money, and foreclosed homes prove impossible to sell. The crisis grows and grows.

By the end of 2007, bankruptcies peak. The housing market collapses and drags down the financial institutions that had speculated in derivatives. Because American securities and derivatives are traded globally, the crisis becomes worldwide, hitting with full force in 2008.

But things do not go that far thanks to the counterfactual Obama. Despite strong opposition within his own party, the counterfactual Obama revises the old Clinton-era legislation so that the housing market is no longer as risky as the 1990s laws had made it. Derivatives trading is subjected to stricter oversight, as are the banks themselves. Here it is not Democrats who protest, but Republicans. Nevertheless, president Obama demonstrates considerable negotiating skill with Congress. As a result, the financial crisis never occurs.

By preventing the financial crisis, the counterfactual Obama administration creates economic stability that secures millions of jobs, prevents social unrest, and averts the growing political polarisation that followed in the wake of the real financial crisis.

In Germany, my counterfactual chancellor Merz is simultaneously cleaning up the German economy. Successive chancellors have neglected to digitalise the public sector and expand digital infrastructure. On the left, many oppose digitalisation in principle, believing it will lead to a surveillance society. But the counterfactual Merz thunders at the left and becomes popular for it. "The war is over. We must move on," he says, to some people's outrage—though many are quietly relieved that someone dares to say it.

To the great anger of both conservative and Social Democratic local and regional politicians, Merz also cleans up the German financial sector. It has been politicised in a deeply unhealthy way, since serving on bank boards is a lucrative sideline for local and regional politicians. Unfortunately, this often leads to losses, because politicians fundamentally lack business expertise and entangle the banks they oversee in unhealthy ventures. This practice is brought to an end, and the German financial sector gradually reaches a scale and level of professionalism comparable to that of other major Western countries.

Chancellor Merz and president Obama work well together. As a result, they succeed in jointly forcing China to comply with WTO rules—despite strong resistance.

Obama and Merz demand stricter oversight of China's trade practices and rigorously enforce WTO rules, particularly in areas such as intellectual property rights, state subsidies, and dumping. This compels China to engage in fairer competition and significantly strengthens Western companies.

The counterfactual Obama never receives the Nobel Peace Prize—simply because the pragmatic, low-conflict world order he inherits makes such an award unnecessary. Thanks to the sensible foreign policy pursued by Clinton in his second term and by president Gore, Obama has no need to act as a peacemaker or appear in global flashpoints.

Posterity remembers him as a capable but somewhat dull president who, in a bookkeeper-like fashion—together with his colleague Merz in Germany—implemented a large number of necessary reforms to both the American and international economy.

Is no one disappointed with president Obama? Yes: the green movements. President Obama continues a technology-oriented approach, in which the green transition is driven not by major behavioural changes, but by new and improved technology.

The counterfactual Obama focuses in particular on massive expansion of renewable energy, modern nuclear technology, and energy-efficient construction. This enables the United States to achieve significant CO_2 reductions without unpopular lifestyle changes.

This produces no eye-catching changes for PR campaigns. But

it reduces the atmospheric burden of CO_2—and makes India and China more willing to cooperate, because they are not required to renounce growth.

Obama's successful economic policy consolidates the Democrats as a party that continues to appeal broadly to the middle class. This prevents radical factions from taking over the party and thereby reduces the polarisation that has characterised American politics in the real world.

Counterfactual event no. 6: Mitt Romney wins the U.S. presidential election in 2012

In the real world, Bill Clinton was elected in the elections of 1992 and 1996. The only counterfactual element of his presidency—in my account—is that, after formally beginning his second term in January 1997, he appointed Samuel Huntington as National Security Advisor.

Counterfactually, I gave Al Gore 538 more votes in Florida than he actually received. He therefore defeated George W. Bush. After a single term, my counterfactual Gore stepped down for personal reasons and made room for Barack Obama. Obama then served his two presidential terms as in reality—just from 2004 to 2012.

In my counterfactual world, therefore, a Democratic president has occupied the White House for five consecutive electoral terms. As a result, the American electorate feels a need for renewal in the 2012 election and chooses Mitt Romney.

President Romney holds a fundamentally different view of U.S. and Western security than Obama. As I have already noted, the real Romney warned the real Obama during the 2012 campaign that the United States' greatest geostrategic rival was Russia. This prompted Obama—uncharacteristically flippant—to respond that Romney was misguided and wanted to reintroduce the security policy of the 1980s.

This uninformed and arrogant attitude toward the Russia question was one of the greatest mistakes of president Obama's real term in office.

With the counterfactual president Romney at the helm, the United States began to exert serious pressure on Germany to abandon Nord Stream 1 and 2. It helped that the U.S. government offered assistance in phasing in liquefied natural gas.

The counterfactual president Romney also began to pressure NATO countries far more forcefully to rearm than occurred in reality. The two-percent spending requirement was imposed immediately upon his inauguration, rather than at the end of 2014, as in reality.

The real Romney wanted the United States to honor the security guarantees given to Ukraine at the Budapest Summit in 1994. Accordingly, immediately upon the counterfactual president Romney's inauguration, the United States began considering what could be done to improve Ukraine's security. This was complicated, however, by the fact that the Russia-friendly Viktor Yanukovych was in power in Ukraine between 2010 and 2014. As a result, there could be no question of deploying military advisers or the like.

Even in a counterfactual world, I cannot imagine that the Russian invasion of Crimea could have been avoided. The power vacuum between a pro-Russian and a pro-Western government was simply too brief. But president Romney immediately offered the lawful government in Kyiv assistance in crushing the uprising in Donetsk and Luhansk. Tensions were significantly reduced by the fact that the two regions were patrolled by the U.S. Air Force.

In the UN Security Council, the U.S. ambassador cut through

the evasions and held Russia accountable for the invasion of Crimea. When China made moves to support Russia, the United States announced that there would be very serious economic consequences if China did not remain entirely passive in the Security Council and refrain from interfering in what was taking place in Europe.

When Russia initially behaved in its customary manner ("deny everything and accuse the other side of doing what you yourself intend to do"), the Romney administration, together with the EU, imposed severe economic sanctions on Russia.

At the request of Ukraine's lawful government, the United States intervened when Russia began constructing the Kerch Bridge. The construction site was bombed from the air, and Russia abandoned the project.

In response to Russia's hybrid warfare, NATO countries went on the counteroffensive in the first half of the 2010s. The military presence in the Baltic Sea became highly visible. NATO countries began locking their radar systems onto Russian aircraft and vessels approaching NATO territory. And through U.S. cyber counterattacks, a very large part of Russia's efforts to jam GPS signals and take down servers in Western countries was thwarted.

A serious crisis erupted when Poland shot down a Russian military aircraft that was illegally present in Polish airspace. Russia could not deny the facts, however, and after the United States made a short-notice decision to have parts of a carrier strike group make a port visit to Stavanger, the Russian news media toned down their rhetoric. Domestic political inconvenience in Russia was, after all, tolerable if the alternative was indefinite aerial patrol of the Baltic Sea by U.S. naval aircraft.

Although there was some initial nervousness among European NATO members regarding Romney's offensive posture, the Western alliance quickly agreed that a clear and unified front against Russia was necessary.

In a Romney-led United States, the response to Russia's hybrid warfare would have been an aggressive combination of cyber operations, information warfare, and targeted counter-propaganda. U.S. forces could have digitally infiltrated and crippled Russian troll factories while Western media actively exposed the regime's extensive corruption and internal power struggles. By systematically challenging Putin's nationalist narratives and exposing Russian military losses, the United States would have undermined the regime's legitimacy and split the Russian elite from within. Putin's authority could thus have been significantly weakened both domestically and internationally.

When Russia began interfering in elections in the West and in the United States, all diplomats in the countries where the interference occurred were expelled. All cultural and sporting cooperation ceased. Individuals acting as agents for Russia were arrested in the interest of internal security.

Toward the end of Romney's second presidential term, he persuaded NATO countries to raise defence spending to three percent of GDP.

Outside Europe, under president Romney the United States enforced the no-fly zone over Syria during the Syrian civil war. In addition, U.S. special forces defeated the Wagner Group in West Africa.

In my counterfactual world, the Iraq War never takes place because of president Gore. President Obama prevents the financial crisis and, together with the EU, presses China to comply with WTO rules. In the 2010s, President Romney contributes decisively to keeping Russia in check and dampening the country's imperialist aggressions—both in Europe and elsewhere.

Because of a more decisive EU—sharply focused on preventing illegal migration—Brexit never occurs. Alternative für Deutschland remains a marginal party of academics with unpopular views. And Donald Trump remains a semi-celebrity among audiences with a taste for reality television.

With Romney in the White House, U.S. policy toward Russia would from the outset have been characterised by pragmatism and resolve rather than appeasement and diplomatic dithering. Consistent realism could have forged a Western alliance that, through both digital and military countermeasures, effectively curtailed Russia's aggressive geopolitical ambitions. Romney's offensive approach could have weakened Putin internally and externally, strengthening Ukraine's defensive capabilities and limiting Russia's ability to destabilise Europe in the long term. Europe's security situation after 2012 would thus have looked different—and more robust.

The last globalists

One of the counterfactual narratives I am most fond of appears in the novel *Out of the World* by Karl Ove Knausgård.[56]

In the novel, the protagonist—named Henrik Vankel—dreams that he wakes up in a world where everything is both deeply familiar and utterly foreign at the same time. Immanuel Kant, for example, turns out to be a physician, and Dante a famous revolutionary. After many compelling pages, it is revealed why the world is both so familiar and so alien at once: in Henrik Vankel's dream world, the Library of Alexandria was never burned.

To round off the story: the Library of Alexandria was founded around three hundred years before the Common Era. It was destroyed in several phases, most extensively, probably, during Julius Caesar's siege of Alexandria in 48 BCE. It is very difficult to assess the extent of the catastrophe. But some believe that 80–90 percent of the written knowledge of antiquity was lost, setting back the development of philosophy, mathematics, astronomy, and many other disciplines by hundreds of years.

The moral of counterfactual narratives is often that very small changes in the course of events can have colossal consequences. Winston Churchill could have been killed in one of the wars he participated in as a young man. Claus von Stauffenberg could have placed the bomb correctly. Lee Harvey Oswald could have missed. In all cases, the consequences would likely have been enormous.

Counterfactual narratives exist to remind us of the relationship between singular events and the world-changing effects they can trigger. But they also exist to remind us that we all need imagination from time to time—even when we are politicians or economists or something else that many perceive as dry, factual, and slightly dull. What would have happened if 538 couch voters across Florida had risen from their sofas? The consequences are almost unfathomable.

Earlier in this book's introduction, I attempted to argue that it is neither true that the individual determines everything—because people sit in shadowy forums issuing orders to their henchmen about how the world should be arranged—nor that the individual determines nothing, because everything is structure and path dependency.

The truth lies somewhere in between (even if that is a banal thing to write). There are few things easier than letting things slide. Or adopting the proposals put forward by the bureaucratic apparatus without altering them—which is more or less the same as letting things slide. Many therefore choose that path.

True leadership reveals itself in the courage to go against

structures and path dependency. Because that usually entails confronting one's own people: party colleagues and other peers with whom one is normally in agreement. The civil servants one usually trusts.

A great deal of what happened between the fall of the Wall and the present occurred because too many people in leading positions let things slide. They refrained from asking the critical questions: What if it turns out that we are not merely agents of historical necessity—even if prominent scholars can be interpreted that way? What if we cannot rely on multilateral organisations to create peace in the world? What if the agreements we enter into with non-Western countries are worthless—because only we care about honoring them? And what if countries outside the West do not become more democratic simply because we trade with them?

Such critical questions have undoubtedly been asked many times since the fall of the Wall up to the present. But they were also filtered out of what ultimately became the official position of Western governments.

Counterfactual thought experiments show us that it would not have taken much for our entire world to have been different.

Over a period of sixteen years, I have allowed myself to change only six things: Clinton appoints different people to his security policy team. Political elites embrace a critical scientist instead of rejecting him. 538 people in Florida get up from their sofas and vote for Al Gore. A power struggle in Germany ends differently than it actually did, so that the current chancellor begins twenty years earlier than in reality. A president serves eight different years than those he actually served. And the losing candidate in a U.S. presidential election—who was right—actually wins.

None of this is particularly implausible. Some contingencies could have turned out differently. Certain things—not cast in structural concrete—simply unfold differently by chance.

In reality, events occur in only one way—namely, the way they actually occurred. We cannot change the past, no matter how hard we try. But we can still use our imagination to envision that things might have gone differently than they in fact did. When we use imagination in this way, it is called a "counterfactual thought experiment."

The reason such a thought experiment is useful is that it helps us better understand why things turned out as they did. It also teaches us something important about how we ought to behave going forward. If, for example, we can imagine a situation in which someone spoke up or acted differently, then it follows that we, too, should not be afraid to speak up if something seems wrong or strange.

That means we are allowed to say aloud when we are uncertain about something others call "received wisdom" or "the correct explanation." We should not be afraid to say that what everyone else believes to be true may in fact not hold at all. On the contrary, it is healthy and important that we dare to be critical and ask questions. That is, in fact, how good leadership begins. It begins when someone has the courage to say: "Wait a moment—perhaps we are mistaken. Let us examine this once more."

For far too long a period after the fall of the Wall, too many people were unwilling or afraid to assume responsibility for subjecting established truths to critical scrutiny. The results followed accordingly.

Perhaps the real problem after the fall of the Wall was that the force one ought to have opposed was the very Zeitgeist itself. The Zeitgeist of the 1990s held that history had ended and that all countries would become democratic—especially if we traded with them. Who dared to oppose that?

It is sometimes said that whoever marries the Zeitgeist quickly becomes a widow. This is a profound truth. Consider Angela Merkel and Barack Obama. Not long ago, these two leaders were the greatest stateswoman and the greatest statesman the political elites could imagine. Angela Merkel was Germany's and Europe's "Mutti Merkel"—the loving, caring mother who loved all her children equally and always had the family's best interests at heart. Barack Obama, for reasons unknown, received the Nobel Peace Prize. All educated people believed that, in time, he would be ranked among the greatest presidents in U.S. history.

That was a very long time ago. If there are still people who have invested in Angela Merkel or Barack Obama stocks, the prudent advice would be to sell them before the losses become even worse. In her memoirs, Angela Merkel convinces everyone, I suspect, that she is a modest and honest person. In his memoirs, Barack Obama similarly convinces all women that he would be the perfect dinner companion—and everyone else that here was a president who truly could do it all: think big thoughts, make big decisions, be humorous, be serious.

In reality, the two leaders were the last of their kind. The last two fully "post-Wall" leaders. Merkel and Obama were the last heads of state who, by and large, believed in the entire ideology that crystallized after the fall of the Wall.

That ideology produced increasingly poor results as the years passed after the Cold War. But as so often before, most of the elite believed most of it—until the moment when they believed none of it. Reality drifted further and further away from the map. Yet the political elites continued to cling to the map—until the moment when everyone suddenly felt that the map was utterly worthless and threw it away.

The harsh legacy that both Angela Merkel and Barack Obama now bear is tied to this split between map and reality. They were the last two leaders of major nations who continued to act as though the map still said something meaningful about reality. And most people admired them and looked up to them.

It is now banal to say that, over decades, reality beneath the map drifted further and further away from what the map depicted (even though only a few years ago many believed otherwise). Such hard realisations come at a price. And that price has been the legacy of Angela Merkel and Barack Obama.

Chapter 8

MACHIAVELLI WITH MODERATION

The peace after the Cold War was lost because, in the 1990s, a mistaken political track was laid out into the future of that time—and because the inertia of those choices led for far too long to bad decisions. Only seven years after Vladimir Putin's Munich speech in 2007 did most people in Western elites finally realise that the man actually meant what he said. And only well into Xi Jinping's presidency did most people realise that he was in fact fulfilling the role he had been chosen for: leader of the world's largest and most effective dictatorial state.

What's done is done. The past cannot be changed, but we can try to learn from it. So what can be done in the future to ensure that the kind of fatal mistakes committed by Western countries are not repeated? That is what I will examine in this chapter, where the perspective is: better leadership.

1. All responsibility begins with realism

Even the greatest master chef will come up short if he or she is working with spoiled ingredients. For that very reason, it goes without saying that it should never happen.

In the world of politics, the equivalent of working with spoiled ingredients is a lack of realism—that is, lacking the ability and the will, without illusions or wishful thinking, to take the world as it is as one's point of departure.

A lack of realism is a recurring feature of politics in the country I know best: Denmark. For many years, while I sat in the Folketing, I was, alongside my work as foreign affairs spokesperson, also spokesperson for education and for higher education (two distinct roles).

In Denmark, people will, in all seriousness, debate whether children and young people make less effort during the school year or semester if there are no tests in a subject. The very fact that such a debate can arise is due to a lack of realism. Anyone who has ever been to school themselves—or had siblings or children of school age—knows (unless they lull themselves into a highly detached daydream) that the impulse to take the path of least resistance is among the most constant and deep-seated traits of human beings.

If one believes that children and young people apply themselves just as much in subjects that do not end with a test as they do in subjects that culminate in an exam, one is, in short, choosing to set aside all practical insight into how people actually are.

But that also hints at how the lack of realism arises. It is often inconvenient to be a realist and to say that, under normal circumstances, no one does more than strict necessity demands. And why is it inconvenient? Because nowadays it is politically incorrect to be even moderately honest about how human beings have repeatedly—across history—shown themselves to behave.

What applies to how people tend to behave also applies to countries and cultures.

It may be politically incorrect to say that, in Europe, the Protestant countries—viewed as an average—have their public finances in better order than anyone else. But you do not have to study the rating practices of the major credit-rating agencies such as Standard & Poor's or Moody's for very long before you are forced—unless your judgment has been ruined by political correctness—to admit that this is how things are. Protestant countries are the most likely to get AAA. Then come the Catholic ones. And then everyone else.

Samuel Huntington was a realist. And he understood perfectly well that Russia and China were not inclined to accept the hegemony and value set of the Western countries—just as he understood that the societal systems of the West, Russia, and China were not likely to converge simply because they integrated economically. The same applied to the Islamic countries: there was a vanishingly small probability that Islamist regimes and movements would suddenly give up and submit to the values and rules of Western democracy. It was therefore utterly unrealistic to pursue a policy premised on that assumption.

Realism cuts across the conventional division into conservatism, liberalism, and socialism/social democracy. That is to say: in one camp there are unrealistic conservatives, liberals, and socialists/social democrats; and in the other, realistic ones. And here I must be honest: I feel significantly more at ease with a coalition of realists that crosses the liberal–conservative–socialist/social-democratic divide than I do with a situation in which it is necessary to make concessions to "one's own" idealists. Politics that has something to do with reality is, after all, better than politics that has nothing to do with it.

For close to 25 years after the end of the Cold War, it was the naïve—or non-realist—politicians and political elites who set the agenda in the Western countries. The lack of willingness and ability to view the world coolly and soberly led, among other things, to Germany making itself dependent on Russian gas; to most Western countries sacrificing astronomical resources in an attempt to spread democracy to regions of the world where it is highly unlikely to take root in any foreseeable future; and to Western countries believing that Russia and China would become more accommodating and more open to Western agendas if they were offered integration into the capitalist world economy.

If something sounds too good to be true, it probably is. That is how a realist should always think, because experience dictates it.

In the best of all worlds, the naïvists would say: "We recognise that we have failed. We regret it. And therefore we will now take a break from governing states and institutions." But people are not like that. Hence it is a constant struggle for realists to keep naïve people away from any forum in which they can make their dangerous and irresponsible decisions.

2. Power is a reality

As I already mentioned in the first chapter of this book, the best definition of power is the one given by Max Weber. Rewritten into something more readily understandable than Weber's own prose, the definition of power is that you can get your way despite what others might prefer.

This also means that there is no one-to-one correspondence between violence and power. Behind the exercise of power there is often violence or threats of violence. But it need not be so. The small child not infrequently gets its way with its parents precisely because the parents love their child and would never dream of using harsh methods to enforce their own ideas of proper table manners or the correct bedtime. In many relationships—but of course not all—it is the most stubborn person who gets their way.

Not because the most stubborn person is necessarily the strongest, but because the lack of proportionality that runs like a common thread through stubborn people's behavior leads the more rational-minded to give up.

An example: A and B are in a relationship in which they have agreed to take turns choosing the restaurant when they go out. But while A readily accepts that this restaurant has been chosen by B because it is B's turn (and then there is nothing more to discuss), B has a habit of complaining endlessly about A's choice—even though it is A's turn to choose.

Here things often proceed in the same way as in the parents' relationship with the child: precisely because one has ruled out the possibility of using hard power for ethical and principled reasons, it is often the weakest—but most stubborn—who gets their way. In this hypothetical case, it ends with B always choosing the restaurant, even though something else was agreed. Because A cannot bear B's endless grumbling. Power is always complicated, and it is local conditions "on the ground" that determine how it is exercised. But to imagine that power does not exist is naïveté in the extreme.

Power is a reality in interpersonal relations, as the examples I have just given illustrate. But it is also a reality in relations between states. And in all cases the same rule applies: power expands until it encounters something harder than itself.

Translated into the theme of this book, this means in concrete terms that Russia's power will expand until Russia runs into someone or something that hits harder than Russia itself does. The same goes for China: until the moment when China runs into something that hits harder than China, China will continue, for example, to claim that the South China Sea is theirs. And the same of course applies to Islamism: until the Islamists are suppressed with a firm hand, they will continue to enforce the—for us Westerners—absurd principle that Islamic rules also apply to people who do not practice the Muslim faith. Here in the West we are so socialised into the Prussian enlightened monarch Frederick the Great's principle from the 1740s—that everyone must find salvation in his own faith—that we can barely grasp that, seen through an Islamist's eyes, everyone must *not* find salvation in his own faith. But that is how it is.

If the Western countries do not want their own annihilation—led by the Russia–China–Iran alliance—they must necessarily establish a counter-power to the power represented by these countries. This is probably the most brutal realisation I have to offer in the entire book—the one that requires the greatest reorientation in relation to how the West has thought since the end of the Cold War.

Concretely, the Western countries should, first, pursue a policy that inflicts so much pain and discomfort on Russia and the regime that controls the country that Russia ceases its hybrid war against the West and recognises every other country's sovereignty. In other words, Russia must get out of Ukraine and Georgia, and it must stop intimidating its neighbors and waging hybrid war against their infrastructure.

That will require very large investments in military equipment and other capabilities, but the alternative is worse: that Russia continues to bully its way into getting a little more than it can, strictly speaking, lay claim to. It will do so if not for all eternity, then at least as long as the Western countries do not establish a counter-power that is sufficiently deterrent.

With regard to China, the Western countries must also establish the necessary counter-power. We should, of course, not tolerate China consistently treating the Western countries in a way that China itself would not accept. Reciprocity must return. If we are to respect China's sovereignty, China must also respect ours. If we are to trade with China on China's terms when we are in China, then China, conversely, must behave according to our rules and regulations when it plays away here in the West.

Achieving this reciprocity requires—just as in relation to Russia—physical counter-power.

Finally, there is the Islamic world. Here, again, we in the West must insist on reciprocity. Islamist regimes and organisations must not have more rights on Western territory than Western countries have on Islamic territory. Put bluntly: for every mosque built in the West, it should in theory be possible to build a church in the Middle East. If, for example, there are zero Christian churches in Saudi Arabia, then zero Wahhabi mosques in the West is the correct number to aim for. If Islamists demand that non-Muslims observe Islamic rules and customs on their home turf, that must be met with a counter-demand that Muslims recognise Western rules and customs on ours.

This is highly controversial in today's political climate in the West. Here, over decades, people have become accustomed to the fundamentally peculiar notion that we must not meet demands from non-Western countries with counter-demands. This lack of symmetry is the engine behind the weaponisation of the United Nations.

It is the lack of symmetry and reciprocity that has led to a situation in which non-Western countries are allowed to criticise Western countries for all manner of misdeeds that they themselves have no problem practicing. A good example is the repeated claims of *islamo-gauchism* about Western colonialism, which entirely disregard that one of world history's greatest empire builders is the Prophet Muhammad—and which entirely disregard the many similarities between the construction of the modern state of Turkey and the modern state of Israel.

The introduction of realism and the recognition of what power is are two of the absolutely most important prerequisites if the Western countries are to regain the initiative after the lost peace.

The practical recommendation is the same for point 1 as it is for point 2: what is needed is "Machiavelli with moderation."

The recommendations for the exercise of power offered by the historical Niccolò Machiavelli are too extreme—which is hardly surprising, given that they were developed in the 1500s: an age that knew neither democracy, human rights, nor respect for minorities.

That does not change the fact that there is a core of truth in what Machiavelli writes. One must think long-term, not short-term. One must be realistic, not naïve. And above all: one must understand the very nature of power to the bottom. It will always expand until it runs into something harder than itself.

That is why there was a touch of genius when Antony Jay and Jonathan Lynn—the two screenwriters behind *Yes Minister* and *Yes, Prime Minister*—updated Machiavelli for 1980s Britain. That kind of updating is still needed.

So when it comes to being realistic and recognising the nature of power, my advice to today's decision-makers is simple: be less like James Hacker. Be more like Sir Humphrey Appleby.

In the world we live in, there is no need for naïveté—not even when it is well intentioned and springs from the best of motives. What is needed is tempered cynicism. And sometimes something very simple: that one starts from the truth—even in cases where it is inconvenient and unwelcome. That is Machiavelli with moderation.

3. Democracy is not created by institutions alone

The best example of how institutions can help build and strengthen a democratic culture is found in the EU. Clearly, the EU is not perfect, and the Union has many flaws that anyone can easily spot. But the most important point is that all the major and important decisions made in the EU must be democratically approved. This means that ordinary citizens, through the European Parliament, determine who occupies the most important posts and how major decisions are to be made. That helps ensure that power is not abused and that the EU remains democratic.

But the experiences from Afghanistan, Iraq, and Turkey clearly demonstrate that democratic institutions alone do not guarantee democracy. Local cultural, religious, and social conditions always play a decisive role. Yugoslavia collapsed after Tito because nationalism and religious tensions proved stronger than the institutions he left behind. Mali fell apart because its democratic institutions were fragile and lacked genuine popular support.

In Turkey, the military historically guaranteed the secular character of the state. But the EU's demand to weaken the military's political role paradoxically contributed to Erdoğan's islamisation of the country. Institutionalism as a universal recipe is therefore risky, though it can work under specific cultural and historical circumstances.

After the Cold War ended, the Western countries—for example the United States and some European countries—behaved in ways that bring to mind classical imperialism: that is, one country tries to rule over other countries without those other countries wanting it. But it was not something the Western countries themselves would admit or think of. They believed they were helping other countries by intervening in their problems, even if they ended up making things worse.

For example, countries like the United States and the United Kingdom entered countries like Iraq and Afghanistan and tried to decide how those countries should be governed. Perhaps they meant well, but in reality they were ruling over other people in a way that resembles imperialism. When Western countries did such things, it was often because they did not think enough about what it would mean for the people who lived in those countries. They were too quick to assume their own solutions were best, without investigating what the consequences might be.

My recommendation is therefore very simple: the Western countries must never, ever do the same again. They must think very carefully before they begin to interfere in other countries' problems. If one does not dare to consider what can go wrong, one ends up doing great harm. Therefore, one must never again pursue a policy that in practice means deciding over other countries and their populations without being willing to admit it. One must take responsibility for one's actions, be honest about one's motives, and think thoroughly about what one is doing before doing it.

4. In a direct confrontation, geostrategy will prevail over geoeconomics

An overwhelming share of the mistakes made by Western elites between the fall of the Berlin Wall and the present day are related to the fact that Western countries prioritised geoeconomics at the expense of geostrategy.

Within geoeconomic thinking, the market economy ought in principle to be extended to the entire world. This would not only lead to a global allocation of resources that is as efficient as possible (a convoluted way of saying that tasks are carried out where they are cheapest). Because there was widespread confidence in so-called "spillover" effects, most Western elites also believed that the market economy would bring liberal democracy and progress in human rights in its wake.

The first thing to say about these assumptions is that it requires a massive suppression of cognitive dissonance even to imagine that they have any validity.

Have the oil-producing countries of the Middle East moved closer to the Western ideal of liberal democracy and improved human rights because Western countries have traded extensively with them since the end of the Second World War? Not at all. Has China moved closer to the Western ideal of liberal democracy and improved human rights because Western countries have traded extensively with it since the 1980s? Not at all either.

There is simply no evidence to support the belief that the hypothesis of *Wandel durch Handel* is correct—unless one is so thoroughly blinded by ideology as to be willing to ignore even the most obvious evidence that the hypothesis is deeply problematic.

I do not believe there exists a single example that disproves the claim that, in the long run, the naïve always lose to those who think strategically. The geoeconomic ideology is fundamentally naïve. And for that very reason, it has suffered a major defeat at the hands of geostrategic thinking.

The most negative consequence of the geoeconomic paradigm's defeat by the geostrategic one is the destruction of competence that has taken place in the Western world.

Viewed very narrowly, it is correct that we as consumers in the West should be pleased that—on average—we have to work far fewer hours to afford a colour television than our parents and grandparents did. This naturally gives us greater freedom in how we spend the rest of our disposable income.

But it is necessary to view this issue in a much broader perspective. If, within a limited area such as Denmark (the example is chosen arbitrarily), one stops building large steel ships, two things happen. The first I have already mentioned: Danes who need a large steel ship can buy one much more cheaply than would otherwise be possible. But this comes at a problematic socio-economic cost: collectively, the competence to build such ships disappears from the country altogether.

With respect to the ability to produce complex and advanced products, once such competence disappears from a region, it can take an extraordinarily long time to rebuild it. In fact, there is no guarantee that it will ever succeed.

The truly great calamity of geoeconomic thinking in the West is that, viewed as a geographical region, we have lost the ability to produce a wide range of highly critical technologies. This applies, for example, to computer chips, advanced batteries, and solar panels. If countries that are hostile towards the West were to decide to cut off supplies of these products, we would find ourselves in the same predicament as when the OPEC countries decided to reduce oil supplies in 1973–1974.

In the real world, Russia, China, and Iran have entered into an alliance whose purpose is to destabilise the West. That this alliance could succeed in its endeavour is due in no small part to the fact that China is practically able to cut off Western supplies of technologies that are critically necessary to sustain our economy and civilisation—and which we have, within the foreseeable future, lost the capacity to produce ourselves.

My practical recommendation under point 4 is therefore this: strategic autonomy matters. It must be fought for. If one does not do so, one will end up being forced to accept diktats from states one would never listen to had one not been so careless as to place oneself in their pocket.

Do not listen to economists who claim that cheap products are the sole path to salvation. There is a certain element of truth in the claim that capitalists would prefer to put out to tender the rope by which they are to be hanged. That is, to a large extent, what they did in the period following the fall of the Wall—willingly assisted by naïve political elites.

But do not fall for the temptation. It is still unfortunate to end one's days being hanged—even if the rope was an excellent bargain and cost only a fraction of what it would have cost had it been manufactured in the West.

5. Do not be afraid to break path dependency

After the Second World War, far-sighted transport policymakers in Denmark decided that the State Railways (DSB) should run on diesel rather than steam. As a result, the state railways DSB acquired the famous MY locomotives, built in Sweden under licence from the United States. They were so robust that, as far as is known, a number of functional examples still exist around the country.

What was courageous about the decision was that policymakers broke with the path dependency created by steam technology. Behind each individual steam locomotive lay an entire infrastructure of coal and large quantities of water for the boilers, as well as a technical organisation in which everyone was trained to maintain and repair steam engines.

When it later became relevant to transition from diesel to electricity—because electrification could one day become an important component of the green transition—politicians of the time were far more hesitant. The first steps towards electrifying Denmark's main railway lines were taken in the 1980s. More than forty years later, the process is still not complete.

This has cost staggering sums. Not only because of the disastrous IC4 project, in which the state decided to purchase advanced diesel trains based on a technology that was already on its way out. The costs of maintaining two parallel technical organisations for diesel and electric traction for more than four decades have also been enormous.

If there is anything to be learned from this debacle—aside from the fact that railway projects have always competed with IT projects for the prize of greatest failure—it is that one should never be afraid to break path dependency. As a general rule, it will be far more expensive to do so later.

Already in the 1990s, dangerous path dependencies were created in Western foreign policy that should have been broken long before they eventually were.

Already in the 1990s—after the failures in Rwanda and the former Yugoslavia—it was clear that the United Nations was not an organisation capable of creating and maintaining peace. In the intervening years, the situation has only worsened. For decades, the Security Council has been paralysed by Russia and China. As a result, the UN has been unable to form meaningful positions or take action regarding the civil war in Syria and the invasion of Ukraine.

Germany broke with path dependency in relation to nuclear power—but immediately entered a new one: Russian gas. Before this dependency was brought to an end, it had come to threaten both German and European security. It therefore constitutes a darker chapter in modern German history than many are willing to acknowledge.

The integration of Russia—long after Vladimir Putin had officially broken with the West in 2007—is another example of a path dependency that later proved both dangerous and intellectually difficult to confront. Romney warned. McCain warned. Neither of them was "Mr Nobody". That only a minority listened is one of the great puzzles future historians may devote themselves to.

The integration of China follows the same pattern. Anyone who wished to know could, since Xi Jinping came to power, have concluded that China was behaving as an adversary of the Western world. But the warning signs have existed at least since China joined the WTO in 2001—and has since systematically violated the organisation's rules. Western countries should therefore never have transferred as much competence to China as they in fact did.

Finally, there are the military interventions in Afghanistan and Iraq—two of the greatest geostrategic disasters for the West since the fall of the Wall. This is not solely because Afghanistan in 2021 ended up exactly where it had been in 2001. The intervening years—beyond the loss of lives and money—also resulted in the West squandering almost all of its goodwill in the region. It will take decades to repair this damage.

The moral is therefore clear: path dependency is not something one should be afraid to break.

My recommendation under point 5 is this: do not allow a single narrow discipline to dictate national policy. Specifically, economists have played too large a role in shaping Western policy since the fall of the Wall. This is not because economics is in and of itself a bad discipline, nor because economists are narrow-minded. It is a bad idea because any single perspective is always insufficient. It would, in other words, have been just as bad an idea to leave the exercise of power in Western countries exclusively to lawyers—let alone to sociologists.

What is needed in the leadership of individual countries is genuine interdisciplinarity. This should not be confused with weak expertise, nor with vague or "fluffy" thinking.

The best way to govern a country is to involve many disciplines in leadership—for example, though not exclusively, economists, historians, lawyers, anthropologists, sociologists, as well as experts in language and culture.

This, of course, is of little use if they lack the real opportunity to stress-test the most popular assumptions of the Zeitgeist (which is usually the most direct route to ruin). But the prerequisite for such stress-testing to yield useful results is—and remains—genuine interdisciplinarity.

6. Culture and history play a decisive role

Samuel Huntington was vilified for telling the truth: Western values are not "universal". They are Western. And as such, they stand in a latent conflict with other value systems that do not originate in Western modes of thought.

The idea that all human beings are of equal worth is a fundamental tenet of modern Western philosophy, deriving in particular from Enlightenment moral philosophers such as Immanuel Kant, who argued that all humans possess absolute dignity because they are endowed with reason and moral judgment. Yet even though this principle seems self-evident to us today, it is by no means universally accepted—neither historically nor in the present.

Similarly, it is deeply embedded in the modern Western worldview that free will and intention are required before we can hold individuals responsible for their actions—an assumption strongly influenced by moral philosophers such as John Stuart Mill, who emphasised personal autonomy and responsibility. But here too, it is crucial to understand that this perspective does not necessarily apply everywhere and at all times.

Finally, the right freely to choose one's religion is a central right in modern Western thought, articulated particularly clearly by Enlightenment philosophers such as John Locke, who argued that the state has no right to determine what people must believe. But again: the fact that freedom of religion is perceived as a natural right in the West certainly does not mean that all societies regard this principle as correct, or even accept it at all. We must therefore not commit the error of believing that our own values and principles are universally accepted.

For this reason, "globalisation" has always been a myth—if the concept extends beyond elementary phenomena such as being able to use one's credit card everywhere or buy a Coca-Cola anywhere. Once one scratches just a few millimetres beneath the "cola-and-credit-card surface", one invariably encounters culture—varying from country to country and from region to region. This is the theme of the excellent film *Lost in Translation*, which—beyond a romantic plot between an older man and a younger woman—explores what emerges when one lightly scrapes Japan's cola-and-credit-card surface.

The sooner Western countries stop believing that their values are universal, the better it will be for their ability to make sensible decisions that serve their own interests.

There is said to be a Turkish proverb to the effect that if you place a clown in a palace, he does not become a sultan; instead, the palace becomes a circus. And even if this is not an authentic proverb, it is in any case well invented—for it captures something true about the relationship between institutions ("the palace") and culture ("the clown").

In Denmark, since mass immigration began forty years ago, we have believed that if we more or less kindly force immigrants to spend time within our institutions, those institutions will have a civilising (which is a euphemistic way of saying Westernising) effect on immigrants.

This is partly true—which is why it has been a counter-strategy for immigrants who wished their children to continue living according to the culture of their country of origin to send them back for "re-education" in the country they had emigrated from.

But only partly. The other side of the truth is that immigrant culture has also contributed to changing our institutions.

This subject is surrounded by an extraordinary number of taboos. Yet despite strong resistance from the many-headed creature known as "the education sector", it has gradually been established as a fact that in some schools immigrants have seized the right to define the "spirit and tone"—including what is considered acceptable to teach. Not least because teachers today are among the professional groups with the weakest grasp of what power actually is.

What rendered the imperial missions to Afghanistan and Iraq impossible was a complete lack of insight into the fact that when one builds institutions based on a culture different from the one prevailing where those institutions are established, it is the culture that prevails—and the institutions that lose.

The scepticism expressed by Per Stig Møller in his memoirs regarding Afghanistan's president Hamid Karzai stems in part from the fact that Karzai was forced to give Afghan culture what belonged to it, and the Western-inspired institutions he headed what belonged to them. This balancing act is almost impossible—and likely the true reason behind the ambiguous signals from Karzai that so often frustrated the Danish foreign minister.

There has been extensive research into the conditions under which given cultures adopt innovations from outside.[57]

There are too many conclusions to review them all here. But if it is possible to adopt a practical innovation without requiring a cultural transformation, there is a good chance it will take hold. In earlier times, this might have been the use of new agricultural tools; today, it includes a range of modern technologies such as computers and mobile phones.

If the culture itself must be fundamentally changed, this will usually require an impulse originating from the very top of the society in question—from a group whose status at the apex of the social hierarchy is virtually impossible to challenge.

Japan was Westernised because the impulse came from Emperor Meiji himself. Earlier still, the Russian elite was Westernised because the impulse came from Peter the Great.

Without such conditions, it is difficult in practice to imagine successful cultural transformation. And even when they are largely fulfilled, success is far from guaranteed. Kemal Atatürk did succeed in "modernising" large parts of Turkey's elite and middle class. But this "class" of modern Turks still constitutes a minority in most parts of the country. That is why Erdoğan loses local elections in most major cities in western Turkey, while achieving success elsewhere with his tradition-respecting political programme.

My recommendation under point 6 is this: read everything that deals with cultural clashes. It clarifies what one is up against when attempting to build institutions based on premises different from those of the prevailing culture. Almost always, it is the culture that wins.

7. Genuine interdisciplinarity is needed in decision-making environments

While I was a member of the Danish Parliament's Research Committee, I visited the University of Oxford. There, several professors emphasised that interdisciplinarity constituted the backbone of the system. I found this puzzling. After all, researchers with academic roots at the university had won more than seventy Nobel Prizes—an achievement that invariably requires rigorous specialisation. I therefore asked what, precisely, they meant.

The explanation was that a very important part of students' academic socialisation resulted from living in a college. It is a collectivist way of life, in which one lives together, eats together, works together, and shares leisure time. The very fact that students are, in practice, encouraged to present their studies and projects to others with entirely different academic backgrounds helps to foster interdisciplinarity.

I could see that the Oxford professors had a point. In Denmark and many other countries, academic quality would benefit greatly if, for example, a sociologist always ran the risk of having to defend grand theories against a historian who—armed with data—could puncture them. Or if one were forced to defend a generalization that had not actually been empirically tested against objections from a fellow student who had command of the numbers.

The reverse would also be beneficial: researchers who rely almost exclusively on data and quantitative methods should likewise be challenged and forced to defend themselves. The criticism might be that their conclusions only make sense if one ignores certain important factors that ought not to be overlooked. In other words, that researchers—consciously or unconsciously—disregard variables that matter in reality, thereby rendering their results less precise or less credible. In short, quantitatively focused researchers should also be challenged on whether their results hold once all relevant conditions are taken into account.

When former Danish prime minister Anders Fogh Rasmussen published the most recent volume of his memoirs, he stated that as a decision-maker one could not have known that invading Iraq and removing Saddam Hussein would simultaneously lift the lid off the pressure cooker containing the Sunni–Shia conflict.

This statement very much deserves to be criticised and contested. The fact that Sunnis and Shias have been in conflict for centuries is as indispensable a context for understanding the Middle East as familiarity with the Reformation and its consequences is for understanding Europe.

If a decision-maker somewhere in the Middle East were to claim that it was impossible to know that Protestants and Catholics in Europe had a long history of conflict, Europeans would clutch their heads and conclude that this decision-maker urgently needed to replace his or her circle of advisers. Anders Fogh Rasmussen's statement is of the same calibre—only with the opposite sign. There is simply something fundamentally wrong with the advisory system if such decisive information is not brought to bear before a final decision is made.

The European Parliament functions somewhat like the Oxford college system as it was explained to me. If one says something that betrays ignorance about a particular country, one is quickly corrected by colleagues from that country. Even if an analysis begins in ignorance, one is rarely allowed to conclude it there.

I have never served on the Danish Parliament's Finance Committee, but my impression is that if one does not employ economic arguments acceptable to the Ministry of Finance, one gets nowhere.

Unfortunately, the same does not apply to the Foreign Policy Committee. There are no minimum requirements for what one should know about the countries and regions one is obliged to address—and this is clearly audible in the Committee's debates.

My recommendation under point 7 is therefore this: it should be just as embarrassing in the foreign-policy environment not to possess broad, substantive knowledge of the countries and regions one deals with as it is in the economic policy environment not to possess broad knowledge of economics and societal conditions.

8. Establish systematic warning systems—take the devil's advocate seriously

I am not writing these lines because I harbor any particular animosity toward the Danish Defence Intelligence Service. It is simply the case that the service has been unfortunately prominent in several of the cases reviewed in this book.

In the run-up to the Iraq War, no one at the top of the system was interested in hearing that analysts had serious doubts about the claim that Saddam Hussein possessed weapons of mass destruction.

After Russia's invasion of Crimea, no one at the top of the system was interested in hearing from the then Chief of Defence that Denmark—and presumably NATO—would stand no chance in a military confrontation with Russia.

And in the period leading up to the Taliban's final victory over Afghan government forces, there seemed to be no one paying attention to ordinary news broadcasts and asking whether it really made sense to claim that government forces would be able to hold out for at least four months.

What these examples have in common is that they point to a systematic failure to accept the necessity of listening to the devil's advocate.

Today, many people believe that "the devil's advocate" is merely a figure of speech. In fact, it runs deeper than that.

Until 1587, the Catholic Church's canonization of individuals was marred by excessive arbitrariness and laxity. Pope Sixtus V put an end to this.

Following his reform, the claim that a given individual was worthy of sainthood was argued on the one hand by the *Advocatus Dei* and on the other by the *Advocatus Diaboli*—the devil's advocate. While the *Advocatus Dei* was tasked with assembling all facts and testimonies in favour of canonization, the *Advocatus Diaboli* had the formal duty to find all facts and testimonies pointing in the opposite direction. Only when both had presented their arguments could a formal decision be made.

Institutionalising the requirement that a formally appointed individual must argue against a widely supported position is close to genius. It ought to be mandatory in all bureaucracies and all governments.

Imagine if Poul Nyrup Rasmussen had been institutionally obliged to hear the devil's advocate enumerate all the weaknesses in the foreign-policy statement presented by Niels Helveg Petersen in 1993.

Or if Anders Fogh Rasmussen had been institutionally obliged to hear the devil's advocate lay out all the weaknesses of invading Iraq—or of engaging deeply with China.

Or if later governments had been institutionally obliged to hear the devil's advocate speak against cutting defence spending to below 1.5 percent of GDP.

Throughout this book, I have devoted considerable effort to explaining the processes that lead states and organisations to cling to the map long after it has become clear that it no longer corresponds to the terrain.

I have done so because I consider this one of the most dangerous things that can happen to a state or an organisation: losing the ability to perceive what is happening around it because it has ideologically bound itself to a worldview that bears no relation to reality.

In the heat of political struggle, it is often claimed that this or that will destroy society. Usually this is an exaggeration. But when it comes to the risks associated with governing a state or an organisation on the basis of what one believes reality to be—rather than what can be demonstrated—the claim is true: it can indeed bring them down.

My practical advice under point 8 is therefore this: all organisations should, as part of their structure and working processes, establish the devil's advocate as a control function—paid at the same level as the CEO and located on the same floor. That is how important this function is.

9. Real-political education of future generations

How does one learn to think in the spirit of *Realpolitik*? How does one learn to understand the concept of power? I do not believe there is a simple recipe. But let us begin by asking the opposite question: what should one do if one wished to misjudge questions of Realpolitik and power as thoroughly as possible?

While working on this book, it has become clear to me that people who lack the ability to think in real-political terms and to understand power often share one trait: they move in very closed environments.

They may socialise exclusively with party comrades or ideological allies. They may remain entirely within their own ministry. Or they may simply have the habit of surrounding themselves with sycophants. In any case, excessive interaction with like-minded individuals is one of the least effective ways of becoming wiser.

Decision-makers should therefore make a habit of regularly entering environments where people disagree with them and where they are openly contradicted.

Power presents itself more as a temptation than as reason. One will never truly understand power if one moves exclusively in environments where rational arguments prevail. If one wishes to approach an understanding of the passion for power, one is more likely to gain insight from novels and films than from the latest peer-reviewed article on calculating the optimal CO_2 tax.

That things went so badly for the Western countries after their victory in the Cold War is, as the preceding pages show, largely due to a lack of insight into how human beings actually are.

We therefore cannot avoid the conclusion that future decision-makers must possess a greater degree of humanistic education than those who have governed from the 1990s to the present. It should not be possible to hold an important political office without a basic knowledge of history—just as it should not be possible to rise to the top without having read the memoirs of major political leaders and without a reasonable engagement with novels or films.

Why? Because one cannot function as a political decision-maker beyond a certain level without a broad understanding of how people think and act—and how the culture we all inhabit shapes our values and prejudices.

I have repeatedly argued that Francis Fukuyama's book on the end of history is far better than its reputation suggests—a reputation based largely on people having read only a few lines from his original article in *The National Interest*. Why is the book so good? Because by turning to philosophy it expands the modern individual's understanding of what it means to be human. A substantial part of the book deals with the need for recognition embedded in the ancient Greek concept of *thymos*—the desire to be acknowledged and respected.

Had more decision-makers taken the trouble to read Fukuyama's book in full rather than a half-page summary, they would have understood that human beings seek not only erotic gratification but also social recognition and respect. Armed with that insight, it should have been obvious how misguided it was for Western countries to trample on this desire for recognition and respect in so many parts of the world beyond our own cultural sphere.

My recommendation under point 9 is therefore this: if we wish to avoid the problems that led to the lost peace, future decision-makers must possess a humanistic education that is both broad and deep.

10. Truth must never become a taboo

While working on the manuscript for this book, it has repeatedly struck me that what prevented Western countries from pursuing a more reasonable and less dangerous policy was an aversion to hearing the truth.

In the 1990s, there was a profound reluctance to acknowledge the truth that countries outside the Western cultural sphere had by no means abandoned their claim to autonomy. There was also a reluctance to admit that the United Nations was not particularly effective at fulfilling its self-appointed mission of preserving peace worldwide—and to accept that even after the fall of the Wall and the onset of globalisation, nationalism and religion continued to play significant roles in the lives of states and individuals.

In the 2000s, there was reluctance to hear the truth that Russia increasingly viewed itself as standing in antagonistic opposition to the West—much like China and various Islamist regimes and movements.

This reluctance persisted into the 2010s and was compounded by an unwillingness to consider the weaknesses of an energy policy dictated by the need for cheap fossil fuels and the desire to implement a green transition.

If there is one thing Western elites have been unwilling to hear from the fall of the Wall to the present day, it is the truth.

And it does not stop there. The truth about why nation-building in Afghanistan and Iraq was doomed to fail; why the Arab Spring could never develop into something resembling 1989 in Europe; and why the refugee crisis of 2015 proved so divisive and problematic—these truths are even more unpopular than those listed above.

They are unpopular because in many Western countries it is a big taboo to say that militant Islamism constitutes a major and persistent problem for Western societies.

This need not have been the case. And here I cannot resist the temptation to recount an anecdote from the Danish Parliament.

Around 2020, the Parliament received a delegation from the German state of Baden-Württemberg. The Social Democrats, the Liberal Party, the Social Liberals, and my own party—the Liberal Alliance—each sent a representative to greet the delegation.

One by one, the Danish panel outlined the main elements of Denmark's refugee and immigration policy. With the exception of the Social Liberals, there was broad agreement.

As we did so, representatives of Alternative für Deutschland sat nodding and expressing their approval of Danish policy in subdued remarks, while representatives of the SPD, CDU, FDP, and the Greens alternated between clutching their heads and shaking them.

It is by no means my intention to endorse Alternative für Deutschland's flirtation with Nazism—that deserves no endorsement whatsoever. But it is striking how great the distance can be between what the political mainstream considers acceptable in one country and in its neighbor.

This is where the question of truth becomes relevant. Almost everything that forms part of Danish policymakers' decision-making basis regarding immigration from MENAPT countries is taboo in Germany. Politicians and citizens alike are not permitted to know what immigration costs society in purely economic terms, how much crime it generates, or how severe the problems in the education system are. These are matters we can discuss openly in Denmark and use as the basis for political decisions. In Germany, by contrast, it is deeply problematic even to obtain a clear overview of this crucial issue.

My final—and most important—recommendation in this chapter is therefore this: we must organise society in such a way that telling the truth can never place one in difficulty.

It is entirely appropriate that one may face consequences for lying, manipulating, or slandering. But it will never be acceptable—subject to ordinary rules of confidentiality and the protection of state secrets—to structure society in such a way that speaking the truth is itself problematic.

That truth was so consistently unwelcome in Western countries from the fall of the Wall to the present day ranks among the greatest failures examined in this book.

The elitist Dunning–Kruger syndrome

The so-called Dunning–Kruger syndrome is named after the psychologists David Dunning and Justin Kruger and was formulated in 1999. It describes the tendency of incompetent individuals to overestimate their competence, while highly competent individuals tend to underestimate theirs.

Among well-educated people, it is common to imagine that someone afflicted by the Dunning–Kruger effect is a somewhat dim individual of low social status—someone resembling the cartoon character Homer Simpson.

Life has taught me, however, that there is also what might be called "high-status Dunning–Kruger." This is a form of self-satisfaction and self-sufficiency that can sometimes afflict elites.

A good example is the Danish Ministry of Finance. And judging from my colleagues in the European Parliament, it is a condition that frequently afflicts finance ministries throughout the Western world.

A large proportion of the Danish state's failed IT projects have been conceived by the Ministry of Finance—often following the same formula: overestimating the system's merits, immediately reaping optimistic savings through rationalisation, and ultimately discovering—yet again—that the system does not work nearly as well as anticipated, while the competent employees who could have mitigated the damage have long since been dismissed or reassigned.

Yet this has never prevented the Ministry of Finance from "advising"—Slotsholmen jargon for "deciding"—on new IT projects with the utmost confidence.

Similarly, one often encounters young civil servants from the Ministry of Finance who hold surprisingly assertive views—based on nothing—about how best to reform secondary education, ensure adequate medical coverage in rural areas, or any number of other complex policy areas.

What is at stake here is high-status Dunning–Kruger: the belief that because one is highly competent in one domain, one must be highly competent in all.

I do not know whether high-status Dunning–Kruger can be cured—but I wish it could be. For it is undoubtedly responsible for many of the policy failures committed between the fall of the Wall and the present day: extremely capable—but narrowly capable—individuals who, lacking meaningful managerial counterweight, came to believe they were not specialists but elite performers in an academic decathlon.

The ten proposals for better leadership outlined in this chapter do not implement themselves. They should be read merely as reflections on what good leadership could and should entail. Because leadership is where everything begins and ends. And here I do not refer solely to how office and department heads manage their staff—important though that is—but to how top leaders should strive to maintain open minds and recognise their own limitations, while demanding the same openness and humility from those around them.

Humility—genuine humility—dissolves quickly when exposed to high status, many privileges, and generous compensation. But it is a virtue leaders should strive not to forget, at least if they wish to avoid falling into the trap of high-status Dunning–Kruger—and all the disasters that may follow from it.

EPILOGUE

The world has returned to normal.

– Robert Kagan: *The Return of History and the End of Dreams*

This book has shown how, after the fall of the Wall, the West lost its ability to read and understand the changes in the world and therefore ended up making decisively wrong decisions. On the basis of this analysis, I present below ten concrete recommendations that may serve as guiding principles for avoiding a repetition of past mistakes. These recommendations are drawn directly from the experiences, analyses, and conclusions set out throughout the book—especially in Chapter 8, which focuses on better leadership.

1. Abandon the notion of the West's universal values: Accept that democracy and human rights do not automatically achieve global diffusion, and adjust policy accordingly.
2. Reassess faith in multilateral organisations: Acknowledge that the UN, the WTO, and similar bodies have been weaponised against Western interests, and refrain from vesting them with decisive power.

3. Substantially strengthen Europe's defence capability: Rearm militarily to achieve genuine strategic autonomy and credible deterrence vis-à-vis Russia and China.
4. Reduce the West's strategic dependence on China: Re-shore critical production, diversify supply chains, and regain control over vital technologies and raw materials.
5. Rethink energy policy on realist grounds: Prioritise stable, proven energy sources and minimize dependence on energy from authoritarian states.
6. Focus on regional alliances in Europe: Develop practical, flexible alliances among countries that genuinely share interests—especially around the Baltic Sea and in the North Atlantic.
7. Build resilience against hybrid warfare and disinformation: Take the fight against disinformation and cyberattacks seriously and extend NATO cooperation to include hybrid warfare.
8. Insist on cultural integration and social cohesion: Prioritize cohesion and shared values to prevent global conflicts from being imported and amplified within Europe.
9. Make decision-making robust against groupthink: Ensure that independent, critical analyses are always included, and be willing to adjust course when the premises of current policy change.
10. Prepare for strategic divergence with the United States: Recognise that, in the aftermath of the Trump era—with its attempts to revise longstanding territorial understandings regarding Greenland and Canada, and its readiness to reopen or abandon established agreements—the United States can no longer be assumed to share Europe's core interests in a stable, rules-based order. Europe must

> therefore define its security, trade, and diplomatic priorities on the basis of its own long-term interests, and build the institutional and military capacity to act independently when transatlantic alignment weakens.

The single most important precondition for rallying around these ten points is, first, that we in the West become better at standing together. And second, that we recognise there is, in fact, something worth fighting for—that our culture and way of life are valuable and worth defending against both internal and external attacks.

I once asked a mayor who had held office for more than twenty years what the secret was. "You must remember that you are also the mayor for those who did not vote for you," was the answer.

That rule of thumb—for mayors and prime ministers alike—that they must remember they also bear a kind of responsibility toward citizens who voted for the opposition sounds simple. In practice, however, it is easily forgotten, and that is to put it mildly unfortunate. For I am firmly convinced that the fuel driving so-called populism is the feeling of never having been consulted—and therefore never having been taken seriously—on issues affecting one's vital interests.

To be quite honest, I must admit that from time to time I myself entertain the kinds of thoughts I imagine form the common thread of populism. Let me give an example.

I find it annoying if I can't speak my native language when I'm in restaurants and stores at home. I know perfectly well that this is something a mature and responsible globalist ought to rejoice in. Is it not wonderful how nowadays we can meet across borders? And is it not splendid that our country offers so much employment?

Yes, yes. Hooray for that. And one is, after all, centre-right and business friendly. That does not change the fact that I still feel everything has been turned upside down. It is not—believe me—a common requirement in the many countries my work has taken me to that natives should switch to a foreign language in order to be served in a restaurant or a shop. It is only in Denmark—and perhaps the rest of the Nordic countries—that the political elite seems to believe the hosts should adapt to the guests.

In everyday life, of course, I restrain myself and politely order my coffee, or whatever it may be, in English. After all, it is not the individual—usually a perfectly pleasant person—standing in front of me who bears responsibility for the state of affairs.

Yet inside me there still bubbles a sense of irritation and disagreement with the people who make all this happen. Because I know that if I were to meet one of them and voice my dissatisfaction, the response would be a didactic lecture about how the nation-state belongs to the past (with the obvious subtext that my views do as well). I find that attitude genuinely provocative. Anyone who has read this far in my book knows why: in my view, it is an argument that expired some twenty-five years ago.

My annoyance at being forced to behave like a foreigner in my own home I can set aside. I live a privileged life, and one should not ruin one's good mood by indulging in first-world problems.

But the feeling of never having been consulted on an issue one considers important, combined with the certainty that those who made the decision over one's head simultaneously regard one's objections as ridiculous and unworthy of serious consideration—that is the fuel that drives populism. Of that I have not the slightest doubt.

"Who, exactly," asks the populist, "ever asked me whether I support our major cities changing beyond recognition?"

Or: "Who, exactly, ever asked me whether I can afford energy prices doubling or tripling in a short space of time to meet a target no one outside Europe cares about?"

Or: "Who, exactly, ever asked me whether I find it acceptable for the public school system to fill my children's heads with left-wing pet causes I do not myself support?"

Politicians like the mayor I spoke with would never, ever have allowed matters to reach the point where a critical mass of citizens thought: "Who on earth ever asked me whether I wanted our city transformed beyond recognition?" He or she would understand that forcing decisions through over people's heads will, over time, solidify into a dangerous division capable of destroying harmony and social peace throughout the municipality.

Yet many contemporary politicians—and this applies across the Western world—have stopped thinking like that good mayor I spoke with. Today, it often brings political tailwinds to pursue politics *against* someone, rather than politics *for* something.

Even if it was not their explicit intention, globalists in practice often ended up pursuing politics against traditionalists. By this I mean that among globalists there was typically a lack of genuine consideration for those who were not enthusiastic about crossing borders, dissolving traditions, and abolishing the national.

Those who wished to preserve national cohesion, national symbols and traditions, and the national language generally encountered little accommodation or acceptance of their viewpoint from globalists. The most glaring example was, of course, Hillary Clinton's description of Donald Trump's voters as "a basket of deplorables". I have never seen a study examining whether Clinton's voters actually thought she was right. But since she received more votes than Donald Trump (though fewer electors), the harsh and sarcastic words did not, at any rate, scare voters away to any significant degree.

It is an extraordinarily serious problem that Western elites over many years pursued policies that dramatically weakened their countries' security vis-à-vis Russia and China, as well as various state and non-state actors in the Middle East. I have devoted most of this book to documenting that fact.

But it is also problematic that Western elites pursued policies that produced so much internal division at home in the West. I have mentioned this in passing throughout the book. Now I want to focus on it in these concluding remarks.

In the United States, globalist policies under Presidents Clinton and Obama—combined with the endless wars of neoconservatism under George W. Bush—led to Donald Trump's rise to power in 2016.

In the United Kingdom, a long-standing policy that was experienced primarily by the English (not the British—the English) as un-national led to Brexit.

In both Germany and France, the traditional elite's reluctance to cooperate with the nationalist right has resulted in between a quarter (in Germany) and a third (in France) of voters being excluded from direct influence over the policies pursued.

With each passing year, divisions in these major countries (three of the four permanent members of the UN Security Council) will become more embittered and radicalised. And let us be honest: it is not only the "populists" who are becoming more radical over time. The "anti-populists" are also often becoming increasingly radical in their unwillingness to accommodate viewpoints they deem categorically unacceptable.

In my view, such division can lead to only one outcome: the countries affected become ungovernable. The United States cannot embark on reforms to improve public finances, even as debt grows ever more alarming. The United Kingdom has no solutions for integrating its underclass—because such an underclass does exist—into ordinary social life. France has no solutions for making state finances sustainable. And Germany has no solutions to the polycrisis that has resulted from persistently poor leadership throughout this century.

The longer these countries appear to their own citizens as manifestly dysfunctional and ungovernable, the more dangerous this becomes in itself—and the more the rest of the EU and the West will miss them when joint solutions are needed.

The core of populist uprisings in all four countries I have mentioned is a disregard for limits—both in the literal and the figurative sense.

First, populist rebels disagree with the idea that their countries should lack real borders vis-à-vis the outside world. They prefer an old-fashioned border that cannot be crossed without proper documentation. Likewise, they prefer to live in a state that enforces its right to guard its borders and determine who resides on its territory.

But they also oppose the absence of limits in the figurative sense. Individuals should not enjoy limitless rights vis-à-vis the community. People's behavior should not be without limits, but should respect existing norms. Long-standing traditions should not be abolished at the first battle cry of "Because freedom!"

It is, of course, painful to write this, because some forms of liberalism—though far from all—advocate far-reaching criticism of tradition. And for many years I myself represented a liberal party, first in the Danish Parliament and now in the European Parliament.

I cannot make sense of any conclusion other than that all populist uprisings in Western countries share the formula: "Mandatory criticism of disregard for limits. Possibly with additional ingredients." Those additional ingredients can be almost anything: historically conditioned grievances in a given country (for example, tensions between the former East and West Germany); concrete mismanagement of specific problems (for example, lack of consideration for agriculture or indifference toward regions that are wasting away).

This is why I also believe that any fight against populism begins with a responsible leader who, in essence, tells citizens: "You should not have to put up with just anything. I acknowledge that, and it will be the guiding principle of this government's work." Populists are not primarily angry about something specific. They are angry because—so they experience it—there are no limits to anything. Not even to what they are expected to tolerate.

Consider the list below. It is not scientific in any sense, but it divides the EU's 27 member states into three groups: countries that are difficult to govern because a substantial part of the population regards the incumbent government as illegitimate; countries that are at times difficult to govern because some parties regard the incumbent government as illegitimate; and countries that are more or less governable.

Group 1: Countries difficult to govern due to a permanent legitimacy crisis

Germany: Political fragmentation;
AfD blocked by the political elite
France: Generalized dissatisfaction with any government;
Rassemblement National permanently blocked
Italy: Frequent government changes;
competing populist parties
Poland: Deep division between Civic Platform and PiS;
EU conflict
Hungary: Deep tensions between Fidesz and Tisza;
EU conflict

Slovakia: High political instability; populism
Romania: Corruption; strong populist currents
Bulgaria: Strong populism; political corruption

Group 2: Countries moderately difficult to govern due to legitimacy problems

Spain: Regional divisions; economic tensions
Netherlands: Strong right-wing populism; unstable coalition
Sweden: Structural problems with gang crime; difficult to remedy
Austria: Rising populism; strong FPÖ
Belgium: Regional division; political fragmentation
Czech Republic: Stable economy; growing Euroscepticism
Greece: Economic problems; growing right wing
Croatia: Moderate populism; stable democracy
Lithuania: Economic stability; moderate populism
Latvia: Economic challenges; Russian minority

Group 3: Countries without significant legitimacy crises

Denmark: Moderate populist currents; stable democracy
Finland: Low degree of populism; stable politics
Portugal: Low populism; stable politics
Slovenia: Low populism; stable economy
Estonia: Low populism; stable economy
Ireland: Extremely low populism; political stability
Cyprus: Economic tensions; moderate populism
Luxembourg: Very stable politics; low populism
Malta: Political stability

This overview makes for worrying reading, because nearly a third of the EU's countries—representing two thirds of the EU's total population—are more or less impossible to govern. Therefore, the political elite in each of the eight ungovernable countries should make it their absolute top priority to strengthen general trust in the political system. In my view, this is best achieved by openly acknowledging the problems identified by populists—while, of course, proposing one's own political solutions.

At the same time, in all countries that operate a *Brandmauer* or *cordon sanitaire* against the far right, it should be recognised that few things are more damaging than this practice. In Sweden, the established parties maintained a firewall against the Sweden Democrats for many years. Nothing good came of it. Now the firewall is gone, and all parties except the far left are moving toward a realistic immigration policy.

Internal division in the majority of EU countries itself prevents correction of the many policy errors committed in the years between the end of the Cold War and the 2020s. But the EU, too, must do better.

The EU should, of course, dismantle the many bureaucratic obstacles that, according to the Draghi report, undermine Europe's competitiveness. It should also break with the version of the green transition that drives energy prices upward and makes Europe dependent on Chinese raw materials and technology. And it should make a concerted effort to restrain itself. Matters that are national competences (including primary education, secondary education, healthcare, social welfare, labor-market arrangements, and gender equality) should be left alone by the EU. Interference has only one effect: it increases EU opposition among centrist voters. And that is the last thing the continent needs.

Above all, however, the EU—together with the European

NATO countries—must adapt to the reality of hard power. Hard power is—as already noted several times—the ability to impose one's will even when others disagree.

The EU should possess sufficient capability and will to defend itself against external adversaries such as Russia, China, Iran, and various Islamist terrorist movements so that they do not dare attack the continent. This costs a great deal of money and requires more streamlined decision-making. But so be it.

Above all, Europe must rediscover its self-confidence. The German philosopher Georg Wilhelm Friedrich Hegel once remarked, in his characteristically enigmatic manner, that Minerva's owl flies at dusk.

It is difficult to interpret the statement unambiguously. But Minerva is the Roman goddess of wisdom. And I interpret Hegel's phrase to mean that wisdom does not take flight until it is almost dark.

If I have interpreted Hegel correctly, now would be a perfect moment for Minerva's owl to take wing. But what might the goddess of wisdom tell us if she were to think that we in the West could use a piece of advice—or three? I believe the first piece of advice would be that we in the West should rediscover our self-confidence.

To be perfectly honest, there is nowhere in the world where it is better to be a woman, to be a minority, to be ill, to be poor, or to be weak than in the West. Everywhere else, women are treated worse than they are here. Everywhere else, minorities are treated worse. Everywhere else, less is done—or can be done—for the sick (unless Western medicine and approaches to illness have been adopted). Everywhere else, people are more indifferent to the poor. And everywhere else, there is a greater tendency to believe that the weak are to blame for their own weakness.

In short: we have nothing to be ashamed of in the Western world. We generally treat other human beings better than any other culture on this Earth.

There is also another reason why we in the West should rediscover our self-confidence: our science and philosophy are vastly superior to all others. It is through Western science that we have ventured into space, to the depths of the oceans, and into the interior of atoms. No other approach can accomplish this. It is through Western philosophy that we have explored every conceivable corner of logic and rationality.

Therefore, we should abandon self-hatred and relativism. Our way of being and of doing things is worth preserving and defending. There is not much we can learn from the rest of the world—unless it is how to cook interesting food. If people elsewhere in the world want a better life, it is us in the West they must copy. It does not work the other way around.

If we can learn anything from the decades following the fall of the Wall, it is that we should not force-feed the rest of the world our values and ways of doing things. We should refrain from that. But we should certainly not be ashamed of who we are.

The second piece of good advice I believe Minerva would offer is that we must find our way back to the Enlightenment and its values.

It is tragic that the very concept of truth has disintegrated. It is difficult to provide a fully satisfactory definition of what truth actually is. But everyone ought to agree that it is the opposite of a lie.

We are able to distinguish truth from falsehood because we humans are moral beings. From our own experience, we know perfectly well that there is a difference between telling the truth and lying—even if no philosopher would be willing to sign off on this or that as the final definition of truth.

Ideally, all human beings should live according to a norm of truth—that is, a norm according to which one ought to speak truthfully, and a norm according to which one must submit to the truth. It is correct that the world can appear different when viewed from different perspectives. But this should not lead anyone to believe that we therefore inhabit separate realities. To a very large extent, we do not: with regard to the overwhelming majority of matters that are relevant to us, we live in the same reality.

At its most fundamental level, the Enlightenment project consists in teaching all people to use their own reason rather than relying on that of others. But this still presupposes that it is possible to become wiser about—and to speak meaningfully about—the shared world we inhabit.

Lies are not the only enemy of truth. Truth also has another powerful adversary: bullshit. On this subject, the American philosopher Harry Frankfurt has written an excellent essay.[58]

As a scientific and philosophical concept, bullshit is—according to Frankfurt—a form of speech characterised by indifference to whether what is being said is true or false. Whereas the liar, metaphorically speaking, builds a fence around the truth so that no one can see it, the bullshitter simply does not care. *If I can get you to follow my instructions by saying something that sounds right to you, then I'll just say that*—so thinks the bullshitter.

We will never succeed in eliminating misinformation and disinformation in a relativistic world. The precondition for that struggle ever succeeding—and indeed for it to make sense to wage it at all—is the recognition that there is a vast and utterly decisive difference between truth on the one hand, and lies and bullshit on the other.

It is a lie and bullshit to claim that Ukraine is governed by Nazis as these lines are written. Just as it is a lie and bullshit to claim that Russia and Ukraine bear equal responsibility for the war. We will never move forward, either as human beings or as societies, if it is not possible—and permissible—to insist on these distinctions. And it is self-evidently catastrophic if those who occupy the highest offices in a society devote themselves to lying or bullshitting.

What has made the Western world as successful as it has been over several hundred years is that we have systematically challenged inferior theories and inferior data and systematically replaced them with better theories and better data. We have done this through a social institution that is unique to the Western world: the modern university.

It is therefore all the more regrettable when universities occasionally abandon their insistence that lies and bullshit are not the same as truth—and that truth should always be preferred. The Western university should always stand on the side of truth. And it should always regard lies and bullshit as enemies of truth.

The final warning Minerva would likely issue to us Westerners concerns our tendency to sow division among ourselves.

For many years now, there has been a powerful current in Western politics aimed at fostering division: division between men and women; between young and old; between city and countryside; between rich and poor; between those with light skin and those with dark skin.

This division—which it has been politically profitable to promote—is, without exaggeration, deadly for us in the West.

It is true that human beings are not identical. It is also true that we have often treated one another worse than we could and should have. But most people are not evil. Most people want to act in a morally good way. We must remember this.

Internal division within Western publics has for some years now been politically lucrative—because claiming victimhood is an effective way of securing advantages for oneself.

We cannot fight for our Western social model and for our Western and humanistic values unless we stand together and remind one another of the elementary truth that although we look different and live under different conditions, we are all human beings—and thus, in a profoundly important sense, fundamentally alike.

The precondition for democracy is, and remains, the insight that we are all human beings, and therefore all possess the same right to life, property, honour, and dignity as anyone else. If everyone were willing to grant others the same degree of respect for their life, property, honour, and dignity that they demand for themselves, the work of judges and politicians alike would be easy. But the very existence of judges and politicians reflects the recognition that although the world does not always function this way, this is how it ought ideally to be ordered.

For decades, the West has tended to underestimate its own strengths and overestimate the intentions of its adversaries. We have forgotten that our civilisation became strong not despite, but precisely because it dared to subject itself to critical scrutiny and to learn continuously from its own mistakes. It is time to rediscover the courage to insist on our values—freedom, truth, and democracy—and to act upon them with the same clarity and self-confidence we once possessed.

We stand at a crossroads. Either we continue to accept a world characterised by disregard for limits, division, and relativism, with all the political disintegration and vulnerability to external enemies that this entails. Or we choose to rebuild Western strength through renewed commitment to our shared values, a revival of Enlightenment ideals, and the recognition that we can meet the challenges of the future only if we do so together.

The choice lies with us. It demands courage, clarity, and determination. The peace we lost can still be regained—if we dare to face reality, listen to one another, and take our own civilisation seriously. This is not merely a possibility; it is our responsibility to future generations.

It is frightening that darkness is beginning to fall. But we must remind one another that this is also the moment when wisdom takes flight.

NOTES

1 German original: Der 24. Februar 2022 markiert eine Zäsur in der Geschichte unseres Kontinents. Mit dem Überfall auf die Ukraine hat der russische Präsident Putin kaltblütig einen Angriffskrieg vom Zaun gebrochen – aus einem einzigen Grund: Die Freiheit der Ukrainerinnen und Ukrainer stellt sein eigenes Unterdrückungsregime infrage. Das ist menschenverachtend, das ist völkerrechtswidrig, das ist durch nichts und niemanden zu rechtfertigen. Wir erleben eine Zeitenwende. Und das bedeutet: Die Welt danach ist nicht mehr dieselbe wie die Welt davor. Im Kern geht es um die Frage, ob Macht das Recht brechen darf, ob wir Putin erlauben, die Uhren zurückzudrehen in die Zeiten der Großmächte des 19. Jahrhunderts – oder ob wir die Kraft aufbringen, Kriegstreibern wie Putin Grenzen zu setzen.

2 Haidt,.J. (2012). The Righteous Mind. Why Good People Are Divided by Politics and Religion. New York: Pantheon Books.

3 Berlingske, 23 April 2025.

4 Giddens, A. (1999). Runaway World: How Globalisation is Reshaping Our Lives. London: Profile Books.

5 Barber, B.R. (1995). Jihad vs. McWorld: How Globalism and Tribalism Are Reshaping the World. New York: Times Books.

6 Brzezinski, Z. (1997). The Grand Chessboard: American primacy and its geostrategic imperatives. Basic Books. Page 55.

7 Fukuyama, F. (1992). The End of History and the Last Man. New York: Free Press.

8 Hobsbawm, E.J. (1994). The Age of Extremes: The Short Twentieth Century, 1914-1991. London: Michael Joseph.

9 Fukuyama, F. (1989): The End of History?, The National Interest, Summer 1989, page 4.

10 Thatcher, M. (1996, 9. March). New Threats for Old. Winston Churchill

Memorial, Westminster College, Fulton, Missouri. Available at: http://www.margaretthatcher.org (https://www.nationalchurchillmuseum.org/new-threats-for-old-speech.html)

11 Friedman, T. L. (1998, 2. May). Foreign affairs; Now a word from X. The New York Times. https://www.nytimes.com/1998/05/02/opinion/foreign-affairs-now-a-word-from-x.html

12 Huntington, S.P. (1996). The Clash of Civilizations and the Remaking of World Order. New York: Simon & Schuster.

13 Samuel P. Huntington, The Clash of Civilizations?, Foreign Affairs, Summer 1993, page 22

14 Brzezinski, Z. (1997). The Grand Chessboard: American primacy and its geostrategic imperatives. Basic Books. Page 55.

15 Op.cit., page 4.

16 Castells, M. (1996): The rise of the network society (Vol. 1). Oxford, UK: Blackwell. Page 3.

17 Official Report of the Proceedings of the Danish Parliament (Folketinget). Written Report on Principles and Perspectives in Danish Foreign Policy. 23 June 1993.

18 Clinton, W. J. (1994, 25. January). Address Before a Joint Session of the Congress on the State of the Union. The American Presidency Project. (https://millercenter.org/ the-presidency/presidential-speeches/january-25-1994-state-union-address)

19 United Nations General Assembly and Security Council, Document A/50/60 – S/1995/1.

20 Blair, T. (1999, 22. april). Doctrine of the International Community. Economic Club, Chicago, IL. (https://www.youtube.com/watch?v=Lqc2MqbhPt0&t=664s) (https://www.globalpolicy.org/component/content/article/154/26026.html)

21 Anghel, V., & Jones, E. (2024). "Three lessons from the 2004 'Big Bang' enlargement". Politics and Governance 12, Article 8358. https://doi.org/10.17645/ pag.8358

22 Taksøe-Jensen, P. (2016). Dansk diplomati og forsvar i en brydningstid: Vejen frem for Danmarks interesser og værdier mod 2030. Udenrigsministeriet. Page 49-50.

23 Kant, I. (2006). *Toward perpetual peace and other writings on politics, peace, and history* (D. L. Colclasure, Ed.). Yale University Press. (Original work published 1795)

24 https:// www.un.org/millenniumgoals/2015_MDG_Report/pdf/MDG%202015%20rev%20(July%201).pdf

25 On peut faire une guerre seul, c'est beaucoup plus difficile de faire la paix seul. Jacques Chirac, press conference after the G8 summit in Evian, 3 June 2003.

26 Clarke, R.A. (2004). Against all enemies: Inside America's War on Terror. Free Press.
27 https: //digital.library.unt.edu/ark:/67531/metadc1228338/m2/1/high_ res_d/9-11Commission_Hearing_2004-03-24.pdf
28 https: //www.kiplingsociety.co.uk/poem/poems_burden.htm
29 https:// www.ft.dk/samling/20042/redegoerelse/R12/185698.pdf
30 https:// www.ft.dk/samling/20061/redegoerelse/R16/376280.pdf
31 Møller, P.S. (2017). Udenrigsminister i krig og fred. København: Gyldendal.
32 https: //digital.library.unt.edu/ark:/67531/metadc1228338/m2/1/high_ res_d/9-11Commission_Hearing_2004-03-24.pdf
33 References are to the Danish translation: Merkel, A. (2024). Frihed: Erindringer 1954-2021 (N. Lund & M. Visby, overs.). Gutkind Forlag
34 English transcript: http://en.kremlin.ru/events/president/transcripts/22931
35 English transcript: http://en.kremlin.ru/events/president/transcripts/24034
36 Bucharest Summit Declaration issued by NATO Heads of State and Government". North Atlantic Treaty Organization. https://www.nato.int/cps/en/natolive/official_texts_8443.htm[](https://www.nato.int/cps/en/natohq/official_texts_8443.html).
37 Kagan, R. (2008). The Return of History and the End of Dreams. Knopf. Page 5-6.
38 Obama, B. (2020). A promised land. Crown. Page 480.
39 https://www.debates.org/debate-transcripts/october-22-2012-debatc-transcript/
40 https://www.ft.dk/samling/20111/vedtagelse/V18/index.htm
41 Dahl, H. (1999). "Halvfemsernes fænomenologi". Kritik, årg. 32, nr. 141, side 1-7.
42 https: //www.ft.dk/samling/20111/forespoergsel/F5/BEH1-37/forhandling.htm
43 Jerusalem Post, 25. February 2011.
44 Intelligence and Security Committee of Parliament. (2020). Russia. UK Parliament. https://www.parliament.uk/business/committees/committees-a-z/commons-select/intelligence-and-security-committee/russia-report/
45 Mueller, R.S. (2019). Report on the investigation into Russian interference in the 2016 presidential election. U.S. Department of Justice. https://www.justice.gov/archives/sco/file/1373816/download
46 Corbet, S. & Surk, B. (2024, 12. februar). "France accuses Russia of a disinformation campaign in a key election year". AP News. https://apnews. com/article/france-russia-disinformation-campaign-macron-ukraine-b345f9c2f0c0d7b7c5d3f0f5a7f0e6c2

47 https: //www.bbc.com/news/business-27503017
48 : https: //docs.pca-cpa.org/2016/07/PH-CN-20160712-Award.pdf
49 : https: //www.nytimes.com/2011/08/13/world/europe/13iht-germany.html
50 : https: //nypost.com/2019/08/17/luxury-beliefs-are-the-latest-status-symbol-for-rich-americans/
51 Dysa, Y., Polityuk, P., & Lee, L. (2025, 26. maj). "Ukraine confirmed Chinese supplies to 20 Russian military plants, intelligence chief says". Reuters.
52 Reich, R.B. (1991). The work of nations: Preparing Ourselves for 21st Century Capitalism, Knopf Doubleday Publishing Group
53 Bob Dylan: Modern Times. Columbia Records 2006.
54 https://www.elysee.fr/en/emmanuel-macron/2017/09/26/president-macron-gives-speech-on-new-initiative-for-europe
55 : https: //www.china-briefing.com/news/made-in-china-2025-explained/
56 Knausgaard, K. O. (2023). Out of the world (M. Aitken, Trans.). Archipelago Books. (Original work published 1998)
57 Rogers, E.M. (2003). Diffusion of innovations (5. udg.). New York, NY: Free Press
58 Frankfurt, H. G. (2005). On bullshit. Princeton University Press.

www.ingramcontent.com/pod-product-compliance
Ingram Content Group UK Ltd.
Pitfield, Milton Keynes, MK11 3LW, UK
UKHW022029190726
13853UKWH00005B/2174